# SOUTH CENTRAL
# SOVIET UNION 1944

Miles

0   100   200   300   400   500

Chkalov

Beforefsk

Orsk

Troitsk

KAZAKH SSR

Lake Balkhash

Tashkent

Issyk Kul

KIRGIZ SSR

ZIK SSR

CHINA

# IN AND OUT OF STALIN'S GRU:

## A Tatar's Escape
## from Red Army Intelligence

# Foreign Intelligence Book Series
Thomas F. Troy, General Editor

BRITISH MILITARY INTELLIGENCE, 1870-1914:
  The Development of a Modern Intelligence Organization
COVERT GERMAN REARMAMENT, 1919-1939:
  Deception and Misperception
ENIGMA: How the German Machine Cipher Was Broken, and How It
  Was Read by the Allies in World War II
GERMAN MILITARY INTELLIGENCE, 1939-1945
IN AND OUT OF STALIN'S GRU:
  A Tatar's Escape from Red Army Intelligence
KLAUS BARBIE AND THE UNITED STATES GOVERNMENT:
  The Report, with Documentary Appendix, to the Attorney General
  of the United States
SOE IN FRANCE: An Account of the Work of the British Special
  Operations Executive in France, 1940-1944
THE WATCHDOGS OF TERROR: Russian Bodyguards from the
  Tsars to the Commissars (Second Edition)

*Of Related Interest:*
DONOVAN AND THE CIA: A History of the Establishment of the
  Central Intelligence Agency
THE FRONTIERS OF SECRECY: Closed Government in Britain
OPERATION ZAPATA: The "Ultrasensitive" Report and
  Testimony of the Board of Inquiry on the Bay of Pigs
THE ROTE KAPELLE: The CIA's History of Soviet Intelligence and
  Espionage Networks in Western Europe, 1936-1945
SCHOLAR'S GUIDE TO INTELLIGENCE LITERATURE:
  Bibliography of the Russell J. Bowen Collection
ULTRA AND THE HISTORY OF THE UNITED STATES
  STRATEGIC AIR FORCE IN EUROPE vs.
  THE GERMAN AIR FORCE

# IN AND OUT OF STALIN'S GRU:
## A Tatar's Escape
## from Red Army Intelligence

### Ismail Akhmedov

University Publications of America, Inc.

Library of Congress Cataloging in Publication Data


Akhmedov, Ismail, 1904–
    In and out of Stalin's GRU.

   (Foreign intelligence book series)
   Includes index.
   1. Akhmedov, Ismail, 1904–   . 2. Intelligence officers—Soviet Union—
Biography. 3. Soviet Union.
Glavnoye razvedyvatelnoye upravleniye—History.
I. Title. II. Series.
UB271.R92A344 1984     355.3'432'0924 [B]     83-17018
ISBN 0-89093-546-7

*To my parents,*
*Huseyin and Fatima*

# Contents

# Foreword

Perhaps the title of this volume should have spoken of Stalin's "G-2" rather than of his "GRU." G-2 has that high-recognition factor favored by politicians and merchandisers. It immediately denotes a military intelligence division of a general staff. GRU, on the other hand, is readily grasped by few beyond the *cognoscenti.* The GRU, in other words, is not the KGB.

The latter is widely recognized as the huge, worldwide Soviet domestic and foreign police, intelligence, and state security service. It has been known as the KGB, the Committee for State Security, since 1954, and before that it was known by different initials—the MVD-MGB, the NKGB-NKVD, the NKVD, the OGPU, the GPU, and the Cheka of Lenin's day—and it has some roots in a Tsarist antecedent, the Okhrana, a pale suggestion of today's powerful KGB. It has been around for sixty-five years. It has been the subject of numerous books and innumerable monographs, magazine articles, and newspaper stories. It is so well known that in 1973 John Barron felt safe in titling his book *KGB.*

Not so the GRU, even though its pedigree is as long, even though it too operates overseas—under cover—and even though it too runs agents and conducts subversive operations in foreign countries. Not so the GRU, the *Glavnoye Razvedyvatelnoye Upravleniye,* the Main Intelligence Directorate of the Soviet General Staff, the Soviet Union's professional army intelligence organization. It has been the subject of only a handful of books, and never has the name GRU appeared in the title.

The first of the handful was by a GRU defector who published his book in New York in 1939 and then two years later was found dead in a locked hotel room in Washington, D.C.—it looked like suicide, but subsequent information indicated a Soviet murder. The book was *In Stalin's Secret Service: An Exposé of Russia's Secret Policies by the Former Chief of Soviet Intelligence in Western*

*Europe,* and its author, Walter G. Krivitsky, had served in various departments of Soviet military intelligence. Experts disagree, however, on whether Krivitsky was not more a KGB man under GRU cover than a genuine GRU officer.

Unquestionably a GRU officer was the late Igor Gouzenko, the young Soviet defector who in 1945 blew the whistle on the very extensive GRU network in Canada and the United States. He told his story in *The Iron Curtain,* which was published in 1948. Gouzenko, whose revelations were a major contribution to western security, nevertheless was only a lieutenant, had been in the GRU only a few years, and, being a cipher clerk, had never been an operational officer.

Then there is *The Penkovsky Papers* by Col. Oleg Penkovsky, a GRU officer. Disillusioned with the Soviet system, he compiled a treasure-trove of notes and commentaries on the operations of both the KGB and the GRU throughout the western world and transmitted them to British and American intelligence. These papers, one of the great intelligence coups of recent times, were published in 1965—after Penkovsky, captured by the KGB, was tried and executed. Valuable as they are, however, the papers are not an autobiography.

Then there are two GRU officers whose stories have been told by other persons. The story of "Ignace Reiss," a Soviet-murdered contemporary of Krivitsky, has been told by his wife, Elisabeth K. Poretsky, in *Our Own People: A Memoir of "Ignace Reiss" and His Friends* (1970). The story of Pyotr Popov, a GRU lieutenant colonel like Ismail Akhmedov and a victim of Soviet justice like Penkovsky, was told in 1982 by William Hood in *Mole: The True Story of the First Russian Intelligence Officer Recruited by the CIA.*

None of these volumes, however, has given us a detailed, systematic description of the history, structure, and operations of the Soviet G-2. More pertinently, in terms of Colonel Akhmedov's memoir, none has given us a genuinely autobiographical account of a professional GRU officer's early life, education, intelligence service, and break with the GRU. This Akhmedov does, from beginning to end simply and clearly, with a sense of humor and tragedy, of loss and joy, of bondage and liberation.

Colonel Akhmedov—he eventually became Ismail Ege when he sought political refuge in Turkey in the district of Ege—was born and reared in a time and space, culturally as well as physically, remote from most current western experience. He was born in 1904, on the outbreak of the Russo-Japanese War, was a lad of ten when World War I erupted, and was only a thirteen-year-old when the Russian Civil War saw Bolsheviks and Cossacks fighting for control of his town of Orsk. That lay (as it still does) at the foot of the Ural Mountains, at the far edge of what is now the Russian Soviet Federated Socialist Republic, and close to what today is Kazakhstan and the Central Asian republics of the USSR.

For the young Ismail, the son of a teacher-trader, it was also a world of Tatars and Islam. Although world events, centering on the Muslim peoples of the Middle East and Africa, have made Islam, in name if not in substance, a household word in the West, the same has been much less true for the Tatars (pronounced "Ta-TARS"). However much western history books speak of the Tatars (mistakenly called the Tartars) and the Golden Horde storming westward out of Siberia centuries ago, today's westerners know little of their descendants. There is even less literature on today's Tatars than there is on the GRU. Akhmedov tells us how a young Tatar, a Muslim, a young Communist, became an officer in the Red Army's intelligence corps.

Fundamental to his rise was a yearning for learning, a talent for languages, and a predilection for the hard sciences. These enabled him, though early put on his own by war and revolution, to move back and forth between school and job, and always to move upward. In twenty years he had gone to a teacher training institute in Orenburg (now Chkalov), a signals communications school in Leningrad, an electro-technical academy, and the high-level Academy of the General Staff. In between those years of study he had been teaching, serving with a radio battalion and running intelligence operations on the borders of Turkey and Iran, working as a research engineer, serving with troops in the Russo-Finnish War, and then becoming acting chief of the Fourth Section of the GRU. His job was the procurement of information on what today would be called "high technology" of the armies of the western powers.

Akhmedov's rise was not without its perils, as the reader will soon discover. He was coming to the top when the Stalinist purges of the late thirties were decimating not only the top political leaders of the country but also the big and little bureaucratic chiefs only a rung or two above himself. It was a time when personal survival was a daily worry, and then the outbreak of World War II added military worries to political worries and left him bereft of his beloved wife Tamara. It was also the war which, as will be seen, caused the Tatar engineer from Orsk, a Muslim and a scholar, to break with Stalinist tyranny.

THOMAS F. TROY

# Introduction

In the name of God, Most Gracious, Most Merciful.

I realize that it may be strange to start a book, especially a book of this nature, with the name of God. Today, talk on something else. Perhaps on existentialism, materialism, philosophy, impressionism, surrealism, psychoanalysis, or sex, where the trend is to neglect the role of God.

But this is a book on Soviet espionage, on civil war in Russia, on the fate of national minorities in Tsarist and Soviet Russia, on Stalin's genocide, on Communist subversion and infiltration, on the blood, toil, and suffering exacted from masses of Soviet citizens in the name of communism. In these areas, even though denied, God is very real, in His mercy and His judgment, the only constant force.

Despite its subject matter, this is not a history. Its deficiencies in literary form are conceded. It is the account of my life. It is written by me, as closely as possible as I experienced it. Even its language, its English, is my own English. It is not American or British English. It is the English of a person who has learned it in the late years of his life.

I start my narration with the name of God because He gave me the determination, the courage, and the wisdom to choose my liberty and my own way to pursue my life. It is only because of my deep belief in God that I could no longer serve like a slave the political system, the dictatorial state, the social pattern forced upon my race, my nation, and others, by a brutal police apparatus and a regime founded on continuous deception, on the denial of people's rights, on the denial of God, the Creator, Cherisher and Sustainer of Worlds. Marxism cannot explain Creation. Marxism does not care about the final end. According to Marxism, we, all life, all the universe, all nature with its wonderful laws and relationships, came from nothing, go through the utopia of an unobtainable Communist society, back into nothing. And while we are alive we are the victims, the tools of our economic environment, deprived of freedom of action and thought. All that, and especially that we came from nothing, for nothing, and end as nothing, I cannot accept. That is why I, one of the first Bolshevik youth, finally determined to break from communism.

Partly because the Soviet Union gave me much of the material things of life, it took me long to come to that conclusion. By profession I am a military electronics engineer and general staff officer. Because of my technical background and my knowledge of several oriental and western languages, I became a member of the Soviet army's intelligence department, now perhaps better known in the West by the initials GRU. That intelligence assignment also assisted my decision to deny communism. Work in that department gave me the chance, rare to most Soviet citizens, to read western writers, especially western thinkers. At the same time, I learned of new western developments in the fields of theoretical physics, electronics and theoretical mathematics that pointed accusing fingers at Lenin's materialism and Engel's dialectics, that contradicted the teachings of the founders of Marxism-Leninism. As a result of that reading, gradually, very gradually, my eyes began opening to many things hitherto unknown to me. For that I am thankful. If I had not had those windows to the outer world, if, for instance, I had worked in a factory or other civilian establishment, I would not have gained that knowledge of what life could be elsewhere, and, most likely, I would not have defected.

In my case, however, I was given the opportunity to learn other than Communist doctrines. And with that I began to understand that something was wrong with the system, to question, to doubt. As is well known, under Soviet rule to think contrary to the official line is considered a crime, and one has to suffer for it. Not only did I not want to suffer for freedom of thought and action, but also I knew from the many terrible experiences of friends and acquaintances that my personal imprisonment or death would serve no really useful purpose. My decision, therefore, was: when the appropriate time came, leave the Soviet Union for good, and be free. That waiting took more than a decade, but the time finally came in the summer of 1942. Then I made my break with Stalin and his lieutenants in Istanbul, Turkey, where as a lieutenant-colonel, GRU, it was my duty to conduct intelligence operations, under diplomatic cover, against Nazi Germany.

Perhaps one might wonder why I have waited decades to tell my story. In the first years, I can truly plead that I was too concerned with the mere matter of physical survival and had no time to put my story in writing. Now, however, after having seen much of the non-Communist world, its recurrent struggles with communism, the cyclical doubts of its youth about the non-Communist ways of life, I feel that the moment has come when I must speak.

My beginnings were as primitive as those of any young people in today's so-called underdeveloped lands, more primitive than those of the youngsters in the underprivileged areas of the West. I, too, once believed that communism offered me and my people the solution. So spare a while now for the tale of an old man who had to travel a false path throughout his youth and the best years of his life. My God is the God of Islam, but He is the God of all, and to Him I pray in gratitude for my fate and in hopes that others can be as fortunate.

# Part One

# 1

## Childhood

I was born on June 17, 1904, the eldest of six children, in Orsk at the foothills of the Urals, where the River Or joins the Ural on its course to the Caspian. By nationality I am a Tatar of Bashkir and Cossack mixture. My name is Ismail Gusseynovich Akhmedov. That is my true name. Later on I had many other names, so complex and secretive a business is espionage. Many times is a person engaged in intelligence forced to change names for security and pure personal safety. I forget the number of aliases I had.

The year I was born the Russo-Japanese War started. At that time Orsk was a sleepy garrison town of some ten thousand people. It still had the aspects of a frontier post, because it had been one of the gateways of Tsarist conquest eastward to Siberia and southward to the lands of my people, the Turkic people. An *uyezdnyy gorod*, as the Russians used to call such places, or chief town of a district; it was not only occupied, but it was also segregated. Russian government, military, and business people lived in the newest and best part of town behind the tall, yellow Orthodox church atop the highest terrain, a bare rocky hill of about 150 feet that dominated Orsk. To the Tatars were left areas along the banks of both rivers and adjoining the commercial quarter at the confluence of the rivers. The only places the average Russians and Tatars met and mingled were the market area, the shops, stalls, and wholesale lumber and hide yards in the commercial district. Paved with cobbles, it was a busy market and trading center, famous then for its bright woolen shawls.

My actual birthplace was a one-floor wooden house on Tatarskaya Ulitza, a dirt street, muddy and rutted during the thaws and rains, but swept and watered down by its residents to lay the dust during the dry periods. I know it must have been well dampened that long-ago summer day when my beautiful mother, Fatima by name, was first in labor. My father, Huseyin, would certainly

1

have seen to that. In those days there was little else he could have done to help.

His domain was not only one floor, but one room. Let me describe that place of happy days. A wooden fence paralleled the street. A gate opened into a small garden of flowers, a summer retreat for the family and visitors. From the garden one entered the combination living room, bedroom, dining room, and kitchen. Facing the street was the only window, paned with glass of which we were quite proud. The main occupant of the single room, some twelve feet by twelve feet square, was a big stove that took up about a third of the area. Made of bricks, it too was squarish, and stood about five feet high. Life would have been impossible without that stove. All the cooking was done in it. All the heating came from it. By evening it also gave some light, although in summer Mother preferred to use the glass-shielded kerosene lamp, which was one of her few household joys. In winter the stove was a special pleasure for us children, for we slept then on top of it. At the time of my birth, the only other things in that room were the big feather bed of my father and mother, several wooden chairs, brass and copper cooking pots, spoons and ladles, clay jars, and wooden bowls. There were also some books in Turkic and Persian tongues because my parents, in the rural standards of those times, were both educated people. With the arrival of us children, the space of that one room was a bit further taxed with our trundle beds. To the rear of our house were several outbuildings. The first was our "refrigerator," a shed covering a four by four foot hole, about six feet deep. Each spring with the coming of the thaws we would go to the Ural at the bottom end of our yard. From there we would haul blocks of ice, stow them in that hole behind the house, and cover the top of the pile with straw for insulation. Thereby, no matter how hot the summers—and in Orsk winters are very cold and summers equally extreme—our milk, yoghurt, and butter were always fresh. Beyond the "refrigerator" were other outhouses for Father's wagon and sledge, several cows and horses, sheep, goats, chickens, ducks, and geese. At the far end of those buildings was our toilet, a simple hole-in-the-ground outhouse, but, since we were Moslems, always stocked with water from the river for washing. At the opposite side of the yard was our vegetable garden, where we raised almost everything we needed. In fact, our family was almost self-sufficient, except for drinking water which Mother bought daily from street peddlers, wheat that Father obtained by barter, and our limited consumption of kerosene. Such was the castle of my father, the bridal bower of my mother, and the happy home of their children.

It pains me deeply that my own children will never have the pleasure and honor of knowing my parents. But they, alas, and all the rest of my immediate family—Father, Mother, a brother, and two sisters—died more than threescore years ago of pestilence and famine, early victims of Communist mismanagement. Only two escaped that disaster, and only by dying earlier. Fuad, the brother closest to me, did not survive what was then called a severe cold, and my youngest sister succumbed to something termed a fever. Both died before I was ten.

My father was the oldest of four children—three boys, one girl—of Zakir, a horse breeder. That grandfather died when I was barely five, but I remember him as a rough and jolly man. He told me first of Ghengis Khan, Tamerlane, Saladin, and the greatness of our people. He had so many horses he did not know their number. And of this, my father was not so proud—Zakir was also a great *kumiss* maker. A dark-skinned man with dark, almost black eyes, Father I remember as being of medium height, about five feet, seven inches, his face badly scarred by smallpox, which he had survived as a boy. He was very proud of his drooping, Ghengis Khan-like mustache as well as of a small goatee he used to grasp when thinking deeply. His hair was usually an unparted dark shock. That was because it was our custom to shave the heads of boys and men twice yearly, otherwise leaving them unbarbered, untrimmed. We Tatars believed that that custom preserved the hair. Although I have used conventional barbering since teen-age, it is my opinion that those twice-annual shaves of my boyhood are responsible for the good head of hair I have today.

Father's health was excellent. He was never sick, never went to a doctor. A deeply religious man, he always prayed the required five times a day, never smoked, never drank spirits. But he did drink *kumiss*, frequently would get a little drunk and sing. *Kumiss*, though, unlike alcohol, is not forbidden to Moslems, and like his father, my father took good advantage of that. Men's participation in sports as it is today was then unknown, but he was very much an outdoor man, liked horses, fishing, and hunting, and never shied away from the chores of chopping wood, tending the animals, bringing water from the Ural for washing and cooking. In the late autumn and winter the wolves used to howl around Orsk, and Father and his friends would delight in hunting them down on horseback, armed only with wooden clubs.

By occupation, he was an *imam*, a teacher, and a peddler, the latter two pursuits depending upon the time of year. Three-quarters of the year, he was the teacher of about seventy boys—

boys only—at a modern Tatar elementary school, modern for those times. His subjects, all in the Tatar tongue, were reading, writing, arithmetic, the principles of Arabic grammar, and *Tajvid*, or the correct reading of the Koran. Father's only certain income came from his teaching, and it never was very much. Every Thursday the schoolboys brought him money from their parents: five kopeks, sometimes ten, never more. We used to await his coming home with the coins wrapped in a big handkerchief and watch him count it out. Sometimes the children brought him presents of butter, cheese, or sweetmeats from particularly appreciative parents. By late spring, with school out until the autumn, Father always loaded up his wagon with goods to barter with the nomadic Kirghiz people to the north and east and would not return until forage and wood-gathering time. In my boyhood, it was among the Kirghiz that he served as *imam*. He was truly an exceptional man among my people, especially for his time.

One of his exceptional points was that he was a one-woman man, rare in those days with the Tatars. I believe that was the result of the influence of the writings of progressive contemporaries of his, Tatars chiefly in the Crimea, who endeavored to awaken my people from centuries of backwardness. As a boy, but with no understanding of the social reasons for and against monogamy, I was always happy that Father was a one-woman man. The neighbor to one side of us had four wives and they were always fighting, while our house was peaceful and quiet. At the top end of our street there lived a well-to-do bookdealer, so comfortably off that he had an enclosed bathing area where his property adjoined the Ural. That man had two wives, but I explained to myself that his house was just as free from screaming and fighting as ours because the two women were sisters.

Despite Father's advanced views on marriage, his bride was selected for him in accordance with the custom of the time, by family arrangement. As it proved in his case, that method worked out much more joyously than often happens under the modern way. Mother too was the oldest of the children of her family—four girls and two boys—was part Bashkir and part Cossack, with many Cossack relatives. Her father was wealthy by our standards then, the heir of generations of merchants who dealt in fabrics, timber, and hides. That grandfather had traveled much outside of Russia, visited Turkey, Iran, and Arabia. Since he had made the pilgrimage to Mecca, he was a *Hadji*, the title given to Moslems who have been to the sacred city. At the end of our street, where it reached the Ural, he had a fine house, the best in our neighborhood, where sod houses were all some of the poor families could afford. That grandfather's house was two-storied—three, really, because it also had a cellar. It was full of good furniture, some brought there from Petrograd, and had shelves full of books in many languages including Russian, a tongue which most of our people resisted learning. As a result of that background, Mother was given an education rare for Tatar women, was taught reading, writing, arithmetic, and the *Tajvid*. She was, however, given no instruction in Russian, of which my father had a rough knowledge.

As I will never forget, in spite of all the years that have gone by, Mother was a very tiny and a very beautiful woman. And let me not forget that she was also very kind and gentle. That was not softness. Mother was a true frontierswoman of her era and area. She could shoot and ride a horse like a man. She also could cook anything we liked. Slim, she must have been no more than five feet two inches. She was blonde with blue, blue eyes, fair skin, and hair of gold. That hair was a wondrous thing to me. She wore it to her hips in two long braids. On holidays, as was fashionable then, she would fasten a score or so gold and silver coins to the end of each braid. And to celebrate more, each arm jingled with gold and silver bracelets set with real stones, not big, but real rubies, emeralds, alexandrites, amethysts. How lovely she was; how proud we all were of her.

When I was a very little boy Mother wore the *chapan*, as did most all our women. It was pretty, usually of the colors of the rainbow, but covering her from head to toe and with only slits at her eyes to see through. It not only hid her lovely face but was bulky and cumbersome. Then when I was six or seven, Father responded to the progressive teachings of the Crimean Tatars in more than word and teaching. He removed the *chapan* from Mother forever. From that time on she wore what Tatar women used to wear before our faith was overridden by bigotry. From then until her death, her clothing for workdays was a pleated blouse of cotton or wool and a skirt of like materials, which of course reached to the ground. For holidays she was a shining thing in bright silk blouse and skirt, with gold coins woven into the pleats of the blouse. And atop her head on those occasions was the *kalpak*, a triangle of velvet fitted just above the brow and also glittering with coins of gold. On those holidays, my father's head was just as bright with his *tubeteika* of many colors and intricate design.

As I said, Mother was a wonderful cook. And all done on spits, in pans and ovens in that huge old stove of ours. She was good at Russian dishes, borscht, soup, *piroshki*, but she was supreme with Tatar recipes. Never again have I tasted—nor will I ever expect to—anything like her *peremech*, made of chopped lamb covered with a flour meal patty and fried in butter, or her *belsh*, a covered pie of rabbit, potatoes, rice, and carrots baked in the oven. And for us children she always had *chekchek*, a baked mixture of various grain meals and honey, very sticky but very good.

Our meals were all eaten on the floor, a wooden one covered with carpets. They started with Mother bringing us warm water and soap and we washed our hands then dried them on a towel she gave us. Next we would pray in thanks. Father usually led the prayer. When he was away on his summer treks Mother did it, until at about the age of eight I took over that duty in Father's absence, having by that time learned some parts of the Koran by heart. Alas, I no longer know it so well today. We had some knives and forks, but did not use them too much. After prayer Father would cut the meat, giving a rib to each child, who would gnaw noisily. Then would come soup which we ate by spoon, then yoghurt, and finally tea. At the end, it was our custom to wash hands once more.

Not only would Mother always cook almost anything we liked, she never really scolded us, and we were not that good. Usually happy, she sang and hummed while she tended for us and worked. Then her favorite song was, "The apple becomes ripe, and when it is ripe, it falls on the throne of the Khan." She was sad and worried only when Father was away, and she would croon, "The horses do not want to cross the river. They are afraid, ayah, a human being needs a friend in the world." And when Father was later than customary coming back, her favorite was, "If you are not coming for me in the spring, my darling, I will await you in the autumn."

My earliest personal recollection, a painful one, is of my circumcision. It happened, I think, when I was about four. If I had been older I would have been suspicious, for not only Father but both grandfathers came in a carriage to the house to take me with them. We stopped at another house in the quarter where I was told I was to take off my trousers and underpants, that I was going to get new ones. Those new clothes I truly did get, but not before I had been circumcised. After it was all over they covered what was left of me with sawdust. That was the antiseptic of those days. It must have worked, though, for in a couple of days I was pronounced recovered. With that I was treated like a local hero, given anything I wanted, as well as the new clothes. At the climax, I was put back in the carriage with the older men. With a sign telling all that I had been circumcised, we toured the neighborhood. The collection of sweetmeats and fruits given me en route by friends and acquaintances of my elders made a small mountain.

When I was five I was sent to the *medrese,* the religious school, right across the street from our house and next to the mosque. Those buildings were the only stone structures in our quarter. I spent almost two years at that school studying nothing but the Koran, but learning it by heart. Once I had done that I was transferred to a Tatar elementary school, not the same one at which my father taught, but with a similar scholastic program.

It was in that period that the girl next door—on the opposite side of the house from the four fighting wives—became my first sweetheart. She was pretty, full of life, about a year or two younger than I was. I liked her. She had an oval face, dark brows, big laughing brown eyes, wore her hair long and loose to below the shoulders. Her name was Bibi-Kamal Masagutova. She was my only girl for years, but finally married a hometown boy when I was far away, at the other end of the country. She had good reason to grow tired of waiting for me. I never returned to stay.

But I did not lose Bibi-Kamal entirely. Her brother Mahmut, the best friend of my boyhood, grew up to marry the daughter of my father's brother, Bakhtiar. So we became cousins, at least. As boys, Mahmut and I were inseparable. We went to school together, fished together, cared for animals together, fought together. We Tatar boys of Orsk fought in pairs or in groups. Our enemies were not other Tatars but Russians, and we theirs. It was an unwritten rule that the Tatar boys kept to their quarter. The same held for the Russians. Even as boys we had no love for the Russians. It had been drilled into us that the Russians were the master race. They had all the administrative and white-collar jobs, the police posts and military positions of value. We Tatars were called the *inoveztsy* or *inorodtsy,* meaning the people of another religion, a different people. To combat that, our families and teachers had impressed us with the facts that all the land from the Ukraine to the Chinese border was once ours, that the Russian occupiers treated us as conquered enemies, that we had no chance for education or advancement unless we Russianized our names and denied our faith. Translated to small-boy level of those times, that atmosphere meant that if we Tatar fledglings entered the Russian quarter we had to be prepared to pay a toll of a piece of candy or fruit to the first Russian lad that encountered us. The same charge was exacted of Russian boys found in our sector. There was no Chinese wall between our peoples, but for us boys that antagonism and resentment amounted to much the same. There used to be some pretty good gang fights along the quarter borders. And woe to those who did not have the toll for passage into the enemy quarter, especially if going singly or in small numbers. After one big gang fight, one which we Tatars had won, our fathers, a bit removed from the small problems of boyhood, gave Mahmut and me the chore of taking the horses to pasture directly through the Russian quarter. Although unable to pay the toll at the time, we made it safely through the Russian area and to the pasture, only to be caught by a gang of Russians on the way back. Mahmut escaped with a black eye and some minor bruises, but I was beaten unconscious. When I came to, I felt something between my swollen lips. The Russians had stuck in my mouth the tail of a pig, the foulest trick possible to play on a properly brought up Moslem lad.

All, however, was far from small-boy tragedies with Mahmut. Our good times together far outweighed our troubles with the Russians. Almost every spring and summer we swam across the Ural from the bottoms of our fathers' properties to a small island in midstream. I learned to swim not long after I was toddling, and by the time I was eight Father had taught me to saddle a horse, to harness them or oxen to wagons, to fish and to trap small animals, especially rabbits. Besides the pleasure I got from all that, I was also of some help to the household economy. But those island swims with Mahmut were for fun only. The island was wooded and we would play Tatar and Russian, stalking each other through the trees. Or we would conceal ourselves in the undergrowth, watching the "master race" at play. The mayor had a *dacha* at the upper end of the island, an area from which we were barred. Probably if it had not been forbidden ground to us, we would have given it no attention. But the case being what it was, we would spend hours spying on the Russian officers from the garrison or important Russian government people strolling the carefully tidied and sanded walks of the proscribed area, playing tennis on the courts, or courting their ladies in more secluded spots.

Mahmut and I had another special retreat as well. That was also in woods and across the Ural, a few miles from Orsk. There in addition to his other activities, Father operated a small mill every year after harvest time. There he ground grain for the small farmers of the area, and the small percentage he received for the work supplied our family's wheat and cereal needs for the year. Mahmut and I would go to the mill with Father to help with the water gate and unloading the grain and bagging the meal. But we had plenty of spare time to scamper off to a small Cossack *sta-*

*nitsa* nearby. In that settlement we both had many "uncles" and "aunts," all really quite distant relatives who nevertheless welcomed their young kinfolk, told them stories, and stuffed them with good things to eat. Part of the delight in visiting that area near the mill was that like the island in the Ural, it, too, was in large part off limits to us Tatars. From the time of the original Russian occupation on, it had been known as the "Commandant's Forest," even though the name of that original commandant was long forgotten and no successor ever claimed it. That place was also of interest to us boys in the early summer. We knew every secret clearing where I still think the finest wild strawberries in the world ripened into an unforgettable sweetness.

Since only the very young and the very old regret the ending of the year, the sole somewhat unhappy season for us boys was the autumn. Then not only was the wide ranging of the outdoors being taken from us once again, but also our chores increased. We had to gather straw and hay for winter forage for the animals. We had to prowl the woods collecting twigs and fallen branches and we were often chased from both fields and woods by angry owners. The worst job of all was making the winter's supply of fuel for our stove. The chief ingredient was cow manure or the droppings of other animals. We would pile ordure of that kind, pour water over it, and then stamp on it, much like grapes are pressed, until it softened. I can still feel it coming up between the toes of my bare feet. And I can still smell it. Next we would mix straw into that mess, let the mixture set for a while, and then form it into bricks. The final work was to stack those bricks in neat, big piles near the door of our house. Disagreeable as the work was for us children, I must confess that those briquets made fine fuel indeed.

Winters for which we thus prepared were very real. I appreciate the tendency of people in arctic and temperate climes the world over to recall the snows of their childhood as monumental, simply because at that age drifts might have been double one's height. Despite that, Orsk, because of its deep continental location, experienced during my boyhood, and still experiences, winter and summer in the extreme. The first snows came early in November. Until late April blizzards howled day and night, often weeks long. Sometimes the snow was so deep, was falling so heavily, that grown people ran the danger of losing their way and perishing in drifts. Usually at those times, it was the custom to put a big red flag up over the mosque. It was also flown when the temperature dropped below minus forty degrees Celsius. That was a warning for everybody of all ages in our quarter to stay in their houses. Even for us, just across the street, praying at the mosque was dispensed with until the red flag came down. In those periods our family and other faithful in our quarter prayed just as regularly and religiously in our homes. But winters for us children were far from matters of just prayer and hard work. True, we fed the animals, cleaned them and their stalls, did not neglect our studies and devotion, even when snowbound. There remained much time close together with the family to make winter for us children more pleasure than hardship. That was when Father told and retold us of the glorious history of our people, of the invincible courage, gallant deeds of the great Khans, of their uncountable wealth and armies and their magnificent cities to the south and east. Over and over, Mother told us the *Thousand and One Nights*, never tiring of my special favorite, "Sinbad the Sailor."

Those long but happy winters always had to end. That time came with the thaws, which we knew had really arrived when we heard the great booms and explosive cracking of the ice breaking on the Ural at the bottom of our land. Then too there was a chore, that of hauling pieces of the ice floes to restock our "refrigerator" for another summer.

Although not easy, that was welcome work, because it meant the coming of spring. From the time that I was eight I did that chore with real joy because I knew that soon school would be out and I would be going with Father on his long and wonderful treks into the hills and valleys of the Kirghiz people. Slowly but surely the days became warmer, the snow started to melt, the rivers to swell. Then would come the day when on return from school, Father would go to the stall to inspect his wagon, a big, four-wheeled vehicle, a sort of prairie schooner of our time and area. He would examine the wheels and canvas, have me grease hubs and the iron turning circles of the front steering. Muttering to himself, he would look over the horses, deciding on their condition and his load and whether to take the usual two or a third to serve as a spare. And just before the start there was the trip to the market, the haggling with the merchants to buy the goods that we would trade. Then came the stowing of pounds and pounds of tea, sugar, salt, gunpowder, rifle, pistol and shotgun ammunition, hundreds of spools of threads of many colors and thicknesses, hundreds and hundreds of buttons, fancy and plain, bars and bars of soap, many, many meters of fabrics, candies, writing paper and ink, flours. Finally, Father would clean and lubricate his rifle, his shotgun, and six-shooter pistol, check ammunition—not all the Kirghiz were simple nomads—clean and repair the fishing gear, check our first-aid kit (no more than a small bottle of iodine and a few pieces of clean cloth for bandages).

By that time, at night I could hardly sleep. I dreamed about sleeping instead under open skies, of fishing, hunting, picking wild berries, making our own fires, preparing our meals, finding new birds and animals, riding, riding, riding, swimming, eating and drinking with the Kirghiz according to their fashion, gnawing lamb and mutton around open fires, drinking with them the little *kumiss*, the man's drink of our people, allowed me. How excited I was.

In the end, just after the first flowers had bloomed, the great day came. I would harness the horses to the loaded wagon. Father would make a short prayer. Mother would cry and kiss me. Little brothers and sisters would wave. From the wagon seat, Father and I would wave back and we were off, to be gone until harvest time.

Father had no plan, no schedule. He just seemed to know where the wandering Kirghiz would be. Sometimes we started east from Orsk, sometimes north. Usually at least once on those treks we would pass through Aydyrlinsky to see Father's two brothers, both gold prospectors. Those two uncles were pretty rabid Socialists, anxious for a way out of Tsarist oppression and calling for open revolution. I remember long nights of their arguments with Father and their telling him, "Comrade, rise up, rise up, there is nothing for us to lose but our chains, rise up." That was the radical side of the family. Generally, we would also visit the conservative side during those summers by passing through Novo Orsk, the home of most of the Cossack relatives of my mother. Those uncles were true cavalrymen—rough, militant, careless, adventurous, and loyal to the last drop of their blood to the monarch, whom they called the "White Tsar." True, they were Moslems and regarded themselves as of pure Tatar stock. But first they were Cossacks. They had the best horses, owned the best land along the Ural and its tributaries, were officers. They had their own *ataman*, ruled their own *stanitsa*, and were ready to fight for the Tsar any time, any place. They treated me generously at their settlements, taught me horsemanship, and hinted with huge laughs that I was getting old enough to have a Cossack girl. At times I was confused, torn by the conflicting ideas of my gentle father who desired only Tatar liberation and Moslem progress, my Socialist uncles urging revolution, and my Cossack uncles and their romantic, easygoing ways. But I did not let that conflict trouble me too much. I was still a boy, healthy and relatively unconcerned with the troubles of a man's world.

In those times there were no roads for those treks with Father, only trails. Nor were there any bridges over the rivers and streams. We forded all waters. If they were too high because of late spring thaws in the higher Urals or heavy rains, we just camped at the shallower spots and waited for the water to go down.

Even though Father had no plan—after all, being nomads, the Kirghiz themselves could not have given their exact location at any given time—he seemed to know where to find them by some sort of extra sense. The first night out of Orsk we would spend under open skies in some wooded valley near a river. After tending the horses we would fish. Our gear might make modern sportsmen smile. The rods were cut from any sapling. The lines were made from the hairs of our horses' tails. The floats were cork or cane bits, and the lures were ordinary flies, hoppers, or worms. But fish we caught and plenty for our needs, usually all coarse: yellow perch, cats, pike, carp, bream, sunfish. Only in the high Ural's streams did we get trout and other game fish. The fish caught, we would make a fire, prepare a tasty chowder, and then to bed under blankets in the wagon, or under the stars if the night were going to be clear.

Father's chief hobbies were hunting, fishing, and trapping foxes and other small animals. As result of that, we ate well on the treks. He was also an excellent woodsman and seemed to know more about weather than many modern meteorologists. It was always interesting to watch that skill of his. Before choosing a camping place he would check the wind direction, scan the skies, look for sites sheltered by trees or overhanging rocks and near clear running water.

Once, well up in the hills, Father camped near an old Kirghiz cemetery, then went to a stream below to fish. Just after he had left me by the wagon a great eagle came swooping low. Being left by the cemetery in the early evening had frightened me enough, but I said nothing. The eagle, however, was too much. I had heard too many stories of eagles carrying children away, and raced down to my father at the stream. Wiping my tears away, he distracted me by drawing my attention to the trout, coursing by in great number. The he told me there was no truth in what I may have heard about cemeteries, eagles, and like terrors I had learned of from other boys and old *mullahs*. I listened and believed. I always believed Father. It was he who had had me vaccinated by a doctor against smallpox, a step regarded at that time as very dangerous, if not in defiance of God. Father had been right then, for me, my brothers, and sisters were the few children in our quarter to escape an epidemic unscarred. The old *mullahs* had spoken against vaccination, had recommended *muskas*, "special" prayers on "special" paper in "special" ink, prepared by them, of course for a fee, then folded triangularly, put in a leather pouch, and worn around the neck. Father, despite his deep reverence for the faith, hated those *mullahs*. I can still hear him hold forth against them: "Those scoundrels. They make cheap our religion. They make sick our children. They make ridiculous our women. They make our people obedient servants of the Tsar. One day they will pay dearly."

Always within the first two or three days after departure from Orsk we would encounter our first Kirghiz settlement. Those encampments were pitched in open pasture land near water. They varied in size from five to fifty *yurts*. The size of the encampments had no relation to the wealth of the groups. That depended upon the industry of the individual members of the various tribes. I have no idea how many people may have been in each settlement because it was the custom then for each Kirghiz man to have at least two or three wives and tens of children. Sometimes an encampment would stay in the same area all summer long if there were enough grass for grazing their hundreds and hundreds of horses, cows, goats, and sheep. At other times a group would move on just for the pure pleasure of going somewhere else. They were a nomadic people and loved their freedom and their life in the open.

Once we had run into the first settlement, we always learned where the next one was and progressed that way by word of mouth throughout the summer. How hospitable were those Kirghiz and how good they were to children. It was their custom to feed and house visitors for days, weeks, months, until the visitors themselves decided to leave. They put food, mainly hunks of lamb or mutton, directly into the mouths of their guests with their own hands. I very soon became acquainted with their goodness. Practically immediately on arrival at an encampment, I would vault off the wagon and run into the arms of the women who petted me and stuffed me with sweets.

Father's affairs were more serious. He would display the goods in the wagon. A barter struck, he would exchange buttons, ammunition, or salt for hides—usually cow, horse, sheep, or goat but sometimes fox and ermine—the preserved butter of the Kirghiz, or their hard, round balls of cheese made of the milk of sheep or goats. Father usually loaded the fine pelts he received on the wagon. For the other exchanges he kept books and had agreements—never broken—with those Kirghiz that they would deliver those articles to him in Orsk once the grazing season was over. Since he was an *imam*, Father would also conduct marriage, burial, and other rites and receive small fees for those services as well.

Such were those wonderful summers of my boyhood. At their ends, back we would go to Orsk to have Mother welcome us, first with tears of gladness because she always feared we might run afoul of the few bad Kirghiz—the highwaymen—next with laughter and smiles, and finally with the most welcome and first real food we had had in months.

A few weeks after our return into town came the Kirghiz bearing the goods they had agreed on with Father. He enjoyed the *kumiss* drinking that was part of those occasions. My poor mother, however, dreaded the flow of Kirghiz. A careless people, they were far from clean, tracked much dirt into her house, and many were full of fleas and lice. She also feared that they did not know that our rule of hospitality did not call for them staying as long as they wanted.

When I was about six, great apprehension came upon our people. The skies flared with a great light—except for the sun, the brightest I have ever seen in the heavens. It was a shooting star that I learned years later was Halley's Comet. My father and other educated people recognized it as a perfectly natural phenomenon, but the old *mullahs* used the comet to frighten further the already terrified and superstitious majority. Those poor people were told that the end of the world or something almost as awful was approaching. Nothing such as that happened, of course, but the warnings of those *mullahs* caused a long period of gloom and dread. That depression continued for several years with the result that the coming of the World War was greeted by many as no more than the final fulfillment of the warning that direful things were to come.

I, myself, as hostilities broke out, was more concerned with entering the Russian Tatar school. That gave me my first opportunity to learn Russian and of the master race. The all-Russian schools of Orsk were virtually closed to us Tatars. Only the few well-to-do families among us could afford the uniforms and other costs of sending children there. Or else we had to deny our faith and Russianize our names. But to me, then, even the second best of the Russian Tatar school was welcome. Father had long drilled into me the necessity of education and I truly wanted one. One of my teachers at that school, Lebedova, and I think her first name was Klara, cast a new light on some Russians for me. Her subject was history, and although she was Russian, she taught us truly of the past greatness of the Tatar and other Turkic people, of our subjugation by the Russians, and all without scorn, more in sadness. Somewhat moon-faced, she was not unattractive. Her kindness and fairness interested me more than her looks, however, and I became her young admirer. Because of her my horizons expanded. I visited a few Russian homes and made friends with some of the Russian boys with whom I once fought.

Father did not have the same distraction from war. Mobilization had started. They were even beginning to round up the Kirghiz—proud, independent people whom the Tsars had never before brought into their armed forces for fear they might turn their weapons on their rulers. They were given no weapons this time, either, but were sent as labor troops to the fronts to dig trenches and fortifications. Thousands of them perished there in misery. Watching all that, Father knew that his time to be called up would come too. In an effort to forestall that he went north to the city of Beloretsk. There he got a job as a laborer at the steel mills, work that he thought would be classed as essential enough to keep him out of the army.

For some months Father would send most of his pay and greetings back to us in Orsk. Then one day a letter came telling that he had been called into the army. He said his refusal to go to the southern front to fight the Turks, related to his own people and of his own faith, had been honored. Instead he was being sent to Galicia. His regiment was mostly Tatars and he told Mother not to worry because he was to be the *imam*, or chaplain, of the regiment, and therefore in less danger than others.

That failed, absolutely, to console Mother. Tearing at her hair and bosom, she rushed sobbing into the street to tell neighbors of Father's fate. Few of them, poor souls, had much solace for her, since their husbands and sons were also leaving for the war. With that there ended forever, although I knew it not then, my happy, innocent days with Father, our treks to the camps of the Kirghiz. And since Father's departure for the front made me the eldest male of our family, so ended my childhood.

# 2

## Revolution

On a cold, snowy day in December 1917, Father returned. Then in his late thirties, he looked ten years older. His hair was streaked with gray. He was still in uniform, still carried his rifle, and had bandoliers of ammunition across his shoulders and chest. Mother cried and cried. She tried to be happy, but she was too worried about Father's gauntness and loss of weight.

After he had eaten and had brought out the *kumiss*, Father told his tale. Until the summer of that year, his regiment had fought in Galicia and well. Then officers began to disappear. Perhaps some of them had been murdered. Next, soldiers' committees were formed, the regiment stopped fighting, and disintegrated. Many soldiers rode military freight trains to Petrograd. He joined some of them. In Petrograd everybody was speaking, holding meetings, marching. There was great disorder. He was afraid that Orsk was having troubles, too, and he worried about the family. He decided to go home, but that had not been easy. No trains were running on schedule. Even the freights were packed with soldiers doing the same as he was, trying to get home. He had stayed in Moscow for a while. Finally, after many freight train rides, some only for a few miles, and much walking, he had squeezed aboard a freight headed for Orsk.

At that time, although the Bolsheviks had already taken over in Petrograd and Moscow, the Provisional Government still controlled Orsk. There were no special troubles in the town, but, as elsewhere, all administration had broken down. That was serious for our family because it meant that all schools were closed. Father had no work until early in 1918, when a friend got him a job as a guard at the factory of the government vodka monopoly. Extra guards were needed because there had been looting.

My school too, of course, had been closed since summer of 1917, but I had not been idle. Until Father returned, my chores at home had taken much of my time, but not all of it. I used the few remaining hours at outside work, small jobs to be sure, but my first work for others and my first earnings. Mother was very proud of me. One job was at the library which had not been closed, where I helped at putting the returned books back on the shelves. But the job I really liked was one as messenger for Tatar nationalists. For a few brief months, those poor idealists were deluded with the dream that with the Tsar gone the Tatar people would be independent. They were of the short-lived Idel (Volga)-Ural group, who wanted an independent state north of the Caspian Sea up to Kazan. Being Tatar myself, my teen-age imagination ran wild and I too believed that we might regain our freedom. Had not the Bolsheviks themselves guaranteed that late in 1917 by their declaration of rights for all people of Russia, the rights of equality and independence, of self-determination and secession, plus the abolition of all national privileges and restrictions, and the free development of all national minorities?

That promise was dangled before us, the minorities, only to get us to support the Bolsheviks. It was broken in the spring of 1918, so far as we were concerned, by their central executive committee decree that proclaimed formation of a Tatar-Bashkir Republic, an act that brought the national administration of the Idel-Ural to an abrupt end, and with that stopped my messenger work. Nor did the Bolsheviks take any steps to make good their second promise, the formation of a Tatar-Bashkir Republic.

Instead, in the spring of 1918, all we in Orsk got was a takeover of the town by the Red Cavalry and the speedy set up of a local soviet. Those Red irregulars with their bobtailed horses descended on us like locusts from across the Ural. For a while Cossacks, among them many of my uncles, held out against the Reds. The Cossacks were units of Ataman Aleksandr Ilyich Dutov, who had controlled all of our area from the provincial capital, the town of Orenburg, to the west. During that Red attack, for a few days, some of my uncles manned a battery of horse-drawn three-inch guns, drawn up at the bottom of our street and firing across the Ural River at Red positions in the woods on the other side.

That was a terrifying time for my family. Red guns, returning the fire of the Cossack battery, sent shells screaming up our street. None of us or our neighbors was seriously injured, as I can recall, but we all expected the worst. During that firing Father collected us in our "refrigerator," the lowest ground available. We crouched there whimpering. Father prayed.

Well-chilled but unharmed, we came out after the Cossacks

surrendered the town to the Reds. Father went back to the vodka factory only to find that it had been shut down and that he was again out of work. That time the plant was really being looted. Father, too, took a dozen bottles. When he brought them home, he muttered *haram, haram* (forbidden), in shame. He also said *haram* when he sold that vodka. To do that was *haram*, too. I also found myself unemployed. With the coming of the Reds the library closed on order, to reopen later with Red personnel. That was a hard time, but we did not starve. We had our garden and our animals.

Terrifying as the time was for my family, it was even more terrifying for the country as a whole. The fighting in Orsk between Reds and Cossacks was but a part of the larger struggle, the Great Civil War then enveloping the land and destined to leave an unforgettable imprint on the history of the world.

The Bolsheviks, having overthrown the Provisional Government under Kerensky, set out brutally to communize the people and the land. They thereby provoked the fierce resistance of the White Armies under Tsarist generals such as Denikin, Yudenich, Kornilov, Krasnov, Baron Wrangel, and Admiral Kolchak. These sought to crush the new Soviet regime and to restore Tsarism.

It was a bloody struggle in which millions were killed or maimed, or perished from hunger; in which fathers fought sons and brothers fought brothers; in which families were separated, properties were confiscated, grain and cattle requisitioned. The whole country was left in ruins, the economy in chaos. But Russia again became unified, to be ruled soon by the Red Tsar, Joseph Stalin, in comparison with whom the White Tsar Nicholas II would look, indeed, like a true saint.

In our part of that Civil War, in midsummer of 1918, Orsk was retaken by the Cossacks. Again an artillery battery, this time Red, was positioned at the end of our street. Again shells, Cossack, whistled above us. Once more we crouched in the "refrigerator" while Father prayed. Nor were we harmed this time either, although a house on our street was badly damaged by an incoming shell. When we ventured forth after the firing had stopped, we found two workers from the vodka factory hanged from lamp posts in the commercial quarter. Why they had been killed nobody knew, although some said they had been sniping at the Cossacks.

The rest of that year with the Cossacks there we had quiet, but life was not normal. There was no work for Father or me, no school for me. Nobody knew what was going on in the rest of the country. There were many rumors, none of them good.

That lull, because that was all it proved to be, ended for good for my family on a day in February 1919. It was a very cold day, and snowing heavily. Toward dusk we heard firing from across the river and to the west of town. Some of my uncles galloped up to our house. They told Father that Dutov had been defeated in Orenburg by the Reds. His Cossacks, they said, were retreating through Orsk, trying to get to Siberia to join other anti-Bolshevik forces. We must come with them, they told Father, unless we wanted more of the Bolsheviks.

By that time it was night. It was still snowing. Father looked very tired and grim, but he agreed to go. He sent me to the sheds to see to the horses. He told Mother to assemble all the warm clothing she could and some cooking equipment. Within an hour we had hitched a *troika* to our sledge, piled ourselves and a few belongings aboard it and were off.

The next day we passed through Novo Orsk. Many of my younger Cossack uncles there had already gone with the main Dutov forces, now many hours ahead of our slow sledge. Most of those had left behind their wives and children. The families were sad and there was crying for those handsome, dashing, brave uncles of mine. None of us expected to see them again, nor did we. Years later we learned what had happened to them. A great horde of some one hundred and fifty thousand—including wives and children—when it swept through Novo Orsk that long-ago winter, that Dutov force had been cut to thirty thousand by sickness, starvation, and Bolshevik irregulars when a year later it crossed into western China and an unknown fate.

When we had left Orsk, our ultimate destination had been Troitsk, more than 250 miles to the north and east, to the east of the Urals. With the handicaps of the slow and heavily loaded sledge, continuing snow, and poor trails, we never made a third of that distance. Day by day we and other stragglers fell farther and farther behind the fighting Cossacks. Finally, more than a week out of Orsk and not far from Aydyrlinsky, where we had argued with those gold-prospecting, Socialist brothers of Father during those happy summer treks of the past, we reached the end of our road. Ahead of us, across a ridgeline at the horizon, raced a troop of cavalrymen. Their horses' tails were bobbed. They were Reds. We had fallen too far to the rear of our Cossacks and were cut off. Without a word Father turned the *troika* around and we headed back.

Next week, again in Novo Orsk, Mother's relatives persuaded my parents to stay there, not to return to Orsk. They pointed out that there would be no work for Father at home and, besides, they needed teachers in Novo Orsk. Dejected, Father was not hard to persuade. He became the teacher at the Novo Orsk elementary school. My Mother, freed from much of her household work by my sisters then approaching their teens, also was given work teaching there on a part-time basis. Even after Father started teaching again I did not feel that he was truly happy, but he tried to adjust himself to the changes. After Dutov left the area the Reds, of course, moved in. Building walls blossomed with a proclamation of amnesty by Lenin coupled with a plea that all return to work for the good of themselves and the country. Father did his best to believe that wall writing and, if not cooperate with it, at least not oppose it.

Being a lad, I was much more hopeful and much more gullible. For me the end of the worst of the troubles meant a return to school. I was sent to Novo Orsk's Cossack Russian school. Called the Vysshaya Nachalnaya Shkola, it was the equivalent of high school. I was greatly pleased that the teaching was in Russian, and that I was thereby getting an opportunity to improve my Russian. I also liked going back to school because, never doubting Father's advice about the value of an education, I had worried that the troubles kept me from school for so long. And more than all that I wanted to be with people my own age again, to join them in the new things opening for youngsters in those changing times. I guess that was mainly ambition that today would better be described as the wish to get in on the ground floor.

And as I said, I was gullible. I believed Lenin's writing, "The tasks of the proletariat cannot be carried out unless the rights of self-determination are championed." I believed his promises of peace, bread, land distribution to the peasants, of equality and independence for the national minorities. Besides, the Bolsheviks promised the young people good educational opportunities and jobs.

Therefore, with that naiveté plus my ambition, perhaps I can be excused joining the ranks of the Reds voluntarily, in fact enthusiastically, at that school in Novo Orsk. One day in the spring of 1919 a young man come to the school. Wearing a handsome black leather coat and a Mauser pistol at his hip, he was recruiting for the Komsomol, the newly formed youth organization of the Bolsheviks. Then fifteen, I was one of the first of the dozen who joined in my class of sixty boys. That evening, however, when I told Father about my joining, he approved it only because he felt I had to. He told me once more about the necessity for education, grasped me by the shoulders and said, looking into my eyes, "Then, after you have learned about the world we live in, become independent and strong, act according to your own conscience and beliefs. That is what I wish for my son. Promise me you will do your best." I did so, with all the solemnity of my youth.

Father rationalized my joining the Komsomol with the hope it would open the road to education to me. But he would have been disturbed if I had told him—which I never did—the whole truth about my joining. When I filled in the application form I exploited my budding knowledge of Red jargon to describe myself as a son of the proletariat, making much of Father's mobilization dodge, his work at the Beloretsk steel mill. I never mentioned, of course, that he was a teacher and a trader. Most of all did I bury the fact that he was an *imam*. Or perhaps Father might have merely smiled at that youthful deceit, but I do know that he would not have liked it, or me for doing it.

My fortunes may have been improving in Novo Orsk, but those of Father went the other direction. By mid-1918 the Bolsheviks replaced the regular *ataman* there with one following Red doctrine. That brought the end of my parents' work at the school, which was Sovietized.

In the fall of 1919, therefore, Father moved the family back to Orsk. He felt that even if he found no work there, he at least had his home, his garden, and his animals. Surprising as it may be to others unfamiliar with our people, our house was in perfect shape. So were our animals. Our neighbors had taken care of all.

As he had expected, Father got no work in Orsk. No Communist had anything for a teacher-trader-*imam*, nor would my father have anything to do with the Communists. In contrast, my horizon continued to brighten.

I was transferred to the Russian high school in Orsk. My Komsomol membership was also transferred, and I became one of the most active of my fellows in proselytizing for new members among my old friends. That work was well noted. The Orsk city soviet was recruiting candidates for the Oriental Institute, the former Tatar Teachers College in Orenburg, taken over by the Communists to spread the movement among the people of Turkistan. I immediately applied for the institute. The Komsomol sponsored my application, which was granted almost on the spot.

On the day of departure Father got out the wagon and took me, plus Mother, brothers, and sisters to the railroad station, in those days some ten miles out of Orsk. This was the first time I had left home alone, completely on my own resources. Mother was almost heartbroken, as if Orenburg were at the other end of the world instead of 150 miles to the west. There was much crying and much final kissing on the parts of Mother, my brothers, and sisters. My Father blessed me, said, "Go and study. Study anything, Arabic, Chinese, but study and be something. It is time for you to be a man. Be firm."

The freight train that was to be my transport finally arrived. Mother passed me a basket of fried chicken, bread, and yoghurt as the train started moving. Then she, my brothers, and sisters ran alongside the track, waving and calling farewells, until they could no longer keep up with the train.

I was sad but I was not alone. In the cattle car with me were nine other Tatar boys from Orsk, all about my age, the other Komsomol-selected candidates for the Orenburg Institute. Like me, they too had had tearful partings from relatives at the trackside.

At that time, in that way, it took two days for the trip from Orsk to Orenburg since the train stopped almost everywhere, not only at stations, but even in the open country wherever a few people had collected alongside the tracks. That was the only "rapid" transit of the era.

For us ten boys, all schoolmates, the dejection caused by leaving families did not last long. We were quickly distracted by the scenery, the hills, and plains we passed by, all of which were completely new to us. Urged on by sympathetic elder fellow passengers, we soon started singing Tatar songs. Regarding ourselves as young revolutionaries, we sang rather more than that which was pleasurable to the others, "Hey, Tatar, arise, awake. Remember who took the last food from your mouth." In between those bursts we also amused others and ourselves with old love songs such as, "Galia, my beautiful sweetheart, I'm so in love with you that I'm just a skeleton. I'm not eating, drinking, or breathing, only thinking of you," and, of course, the songs our mothers had taught.

At Orenburg our ten walked the mile or so from the station to the institute. For me, at least, that walk was a fascination, not a chore. Under Tsars as well as commissars, Orenburg was regarded as the gateway to Turkistan, and special efforts were therefore made to improve its appearance. On that walk, I, then a pure country boy, with mouth literally open, saw my first electric lights, my first paved streets, my first fine administrative and dwelling buildings.

Mustered in at the institute, a boarding school, we were assigned bunks, blankets, small night tables, and were given books. Our studies were mathematics, physics, chemistry, plus— since the purpose of the institute was to train teachers and propagandists to be sent to Turkistan on graduation—much political indoctrination. Before our studies actually started we were all assembled and told, "You will be messengers of Soviet goodwill to Turkistan, the Caucasus, or wherever you will be sent, on whatever mission." The curriculum also included some emphasis on the history of the Tatars and related peoples, on Persian, and elementary Arabic. The latter because we were told we were at the gateway, not only of Turkistan, but of the whole Middle East, so much did the old imperialism continue under a new name. And of course we spent considerable time on Communist economic theory and the history of the Party.

Concentrated as our work was at the institute, it was not all study. On weekends we would go in groups out into the countryside to help in potato harvesting or work on new roads or other reconstruction projects. Thus we were among the first of the now so common Communist youth brigades, the same device later used by Hitler and other dictators to win over and control the youth. At my age then, I, of course, attached no political significance to those outings; in fact, as did most youth later elsewhere, I enjoyed them very much.

My particular pleasure during that year at the institute came when the Komsomol nominated me a candidate member of the Russian Communist Party. At the age of sixteen I had attained political majority and recognition. I was so proud that I almost thought of myself as an old Bolshevik.

Later that year shortly after graduation, my class was informed that we were to be sent to the Tashkent area for our first work with the people, a sort of probation. My group was headed by a tall, skinny Tatar lad with blue eyes and red hair, who, for a Tatar, had the unusual name of Hay. I remember him distinctly because he was not only secretary of the Communist Party organization of the institute, but was also very much the activist.

Upon our selection we were told we were to consider ourselves the advance guard of the Party, with the sacred duty of accelerating the Sovietization of Turkistan. We were briefed to conduct ourselves cautiously and direct our efforts and agitation towards inducing the peasants and the lower ranks of Moslem clergy to side with the Bolsheviks. Our instructors read us this from Lenin's letter to G. K. Ordzhonikidze, Caucasian Bolshevik leader: "Once again I ask you to act cautiously, and not to fail in showing goodwill towards Moslems, especially when entering Dagestan. Stress in every way and moreover most solemnly your sympathies for Moslems, their autonomy, independence, and the like."

Lest we be naive about that Lenin advice for the takeover of the Moslem area of the Caucasus, our leader Hay then took the floor and said substantially this: "Comrades, of course all of you realize that any religion is an opiate, and as such is incompatible with Marxism. No one formulated this matter more precisely than Lenin. You must not be confused with the Party's demands to win the confidence of peasantry and lesser clergy in Turkistan by whatever artifice necessary, and the incompatibility of Islam, the most reactionary of all religions, with communism. You must understand that our effort to win confidence is a temporary, tactical move to gain allies. If the devil himself is of some interest to us, we must win his confidence. The incompatibility of our movement with religion is a matter of strategy." That was my first introduction to Communist deceit, and I have never heard it expressed more clearly, even later in life.

Instructions and briefings completed, we were given a few days' leave for farewell visits to our families before departure for Tashkent. Again by freight train I went back to Orsk. To my surprise, I found our house closed and vacant. I have never been a faithful letter writer, and I was a very poor one indeed during that year at the Orenburg Institute. I admit now with great shame and regret that I never wrote home once in all that time. My family, I understood later, believed that my silence meant that letters from them to me might embarrass me. The empty house there told me something, that my Father had not been able to make a living in Orsk. I had hoped to please him with announcement of my candidate Party membership and an account of my new work. Abruptly my little successes had become trifling compared to the troubles of my family. Depressed, I went down the street to the fine house of my mother's father to find out what had happened. There I met misery, too. That once busy, happy place had only two occupants, my grandfather and one goat. His beard and hair pure white, long, and unkempt, the old man was crying and reading the Koran. Gone were his sons with Dutov, forever. Gone, too, were his daughters and his other grandchildren to the *stanitsa* at Novo Orsk. There, too, he told me, had gone my family, where Father had found some work as *imam* to the few faithful who remained. My grandfather had been keeping a vigil for return of his sons and had reached the end of his strength. He gave me a few books for Father which I took with me to Novo Orsk.

Despite my thoughtlessness of the intervening year my family smothered its anxieties and received me with joy. Both crying and smiling, Mother took me in her arms, exclaimed at how I had grown, then cooked me *belch, peremech,* and *chekchek* until I thought I would burst. Father blessed me, shared *kumiss* with me and listened to my small accounts of myself. At the end he said only, "God bless you. Perhaps it is necessary that you go." Of course I did not know it then, but that was the last I was to see of my family. I wish I could remember more, but I cannot. Three days passed, then my father got out the wagon, the same wagon of our treks, and took me to the railroad station outside Orsk. That time the rest of the family did not accompany me. True, the round-trip ride was long, but the absence of my mother, brothers, and sisters, reduced to little more than wards of the old Cossacks, should have shown me how much our ways had parted. At the station Father blessed me on departure. For the first time, however, he gave me no final advice. Probably he thought I was beyond his reach.

Shortly after return to Orenburg, whatever qualms of conscience that may have affected me in Novo Orsk were forgotten. I was too excited, too distracted with the voyage into new lands, with the departure for Tashkent. Packing certainly was no problem. All I had was a small wooden "suitcase" for change of shirts and underwear. With our group of twenty we carried a communal tea kettle.

That great trip to new worlds started on a warm August morning in 1921. For me it was a luxury voyage, and the first time I had ever ridden in the passenger car of a train. Our compartment was a "hard" one, with wooden seats and bunks above for eight passengers, but to me then that was wonderful. And although the train went at a speed of never more than thirty to thirty-five miles an hour, that was the fastest I had ever travelled. I fought for a place at the window to feel the wind streaming against my face and through my hair.

The two days of crossing the great steppes of Kazakhstan would be dull to me now. For a seventeen-year-old, however, every station, every stop of the many we made was a new and intriguing experience. Even before the brakes had stopped grinding, out we would pile into the stations to look, to ask questions, to buy fried chicken or lamb, bread, cake, or hot water for our tea kettle from the peasants who used to throng to those places before they were put out of business by Sovietization.

Near the halfway mark we touched the shores of the Aral, my first sea. At the end of the third day we saw glimmering far to the east and south, on the very edge of the horizon, the snowcapped peaks of the Tien-Shan range, my first sight of perpetually snow-covered mountains. So many firsts in so short a time. On the morning of the fourth day we saw Tashkent Valley, brilliant with huge green fields and gardens in the rainbow of colors of the south. What pleasure and beauty after the bleakness and sameness of the steppes! The air was cleanly fresh and filled with the aroma of fruit trees and flowers. There were vineyards heavy with grapes and there was water rushing everywhere along countless *ariks* or into an occasional big *havuz*. We were entering the land of cotton, of fruit, of silk, of the best *karakul* in the world. We were entering the heart of Russian Central Asia. Overcome with the richness, I said, and will always say: "Salute to you, sunny Uzbekistan."

We were met at the Tashkent station by a representative of the People's Commissariat for Education and taken in a horse-drawn wagon to the old part of the city called Sheikhan-Tavur, unfortunately since razed by the Communists. En route we passed through the new or Russian quarter, which seemed to us a most beautiful city with fine shops and buildings, with broad avenues, bordered at either side by open ditches of running, clear water, and tall poplar trees. Sight of that area made Orenburg, which we had thought a considerable place, seem like a village. Compared with the scarcities of food and other commodities caused in the north by the Revolution, Tashkent looked like a paradise. So much fruit in the stalls, so much to buy. Private trade was flourishing. Nationalization had not yet reached the south.

It was plain that the new town had been designed for the Russian masters who conquered the region in 1865. Comparatively, Sheikhan-Tavur, although colorful, was a sorry place, left as it had been almost since the seventh century for the original masters, the Uzbeks. The old quarter had no electricity. Its streets were winding, narrow, impassable at many places for modern traffic. The houses were of sod or of baked mud bricks, were flat-roofed and looked, windowless, onto the streets. And the fact that we arrived there on an afternoon in the month of Ramadan, the Moslem month of fasting from sunrise to sunset, did not improve our impression. The streets were empty, shops closed, as we were taken to our quarters in a *medrese* near a mosque.

At sunset, however, that quiet ended crashingly with the boom of the cannons that marked the end of that day of fasting and withdrawal from the public. Stores and shops were flung open, peddlers hawked their wares. Seas of people surged onto the streets to spend the night eating, talking, buying, strolling. There were men on horseback, on camels, on donkeys, many in costumes from areas I did not then know, costumes which have long since disappeared under Soviet rule.

Since the Uzbeks then were very devout, our group too did not go abroad until after sunset. Even though we had been told religion was an opiate, we had also been told to behave ourselves properly and not offend the beliefs of the local populace. We also strolled and gawked during the night. We too sat in *chay khanes* or tea houses sipping green tea, lulled by the musical murmur of the water coursing through the *ariks*. For the first time we saw and tasted many delicious things. There were apricots, peaches, cherries, watermelons, other melons with white, aromatic, juicy meat. There were those Uzbek culinary delights, tasty *pilaus* and kabobs. And there was much also good which I did not know. Within a very short time we started to appreciate the southern way of life. Despite that enjoyment we experienced great discomfort at first. We, accustomed to hard winters and cool nights, even during the hot summers, had difficulty sleeping in the hot nights of Tashkent until we acclimated ourselves.

We did not, however, stay long with that conglomeration of humanity among those many mosques, minarets, and covered bazaars. Tashkent proved to be only one of several way stations. Within a few days after arrival there we were again put on a train, that time for Samarkand. We passed through narrow gorges, with dark, rugged rocks towering on either side, then burst into the fertile valley of the River Zaravshan, meaning Shower of Gold. That stream is fed by the mighty glaciers of the Kuhistan Mountains, whose peaks loom down on Samarkand from the east. That city of Tamerlane, that we had heard so much about from our families, that city once made a center of arts, sciences, and poetry by Tamerlane's grandson, Ulu-beg, was a vast disappointment to us. Overrun by the Russians in 1868, it was merely another Russian city. True, Ragistan, the spacious *maidan*, or square, and the great buildings surrounding it were still there. So was the tomb of Tamerlane, which we stood by silently, unable to conjure up the past because nothing else remained of it. Disappointed, we roamed the rest of the town visiting shops filled with fresh and dried fruits, bright fabrics, hides, carpets, all still privately run. Uzbekistan was not then a Soviet republic. It was not even a Socialist republic, just a plain peoples' republic.

As in Tashkent, our stay in Samarkand lasted only a few days. We were once more put on a train, that time for Bukhara, which was to be the final destination of our group. On arrival at the ancient city, second only to Mecca as a holy place for Islam, I learned the facts behind our stopovers in Tashkent and Samarkand. We would never have had the pleasure of seeing those two other cities had not the Bolsheviks been having trouble elsewhere in what had been the Emirate of Bukhara. The Emir himself had been driven from the city only less than a year before. Several of the gates of the old walled capital still showed signs of shelling when we arrived. Bands of irregulars were still raiding to the east.

Our home there, again, was in an old, old *medrese* in the very heart of the city. The balcony of my room looked out over a large, circular *havus*. The stagnated water in that pool was literally alive with all kinds of bugs and wriggling creatures. It smelled bad, too. That was the water in which the faithful made ablutions before praying in the many mosques round about. That was the water used by the people of the neighborhood for drinking, for making tea, for washing. From the pool radiated a network of streets, some long and straight, most crooked and narrow, but all covered: the once-famous covered bazaar of Bukhara. Behind that were ancient cemeteries. Those took up a fifth of the city. For centuries all burials had been aboveground. As a result, with bodies stacked one upon another, some of the cemeteries were close to ten stories in height. The stench from them all was unbearable. When it rained, decomposition from the bodies washed into the streets. It was debatable whether it was worse to be near the cemeteries when it was hot—and temperatures over 110 degrees in summer were common—or when it was raining. Beyond the cemeteries was the rest of the town, a maze of hundreds of narrow, crooked, nameless streets, frowned on by fortress-like houses of baked brick or sod and with no windows to the streets. That composite of bazaar, cemeteries, and dwellings was ringed by high and thick walls. There were eleven gates, closed from sunset to dawn and guarded night and day by armed men.

Each morning the city returned to life. The gates were flung open. In would stream horsemen, camels, and donkeys, as Uzbeks, Afghans, Persians, and Turkomans began their daily pursuits and the shops and bazaar filled with customers. It was very colorful, but it was also very noisy with the calls of children and the haggling of buyers and sellers of goods. I never saw a single woman with an open face. All the females except the very young were tightly wrapped in black *paranjas*, their faces covered with black veils made of horsehair.

At night it was dangerous to be abroad. There was no electricity, no light of any sort on the streets. In those hours they were roamed by hundreds and hundreds of homeless dogs, horribly dirty, hungry, and diseased, and a few thieves in not much better condition. The few times we did venture out of the *medrese* after dark, we always went with an armed escort and with a lantern.

We got a somewhat better impression after we had been in Bukhara a while and made friends with a few residents of that strange city. Invited to their homes, we were surprised to find out how nice they looked from the interior. Most houses had some kind of pool, small or large, depending upon the wealth of the owner, pools with far fresher and cleaner water than the one below our balcony. Around the pools were gardens of fruit trees and beautiful flowers such as roses, marigolds, daisies, and many others whose names I can no longer recall. Rooms of the houses, the windows and doors of which opened on to those pleasant vistas, were delightfully cool after the heat of the streets. Most were furnished with low sofas and extremely handsome carpets, the famous Bukharas.

The pleasure of those visits did little, however, to remove my depression caused by the general state of decay of the city. What a terrible fate to have befallen great Bukhara, once the capital of the Samanids, once the intellectual center of Islam and second only to Mecca as a holy place. Bukhara, I almost cried, once a fine city with paved streets and gracious *caravanserais*, with famous libraries and universities, even with adequate sanitary facilities. I felt how the spirits must have mourned: of Rudagi, the great Tadjik poet; of Nizamuddin Ali Sher, the great Uzbek poet; and of Abu Ali Ibn-sina, the remarkable Tadjik scientist and philosopher, a native of Bukhara and known in the West under the name of Avicenna.

True, beyond the wall things appeared better. From the city stretched in every direction acres and acres of fertile soil, the famed Bukhara oasis. There, the *dekhans*, or peasants, were busily farming their lots, growing fruits, vegetables, and cotton in great abundance. Everywhere there was acacia, walnut, huge mulberry trees, chestnuts, elms, oaks, almonds, apricots, cherries, and plums.

But all the land, countryside as well as city, was oppressed with illiteracy, superstition, malaria, skin and intestinal diseases. Those were the chief enemies of that people of bygone grandeur who once gave the Moslem world great poets, scientists, and thinkers. That was the legacy of Russian colonialism, a colonialism made worse by the selfishness of local *begs* and *khans*, interested only in the exploitation of their own people with aid of the conqueror.

To be sure, I thought, Bukhara and much of the rest of Russian Turkistan badly needed a new order. Long overdue was a kind of revolution, the establishment of some new system, the promulgation of education, of sanitary installations, the building of roads and new houses, a reformation, a national movement, and independence. Gentle, hospitable, industrious Uzbeks, known abroad for their kindness to children, their good taste, and appreciation of artistic form and flowers, were not a bad people. All they needed was enlightenment of their leaders ready to fight for a new order. But in those days of my innocence, I did not know that Uzbek progress was to be gained at the terrible cost of collectivization and Sovietization.

My small part in that woeful process came soon. After a few days of rest and sightseeing we were called to the office of the *nazir*, or minister, of education. Once seated and after green tea, candies, and fresh fruit had been served, we were told that our group was to be disbanded so that each might be sent out on individual assignment. We were the first of young activists who would be spread over Turkistan and as far north as Alma-ata. Some of us were sent to Tezmez. Others were to stay in Bukhara. Our leader, Hay, was assigned to Khiva, which must have been in a very bad way, indeed, for such a fanatic to be ordered there. I was sent to Chardzhou (now one of the several Leninsks of the Soviet Union), some sixty miles up the Amu-darya (Oxus) from Bukhara. My mission was to be an instructor at the teachers' college that the Communists had just opened in that small Turkoman city.

That Chardzhou school was a most unusual and makeshift institution. The entire staff was Tatar. The director was a Tatar from Kazan. The administrative officer was a Tatar from the Crimea, a former merchant marine sailor. The students were quite exceptional, too. Their ages ranged from the midtwenties well into the fifties. All had been rounded up in their villages and sent to Chardzhou, selected on the basis that they were the best educated. That education, however, had been pitifully meager. It had consisted mainly of sitting a required number of years in the cells of the old-style schools learning by rote Arabic words whose very meaning they did not know. They knew nothing of the basics of arithmetic, physics, chemistry, let alone history, foreign languages, or sciences. They had been sent with their few belongings to live on the school premises, to sleep on floors with their own blankets in overcrowded rooms. Our job was tremendous to impossible: to give that sorry lot not only elementary education, but also to make them politically aware, to Sovietize them for use back in their villages.

I found myself at the age of seventeen a professor of mathematics in that strange place. That, despite the fact that my own knowledge then went no deeper than logarithms, the binomial theorem, geometry, and trigonometry. But that was more than enough for my students. For them, my task was completed once I had driven basic arithmetic and elementary algebra into their unwilling heads.

It was a fearsome day when I faced my first class. Before me I found some fifty bearded men in colorful Uzbek robes with either turbans or beautifully embroidered *tubeteikas* atop their heads. All were forty, at least. Their expressions were far from friendly. They were waiting for me to make some mistake, some slip of the tongue, or to show some sign of weakness. On some faces was written, "What do you expect from a boy of seventeen?" On others I could read, "He is a *Kafir* [unbeliever], or maybe a Russian." Probably to their disappointment, I did not falter. I had been toughened by what I had seen of the Revolution and by my membership in the Komsomol. I had been put through basic military training with the youth group, knew how to use a pistol, rifle, and grenades. My confidence was also based on my knowledge that my education was superior to theirs and by my determination to teach them. I was accepted by them as their instructor, at least by the majority.

Sometime after that initiation, a quite intelligent man joined my class. He was about twenty-five, my youngest student, was cleanly shaven, and affected a white robe and a white turban. His name was Hamza. One day after class he approached my desk. I could tell he wanted something. Without a word he gave me a little bunch of straw and a piece of charcoal. "What is this, Hamza?" I asked. "*Yoldash Muallim* [Comrade Teacher]," he explained, "my home is in a nearby *kishlak* and I have a young wife. Our women do not know how to read and write. The straw and charcoal are a message, a letter. They mean that left alone without her husband she is badly missing me, is becoming as yellow as this bunch of straw, while her mood is growing as black as this piece of charcoal. Please, *Yoldash* Director of the Class, grant me a few days to visit my wife." Amused by his flowery presentation of his case and sympathetic to his love for his young wife, I did my best for Hamza. That was far from difficult. The director of the institute was not a Communist and knew that I was. He quickly agreed with my suggestion of a short leave for Hamza.

That favor to Hamza literally almost caused my death. Shortly after Hamza had visited home, an elder student, a man in his fifties, also asked leave. "*Yoldash*," he said, "a home with children is like a bazaar. A childless home is like a *mazaar* [Uzbek word for tomb]. I have seven children; I am homesick for them. My *kishlak* is not far from here. Please arrange for my leave. I will be back in a week." I felt sorry for him. I knew he had been sent to the college by force, so I got him his leave. With that there started a small flood of similar requests, most of which I granted on grounds of sickness, family problems, or like troubles. Finally, a rough and bearded student in his thirties demanded leave and gave no reason whatsoever. He shook a finger at me and said, "You have arranged leave for others. I have the same rights." I became angry, told him to see the director himself and refused him any help. He became very angry, too, and left shouting, *"Yoldash*, you will be sorry for this."

Several weeks later I went to bed early, dead tired. I had had a hard day, not only with classes, but also with military drill, and a lengthy Party meeting. Weary as I was, I could not sleep. I sensed trouble, but could not define it. Perhaps it was merely that a full moon was shining somewhat eerily into my room and the night was very hot. Just the same, I was disturbed enough to get up, find my pistol, and place it under my pillow before finally dozing off. I awoke suddenly shortly after midnight. Perhaps I had heard something rustle while still asleep. I rubbed my eyes, saw a man's figure inching slowly along the floor toward my bed. The moonlight glinted off the blade of a dagger gripped in his teeth. There was enough light that I could see he was wearing a long, white robe, but not sufficient for me to make out his face. In a split second I jumped from bed, pistol in hand. I shouted and dove for the man, but he was too fast. With almost incredible speed he bolted out of the door and just disappeared into the darkness of the building corridor. My shout as I awakened had aroused other teachers. We searched the entire building and grounds, but found no one. In the morning we had a roll call of the students. One was missing, the insolent fellow who had shouted at me, "You will be sorry." We never saw him again. Perhaps he joined the *Basmachi*, the irregulars and insurgents then roaming the hills and countryside, striking at isolated Communist units. Perhaps he had been one of them before he was enrolled.

In those troubled times the *Basmachi* had made a mess of the whole military and political situation in Turkistan. From the fertile valleys of Fergana to the mountains of eastern Bukhara, organized groups of armed men, recruited from the local populace, were raiding Red garrisons, destroying supply depots and communications, killing pro-Soviet elements. Although called bandits by Moscow, that anti-Soviet movement in reality was composed mainly of Turkic nationalists seeking that same autonomy from Russian rule always promised by the Communists, the same autonomy with which the Reds had deluded the Idel-Ural group in my home area.

In my first few months at Chardzhou the *Basmachi* movement mushroomed to the extent that regular Red Army forces were called in to liquidate it. Even I was put on sort of special alert. Together with other Party members in the city I was put into ChON, or *Chasti Osobogo Naznacheniya*, special troops to guard against *basmachi* attack. Formed into units, we were armed with pistols, rifles, and hand grenades, and were given military training. It was from one of those exercises that I had returned on the night the attempt was made on my life.

Exhaustion was not the only thing that had made me restless that night. I was also disturbed, deeply, by a personal and first-hand report I had just received of how really badly things were going under the Communists. With winter approaching I had become somewhat accustomed, somewhat hardened, to the hordes of refugees fleeing from Russia into sunny Turkistan, trying to escape epidemics and hunger, to find some food. Because of the troubles with the *Basmachi*, all communications with the north had been cut and the local papers in the south printed pure Communist propaganda, not news. Nevertheless, I had heard vague reports of very hard times in the Orsk area, rumors of epidemics and famine there as well. On that very day those reports had been confirmed to me, and very directly. Our neighbor from up the street in Orsk, the book handler married to the two sisters, somehow got south in search of food, somehow found me at the teachers' college.

The neighbor was well past middle age, but he looked years older. He cried on seeing me, told me that my father's garden plot and animals had been exhausted. Father had been maintaining not only his own family, but Cossack relatives from Novo Orsk, who had no source of food, having lost their range lands and horses under the new system. Concluding his account, the old man said, "Your family's situation is truly very critical. Please help in some small way, at least."

I was terribly embarrassed and much ashamed. First making the old man comfortable I took my only spare possession, an extra pistol, to the bazaar. Still only a boy, I treasured weapons then and was loath to part with that miserable pistol. But it was all I had, and I traded it with an Uzbek for some fifteen or twenty pounds of rice and a few pounds of dried grapes, gave the sorry lot to the old man. That was the last direct contact I ever had with my family, the last, small thing I ever did for those dear ones.

Party activities at Chardzhou were much more than organiz-ing against possible *Basmachi* attack. Shortly after arriving at the college I reported to Party headquarters and was assigned to the Party cell of the city educational department. That cell had eleven members, all Russians. I became Number Twelve, the only Tatar, the only non-Russian. I recall three of that cell: a scholarly professor of mathematics from the University of Kazan; an elderly, heavily moustached and nervous professor of physics; and a representative of the dreaded Cheka, the Extraordinary Commission to Combat Counter-Revolution and Sabotage, as the Soviet security police, now the KGB, was then called. The Chekist was a tall, dark, strong, and handsome Latvian in his early forties. He affected the leather jacket of his kind, and beneath that black leather he carried a Mauser in a wooden holster at the hip. When he smiled, and he did that frequently, he displayed two rows of fine golden teeth. I often wondered about the reaction of people he had under interrogation to that gleam of gold.

Almost from my initiation into the cell, our discussions centered on the increasingly varying views of Lenin and Trotsky. One evening during a closed session, the Chekist gave us details of the differences between the two leaders in some detail and then demanded that each of us express his view. Those were the good old days when we had the luxury to agree, disagree, or abstain in free discussion. The first purge was yet to come. At that particular session the professor of mathematics supported Trotsky and the majority sided with Lenin. A few including myself abstained.

That liberty was very short-lived. Later in that year of 1921, the Bolsheviks started the first *Chistka*, or purge, and it reached us too, way down south in Turkistan. The object was to rid Party ranks of Trotsky supporters. In Chardzhou that was accomplished at open, mass meetings of the Party, meetings which non-Party members were also forced to attend. Party members took the platform in turn, gave their biographies, explained their position on Trotsky, answered multitudes of questions from the audience. Those were very monotonous affairs. There were so many Communist candidates or full members to be heard from that the audiences soon tired of their role of questioning. From that point on, those who backed Trotsky were simply read out of the Party and the purge was quickly over.

When my turn came I took the stand, told my brief life story, and declared my opposition to Trotsky. Why, I so nimbly said, should I support the crazy idea of a permanent revolution for the survival of communism. Lenin's promises, I mouthed, of the right of national minorities for self-determination were so much more reasonable than those ideas of the ultrarevolutionary Trotsky. True, I was still too young to understand that Lenin's position on nationalism was a tactical fraud. So, I concluded my little piece with ringing words about one revolution being enough for Russia and the demand for those who wanted world revolution to stand up and be counted. The audience cheered and I was cleared.

The very next day I became a full member of the Russian Communist Party of Bolsheviks, and was given Party membership identification. That, at the age of seventeen. Ha! I did not understand even the ABC's of communism. I was a young man carried away by adventurous aspirations. I needed some outlet for my energy and there was a sense of power in belonging to the Party. Ha! What dreams!

Somewhat simultaneously with my soaring to that political height, I had a pair of economic props pulled out from under me. The college where I had been teaching was completely reorganized, and I must admit for the good. Even its name was changed to the Uzbek Pedagogical Institute of Chardzhou. Similarly reorganized at the same time was the Orenburg Institute, which had sent me and my group to Turkistan. All ties between that institute and us were cut. We were no longer its responsibility, since it, too, had been made into a pedagogical school. From that point on, for it we simply did not exist.

All that saved me from financial disaster was the director of the short-lived college. He was made chief of the city educational department and he took me along as his administrative assistant. My only connection with the old place from then on was a purely physical one. I was allowed to sleep in my old quarters there.

At the newly established institute both the staff and the student body were completely changed. The director was a former Turkish colonel, Necmi Bey, who had been captured during the World War. Set free during the Revolution, he had married a young Russian girl and had settled in Turkistan. He spoke fairly good Russian but he was not a Communist. All his instructors were Turks too, professional teachers and university graduates invited to the Bukhara area by Communist authorities. Compared to that staff our deposed one was little more than a bunch of trained agitators.

All my former students, mature to quite old men, were sent back to their *kishlaks*. In their place came youths, no less than seventeen and no more than twenty-one years of age, all who had to pass entrance examinations and all who had to have had at least six years of elementary education. Those youngsters were required to spend three years at the institute. For them real, new dormitories were built and cots and bedding were furnished. The Turks introduced paramilitary uniforms for their students, a system of saluting teachers, enforcement of discipline, even daily drilling in formation, and marching like soldiers. The institute became almost a military school and its students cadets.

Naturally I gravitated toward the Turks. Not only were they my first real foreigners, but they were also my own people. Evenings after work I would seek them out. Necmi Bey himself had time for my youthful eagerness, would tell me about his war experiences and about Turkey, especially about Anatolia where he came from.

My particular heroes among those Turks were three instructors. There was Necib Bey, a resident of Istanbul, a graduate of Istanbul University's faculty of mathematics. Young and handsome, he knew well the business of teaching math, and I blushed when I remembered I had been his predecessor. Of Tatar origin, he was also more friendly to me than the rest. Then there was Ahmed Muhlis Bey, a tall, dashing young fellow, a real lady's man, who succeeded in finding two sweethearts, one blonde, the other brunette, on the very first day he arrived in Chardzhou. He played the piano, danced, sang, rarely spent an evening at the institute, usually disappeared into the city. The third was Mustafa Durmush Bey, a kindly gentleman in his late forties and also a former Turkish officer. He was thoughtful and serious, always seeming to say less than he thought, and I liked to fancy the idea that he may have been an agent of the famous Enver Pasha. How I admired those Turks, their way, and knowledge of life! All had nice suits, dozens of clean shirts, bunches of neckties, nice shoes. Our poor clothes were no match for theirs. And they looked well fed and healthy and were full of life and humor. They were human, modest, and kind. They were not the foreigners ridiculed in the Communist press, until then my only contact with the world abroad.

The reason I toyed with the idea that Mustafa Durmush Bey may have been an agent of Enver Pasha was that it was then the fashion among Communists in Turkistan to suspect that that redoubtable Turk or his men were under every woodpile. Sent by Moscow to Bukhara as an advisor, the former Young Turk broke with the Communists, took to the mountains, and declared himself leader of the anti-Soviet movement in Turkistan. His dream was to create a new *Turan*, or a union of Turkic peoples from the Bosphorus to Oceania. He never succeeded, but until he was killed in a clash with a Red patrol, he worried the Communists more than the *Bashmachi*. And to me he was always a hero.

In the spring of 1922, at the height of an Enver Pasha scare, Mustafa Durmush Bey came one evening to visit me in my room. "Ismail," he said, "I feel trouble coming. It is possible that the

Cheka will arrest me. Here is something they may use against me as material evidence. Please keep it for me for a while." He handed me a bag with many gold coins, real gold, and a revolver. I forgot completely my suspicions about him and took the money and the gun. "You are a good boy," he said. "If nothing happens to me, you can give this back to me. If I am shot, it is yours. I have no family." He had tears in his eyes as he left.

I hid the gold and the gun under a board in the floor of my room. The next night Durmush Bey and Ahmed Muhlis Bey as well were arrested by the Cheka. A few hours later I was summoned to Party headquarters. There I was confronted with the same Chekist who attended our cell meetings. He asked if I had noticed anything peculiar, anything counterrevolutionary about the Turkish teachers. "Comrade," he said, "you are the only Communist at their institute. Please indicate something against them, even something which might seem insignificant to you. If you help us you will be making a great contribution to the Party." That showed me he had really uncovered nothing against my two friends. I answered, "Comrade, those two Turks are very nice fellows. They just teach. They have no interest in politics. In their free time, all they do is play cards, chase women, and drink." That ended my interrogation. Later I learned that my chief, the former director of the college, had also undergone Cheka questioning about the Turks and likewise defended them.

After a week or so my two friends were set free. I gave the gold and the revolver back to Mustafa Durmush Bey and soon forgot the whole affair. But as with most Turks, Durmush Bey's memory was much longer. That summer he called me for a long talk with him. He spoke of the unsettled conditions in Russia, of the famines, epidemics, and chaos, then said I should go to Turkey, enter Istanbul University, and get off to a fresh start. When I asked him how, he said his friend, the Turkish consul-general in Baku, had powerful and influential acquaintances in Ankara and could help me. With that Durmush Bey gave me a letter, already prepared, to his friend in Baku, asking him to intercede for me.

To go to Turkey was not a completely new idea to me. My curiosity about the country, my desire to see it, had been well aroused earlier by talks with other Turks at the institute. Durmush Bey's kindness not only offered actuality to that hope, but also coincided with my increasing worry about my future. Working in the city educational department gave me a living, but did nothing to advance my education itself. My contacts with the Turks had most clearly shown me how much I needed further schooling. But until Durmush Bey stepped in I could conceive of no way of accomplishing that. To have gone home would have been going to nothing and an acknowledgement of failure. To have returned to Orenburg and to famine there too would have served no real purpose. And to have stayed on at my small job in Chardzhou would have been no more than marking time, at the most. Besides, I was only eighteen, in good health, and with an unquenchable desire to see the rest of the world and its people. I was more than ready to leave Chardzhou, for almost anywhere. Baku and Turkey was the only possibility open.

True, wanderlust played a large part in my decision to go. With youthful self-confidence, I attempted to put some security in my direction by a sort of rationale. I established a "program maximum" and a "program minimum" for myself. According to my "program maximum," my ultimate goal was to get away from Soviet Russia to Turkey, to resume schooling in Istanbul, and learn some real profession—engineering was my preference— with which to earn my living. My "program minimum" was to enter some technical school in Baku to learn some industrial trade. I certainly was far from realistic in those troubled times, but I felt sure I was doing the right thing.

So, full of dreams, hopes, and determination, with little more than Durmush Bey's letter in hand, I said quick farewells to the Turks and other friends in mid-August of 1922 and boarded a train for Krasnovodsk on the eastern shore of the Caspian. I had quit my job with due formality, but foolishly had told Party headquarters nothing of my intentions. I dropped Chardzhou from my thoughts the minute I left the station.

The route, so important to Russian conquest of Turkistan, fascinated me. Most of it was across the Kara Kum, one of the world's most formidable deserts, with hundreds of miles of track paralleling the fairy book shaped peaks of the Kopet-Dag range. To one side of the tracks I saw desert as far as the eye could reach. To the other side the mountains presented no barrier to my thoughts. I knew that just the other side of them was Persia, and beyond that Bagdad, Turkey, and all the places of the fabulous battles of Said Battal Gazi, Saladin Eyubi, and of marvelous stories of the *Thousand and One Nights* of my boyhood. I felt sure that I was going to see those places sooner or later and pay my respects to the memories of heroes of my people gone forever.

It was a very hot and humid noon when the train reached the end of its run at the port of Krasnovodsk. It was the first time I had ever been below sea level, let alone on foot at the shore of a sea—my earlier sighting of the Aral had been only a fleeting, distant glimpse. I was very thirsty and looked for a water tank at the station. All the stations I had been in elsewhere had drinking water for passengers. The Krasnovodsk station was my first exception. It had no tank, no water. Being at the edge of the desert, the port imported water from more fortunate areas by boat and by rail. When I finally found a water tank in the city, I learned that I had to pay for drinking water. I was shocked; still am.

The daily boat for Baku had already left several hours before my train arrived. I killed the long afternoon and evening ahead of me by going to the docks and the seashore, as if on a voyage of discovery. The cranes, the loading and unloading of ships, I absorbed in full before going to the beach to smell the sea more closely, to wade in the surf, and to inspect jellyfish and other little sea creatures at firsthand.

That night I slept, as did the hundreds of others awaiting the next boat, in the open air near the pier. Long before dawn people awoke and formed a line in front of the ticket office. I joined the line but when the office opened in early morning, we private citizens got no attention until a swarm of military men and Party and government officials were given their reserved place. Then when the line did start moving, the ticket window closed just as I got to it. The last place for that day's boat had been taken.

I had no liking for another wasted day and night or for spending more of the little money I had on drinking water, so I stayed at the pier even though I had no ticket. At midmorning passengers started to board. The process was much like a riot. Each of the hundreds there was struggling to be the first aboard. They were pushing each other, cursing terribly, shoving tickets and all kinds of documents and warrants under officials' noses. Some of the stronger ones were working their way aboard by full use of elbows and shoulders. I was as strong as most of those and realized that my solution was simple: to shove my way aboard, too.

Picking a peak of the struggle at the pier, I pushed my way past ship's officers involved in a big argument with other would-be passengers and got to the lower deck. I was a stowaway, but my conscience was clear. Many other "experienced" travelers did likewise on ships and trains in those troubled times. Besides, it was the system, not me, that had made the transportation mess. Also, I had saved a little money to help me on my way in Baku. Within a few minutes after I had exploded onto the deck, we sailed.

# 3
# Youth

It took little more than a day to make the crossing to Baku. Slipping off the boat without attracting attention was much simpler than boarding it, so finally I made it ashore at the Apsheron Peninsula. I was almost burbling with excitement. Hail to the Caucasus, I said to myself, hail to the Trans-Caucasus, hail to the lands so wonderfully sung of by the great Russian poets Lermontov and Pushkin and so excellently described by Lev Tolstoy.

But my joy was to last less than twenty-four hours. In that short time both my "program maximum" and my "program minimum" came crashing to the ground. My first disappointment occurred at the Turkish consulate, where despite Durmush Bey's letter, I was told that there was nothing they could do to get me to Turkey, let alone to a university. Stay instead in my homeland, they recommended, and become a good citizen. Knowing of no way of crossing the border illegally, I accepted the advice.

The second blow came when I called at the educational department and asked to be enrolled in a technical school. There I learned that no such school was open to me unless I had been sponsored by a recognized institution or organization and had full recommendations. I had need of an institute or the Party to back me and all that I had abandoned by leaving Chardzhou and not returning to Orenburg.

With both programs wiped out, I knew that my few roubles would quickly go as a little lump of snow melts under the rays of the hot sun. I had to find work and fast, so I went to the labor exchange office.

My thoughts had been so much centered on myself after my arrival in Baku that I had thought little of the fact that the city's streets and parks were jammed with hungry, tired people, men, women, and children just walking or sitting, doing nothing. What that was all about I learned when I tried to register for work.

It was a shocking scene at the labor office. There I found literally tens of thousands of poor devils who had been waiting in lines for weeks and weeks for some job, any kind of job, just in order to exist. Some had been waiting by night as well as day in those lines so as not to lose their turns.

Now in those lines myself, the 1921-1922 famines, epidemics, and civil war that had befallen the Ural and Volga regions, many places in Kirgizia and Kazakhstan, and in the foothills and mountains of Dagestan and Azerbaidzhan, at last became more than hearsay. How I shuddered to think of my heedlessness to my family that must have suffered much the same. How ashamed I was to know that my only help to them had been a miserable few pounds of rice and dried grapes, and that had been asked of me, not volunteered. The people standing with me in those Baku lines of unemployed were the survivors of those terrible troubles over that vast area. I shuddered to think that among them could also have been my father, also hoping to find work of any kind.

Most of my fellow standees came from nearer by, from Dagestan and Azerbaidzhan. Their stories were awful. Like my Tatars, they too had believed the Revolution meant freedom from Russian rule. Proud peoples, they fought when the Communists tricked them with false promises. Although very brave they were defeated by the Soviets, who recognized the economic, political, and strategic value of the area around Baku just as much as had the Tsars. With defeat, roads, bridges, irrigation systems, whole settlements, and local industries were completely destroyed and people were put to the sword. In Derbent alone, a pretty little town on the west shore of the Caspian, three-fourths of the buildings were burned to the ground by the Soviets. On the heels of defeat came the famine, malaria, and typhus. After that a cattle plague wiped out the last remnants of the herds. As if that were not enough, next the crops were invaded by locusts and field mice. Finally what was left was ruined by terrible wind and hail storms. All that remained for those afflicted people was to go to Baku or other big industrial centers and hope for work.

Every day we stood in front of the labor office an announcement would be chalked on a big blackboard on the doors saying: "Wanted immediately—one graduate electrical engineer, two graduate mechanical engineers with long experience," or, "three graduate designers." I had no such qualifications, nor did anybody else in those sad lines of unemployed. I swore to myself that someday I would become a graduated, qualified expert of some kind. There were no blackboard calls for unskilled, untrained labor such as we were, and I was thus taught early the lesson that educated personnel were always in demand, in bad times as well as good. My father had long tried to tell me that, but I had to learn he was right by personal experience.

As time went by in those lines, my money ran out, no matter how carefully I had hoarded it. I next sold every possession except the clothes I stood in at the marketplace. Inexorably the day at last arrived when I had no more money and had to leave my cheap hotel.

On that grim day I turned to the Party as last resort, went jobless, roofless, and increasingly hungry to the Azerbaidzhan Central Committee. There my frayed and greasy Party membership card that I had once regarded so highly was examined disdainfully. A minor official flipped it back to me, said it bore no stamps to show I had gone through the purge or had paid recent dues. He was right. In my hurry to leave Chardzhou for greater promise in Baku I had not bothered to have my card brought up to date. I tried to explain that and argue that being jobless I could not have paid dues. That only angered the official. He grabbed my card back from me, tore it up, called me a non-Party scoundrel and imposter, told me to get out and never return.

That was the bottom. Unemployed, unfed, unhoused, and out of the Party, I was completely free to starve or die, as free as millions of others were then under the new Soviet system.

That night and many another I spent on a bench in a city park at the seashore. Nights get cool at the end of August in Baku. I shivered more than slept. Often I would be cuffed awake by a policeman as well, and warned with arrest if I returned to the bench. I always went back. I would have liked to have been arrested. At least I would have been given shelter and food. Nothing mattered much any longer. I was a tramp, an outcast, and so very, very hungry I dreamed of all the food I once had at home.

By day, acting on advice of others in the lines at the labor office, I went to the railroad station. There some money could be earned for food by carrying passengers' baggage between trains and their homes. If others could do it, so could I. Young and strong, I could carry a lot of things.

At dawn after my first night in the park, I ran the five miles to the station, joined the gang of volunteer porters in time for the first train. Almost before the wheels stopped rolling I raced to a group of passengers getting off and shouted at the top of my lungs, "Please, let me carry your baggage for any price you can pay. I am jobless and hungry." I had luck. A good fat fellow with a small mountain of bags and parcels hired me. I was so glad.

Never mind that the baggage was heavy, the sun was getting hotter and hotter, and the distance quite far. None of that bothered me. I was going to eat. At his home, the good fat fellow paid me enough to buy breakfast and even have a few kopeks left over for lunch. After profuse but hurried thanks, I made it as fast as possible to the nearest market, bought a whole pound of hot bread, a pound of grapes, and a piece of cheese. I stuffed myself and washed it down with water from a fountain in the square. That was the best breakfast I have ever had. Life no longer seemed so bad.

Going back to the station for more work, I soon learned that some know-how and risk were involved in the business of being a volunteer porter. It was necessary to have an almost split second knowledge of the schedule of incoming and outgoing trains. The volunteers had to arrive just before the trains arrived or departed and melt in among the passengers. Otherwise we ran afoul of the official railroad porters, the local police, and the railroad Cheka men. True, a very few of the volunteers proved to be thieves, but their main offense was that they endangered the livelihood of the official porters, who had their own uniforms, identification numbers, and most important, their own union, and therefore a standing with the authorities. I sympathized a bit with the official porters. They had to exist, but so did we. I was beginning to understand some of the facts of life of which I had been totally unaware as a Soviet propagandist in Turkistan. Naked life, Father had once told me, was a good school, too.

Nimble-footed and alert, a good volunteer could escape the official porters and police and eke out enough food for himself and his family. There always were passengers willing to give us work, either to save money or out of pity. So, my profession became that of a volunteer porter. I was well aware that I could make no fortune that way, but I had to keep alive while I waited for some miracle to happen.

After becoming experienced, I developed a system of working only long enough each day to earn my food. Rather than work myself into ill health for a few more roubles, I decided it would be better to spend some of my time between the labor office, looking for better opportunities, and the city library, reading and improving my knowledge. I never found better opportunities there in Baku, but I did see other worlds in translations of Schiller, Jack London, Cervantes, Dickens, and the Russian classics of Tolstoy, Pushkin, Gogol, Lermontov, and Chekhov. I also escaped a little from my mean life by walks to the oil refineries, to wonder at the mystery of their operation and to Baku's fine harbor to marvel at ships carrying raw cotton, rice, fish, dried fruits, and timber.

As autumn followed summer, it became too cold to spend the nights on park benches. Instead I sought out the sides of big buildings, sides that had been heated by the sun during the day and kept some of that warmth into the night. I tried to find walls in less populated sections, because it was painful to be awakened by people returning to homes nearby after a night with friends or at the theater. I was tormented by visions of their going into the warm rooms and into beds.

In late autumn even those sun-warmed walls became too chill for sleep. I had heard from volunteers and other homeless people of common lodgings run by the city and found one near the station.

My spirits were low as I approached that building and dropped even lower after I had entered. It was a terrible place. It had an earthen floor and sod walls. It had no windows, no lights, no water, no heating system, no toilet, no washing place, no cooking place, no furniture. It was filthy beyond description. It had no bedding, only tiers of bare, plank bunks. The first row of occupants lay on the earth floor. The "aristocrats" had the first and second tiers of the planks.

Horrible as that was, it was better than the street. No one offered me room and some were ready to fight for their places. I shoved and pushed myself into the first tier between two men weaker than I was. The seventy-fourth occupant of that horror, I lay back and looked at my new home. It was an abandoned shed, fifteen by twenty-four feet in area and about six feet high. I estimated that it offered about thirty cubic feet accommodation for each occupant. That was a sample of how well the Soviets cared for the poor, the homeless, the jobless.

Because of the stench, I fled that place whenever it was warm enough to sleep outside on a park bench or along a wall. With the coming of winter, of course, that escape became impossible. I had to suffer the "Hotel Orient" as we sorry occupants called the place, even though the violent northwest winds of the area, the rain, the snow, and the slush found the leaks in its walls and roof. Unable to sleep in the effort to keep dry, that miserable crowd of humanity would talk, and loudly, in many languages and dialects, recalling happy earlier times. Some were men in their forties and older who had once had their own families and decent lives. It was heartbreaking to listen to their accounts of lost children and wives, of businesses and homes gone forever. Most of these older men were persons who had either refused to accept the Soviets or had joined them and then become disillusioned with communism and sought a better future.

Besides us grown-ups, there were also thousands of homeless children, real orphans, roaming the streets of Baku in those times. Periodically the police would round up those waifs, mainly boys, and send them under heavy guard to so-called special colonies, in reality concentration camps under Cheka management. Of course those children were fed better than when on the streets and were sheltered from the weather, but most of them hated the colonies. Many fought desperately to avoid being picked up. Some escaped from the colonies, and the stories they told of life there under the Cheka made their existence as waifs seem much preferable, miserable as it was.

With the coming of winter, either the Cheka improved their methods at the railroad stations or we volunteer porters became less agile from malnutrition and exposure. Both factors probably were responsible, but the result was that we could get very little work. Our hunger approached starvation and we envied the dogs and cats, for they at least had food, shelter, and protection. We were also barred from the streetcars and public places. After months of steady wear, my clothes had become filth and rags. And with no hot water, soap, or change of clothes, I myself became even filthier. In fact, I was so dirty and in such awful condition that I was no longer allowed in the library. Despite all that, we occupants of the "Orient" knew that things could be worse. There were only two other such "hotels" in the entire city. That meant that thousands and thousands of poor creatures had nothing more for shelter than the streets and parks, an occasional steam boiler or paving mixture cauldron for warmth. The Soviet press was blind to all that, of course, and continued its propaganda about how the Party and Communist organizations were mobilizing for care of the homeless and jobless masses.

The packs of orphans suffered the worst in that terrible winter of 1922-1923. Their rags, their hunger, could not cope with disease, especially with typhus that came in epidemic proportion. They started dying in the streets and parks, first in tens, soon in the hundreds. In the early mornings police would come in wagons to pick up those little bodies wherever they had fallen, while happier children were warm abed. The dead children were then taken outside the city to be buried in mass graves or cremated.

One early morning that winter, after watching the police making a grim harvest of dead children, I felt very sick, not only in my heart, but physically. It was all I could do to make it back to the "hotel" I had left a few hours earlier, unable to stand the stench there. My head, my whole body, ached terribly, and I knew my temperature was high.

I collapsed onto my planks and almost immediately lost consciousness. I do not know how long I lay that way, but when I awoke it was dark. I could hear it raining. My whole body was burning. I had a terrible thirst and I wanted to drink and drink. Slowly I forced my way from the planks to the floor and just managed to creep to the door. My neighbors watched me without making a move to help. They were perhaps hoping I would be gone forever and they would have more space.

Once outside the door of the "hotel" I crawled to where water was trickling from a drainpipe on a neighboring house. Clinging to the base of the pipe, I began to drink and drink. . . .

Later, I do not know how much later, I came to. Slowly, very slowly, I opened my eyes. I could not believe what I saw. I bit my hand. I felt pain, therefore I was not dreaming. It really was a bed that I found myself on. Yes, a real bed, after all those terrible days and nights, after all that nightmare. It was not as good a bed as I was used to at home. It was a hospital bed, but nevertheless, it was a bed.

Coming fully awake, I also found I had clean, white underwear on and was covered with an army blanket. Beside my bed was a little table and on that several pieces of bread, a full water bottle, and a drinking glass. What luxury! Somebody cared for me.

The room was little, held only two other beds, to the right and left of mine. A pair of bodies lay on the other beds, with blankets covering them from head to toe. They were two for whom no one could care much any longer. They were dead.

I was frightened. I tried to forget the dead by staring out the room's only window into a gray and rainy sky. Eventually a man in a white smock looked into the room. An orderly, he was surprised that I was alive, let alone conscious. He said that I was in a charity hospital, that I had typhus in an advanced stage, and the doctors had not expected me to live. The epidemic had greatly overcrowded the hospital and that was why I had been put with some of the dead. Some unknown good soul, the attendant told me, had found me unconscious under the drainpipe and had notified the authorities. God bless that kind person who had saved me.

A few days later I began to recover. My youth and strong build were fighting death for life. I was taken off the critical list and transferred to a big ward where there were some thirty other patients also recovering from typhus. There I spent several months before I had gained enough strength to walk short distances slowly. Sundays and holidays were the most painful periods of that convalescence. On those days the other patients, all from the Baku area, were visited by their relatives and close ones. My relatives, my friends, were hundreds of miles distant so I was left to myself. At first during the visiting hours I would pull the blanket over my eyes to hide my loneliness and the tears that welled into my eyes. A good fellow in the bed next to mine understood my despair and sent his wife to me to say warm words and give me encouragement. Other patients soon followed that example and I got much kind attention from the visitors. Many of the cakes and other good things brought the sick relatives were shared with me. Much as that improved my morale, I was sad at the failure I had proved to be. I would swear silently to myself that if I survived and found my place in life I forever would try to do good for my fellow human beings and avoid any kind of evil.

At last there came a day toward the end of that awful winter of 1922-1923, a day when one could almost smell that spring was not far off. Several doctors came to my bed for a routine checkup. I told them that something was wrong with my back; I felt acute pain and it also hurt to breathe. After tapping and listening to my chest and back, they exchanged frowns and left.

The next morning I was moved to another hospital in Bibi-Eybat, the oil producing area of Baku. There I was told that as result of the typhus I had developed a complication as well, pleurisy. It was bad news. Without proper care and food TB could have come next.

After a general examination, one of the doctors, a young woman of German origin, paused a moment by my bedside. She said that if it were possible after leaving the hospital, I should go to Abastumani, or some other mountain resort for pulmonary patients in the Trans-Caucasus to regain my strength.

I am afraid I almost sneered at her suggestion. Ha, me, a jobless man go to a mountain resort? I asked. The doctor flinched, but her eyes, a beautiful dark blue, remained kind and understanding. I seized on her sympathy to blurt out everything about myself and what a mess I was making of my life. She heard me out then left without a word, avoiding my eyes.

The next day on her regular round, she came to my bed again. That time she was smiling like an angel. She told me to forget my worries, to think only of getting well, that I would get good care in the hospital and would be kept there until I had recovered completely.

That fine woman more than kept her word. My food was improved. I was put in a cheery ward with windows to the seaside. By day I could see the wind in the green trees outside the windows. By night I would fall asleep to the sound of the surf. Often she would bring me good books to read and she always had cheerful words for me. As I became better, I became a little impertinent, impertinent enough to ask her once if she was a Communist. She was not amused. She said a simple "no," and left me. I did not believe that wonderful creature was a Communist, but I had to make sure.

Week followed week of that excellent care and attention. Real spring came with green grass, blooming trees, balmy days, and wonderful sunshine. I had never felt better in my whole life, and I was itching to get out of the hospital and see the world again.

The staff must have agreed with me. There came the day when the kind woman doctor called me to her consulting room. She told me I had no more traces of pleurisy, that my general health was excellent, and that I was to be discharged from the hospital. In a little talk she advised that I leave Baku where thousands were still unemployed, that I try to find work in the countryside, which would also be good for my health. She recommended that I take things easy for a while, then told me that there was a package for me in the dressing room for discharged patients. In leaving I tried to thank her, but stumbled for words in my deep gratitude and admiration for her. Instead, I reached for her hand, kissed it, and went out of the room without letting her see my eyes. I wondered if I would ever see her again, when I would be on my own, be a man. Years later on a trip through Baku I tried to find her again, but had no luck.

In the dressing room I found a bundle with my name on it. Within was a suit, underwear, socks, a pair of shoes. Everything was my size. My astonishment became joy. Then in a pocket of the suit I found a little wad of roubles, enough to feed me for a week or so. All that was my doctor's gift. God bless her and protect her.

I almost ran from the hospital, straight to the railroad station. I boarded the first express, a passenger car, a first-class one. I had no idea where the train was bound. I had no ticket. I had no definite plan. All I wanted was to get out of Baku. I did not want to stay there even one day more.

Finally the train started to move. Once it reached normal speed I looked out the window and said, "Goodbye, angelic doctor, goodbye Baku. I suffered too much on your streets, Baku." I had wasted away about seven months there.

Yet in my own way, I was proud of myself there. In spite of all those black days, hunger, gangs, the "Hotel Orient," no real work, I never had a desire to steal as some others did. I never tried to beg money or food, as some others did. I never used force to get something that did not belong to me, as some others did. I had arrived in Baku a decent human being and I was leaving Baku a decent human being. I had been poor, shabby, and dirty, I had seen human misery, but I had been honest. Thus everything was easy in my heart, and life began to seem good and even wonderful again. I also knew I had learned much. I had seen and talked with people at the bottom of the newborn Soviet society, with peasants uprooted from their homes, with workers made jobless, with others who became tramps rather than accept the Soviets, with children made homeless and orphaned by the system. I was no longer starry-eyed about the Soviets and communism.

Boarding a train without a ticket was not unusual in those times, in fact it was almost the fashion. Everybody tried to avoid paying fares and those ticketless travelers were so common that there was a name for them, *zaytsi*, or rabbits. Some rode on the roofs of the cars, others on the rods beneath. The worst penalty they faced, because many of the railroad men felt sorry for them, was being put off at the next station.

A first-class rabbit myself, I learned from fellow passengers that the train I had boarded was going all the way to Moscow via Rostov-on-Don and Kharkov. En route it would pass through northern Azerbaidzhan and Dagestan. The destination I picked for myself was somewhere between Khachmas and Derbent, a forested area along the coast where somebody in Baku had told me that woodcutters were wanted.

I never got there on that trip. A score or so miles north of Baku, my car was visited by a ticket collector and a Chekist, the latter a hard-eyed character in the usual black leather coat with the usual naked revolver on the hip. Hardened by my months in Baku, I smiled as I told them I had no ticket. When they asked my destination, I told them I was following my nose. With that, they ordered me to get off the train at the next stop or face arrest.

Both officials seemed quite serious, so wanting nothing of a Soviet prison, I obeyed and left the train at the very next stop. It was about noon, the sun was high, and it was hot. I found myself in a little country station. It was graced by a few sad, unsmiling railroad officials and workers, a few scraggly trees. It smelled of oil, empty freight cars, camels, and donkeys.

After about an hour a long freight pulled in, headed north, and stopped to change a few cars. As it got ready to leave, I sauntered casually away from the station and up the tracks to avoid the attention of the station master. Then as the freight started to roll again, I jumped aboard an open car.

Within I found I had a pair of fellow passengers, a redoubtable looking Azerbaidzhanian about thirty, with a big dagger at his belt, and his wife, some ten years younger. The man merely grunted a reply to my *Salaam Aleikum* while chewing on his lunch of cold meat, bread, and cheese. Watching him, my mouth watered since I had had no food since early morning. Suddenly he smiled and asked me to share the meal with him. That was mountain hospitality which I dared not offend. It was a very good lunch, too.

When we had finished, since people everywhere are in a good mood after a meal, we started to talk. My Turko-Tatar was close enough to the Azerbaidzhanian tongue for us to understand each other easily. I told him something of my troubles and that I was looking for work.

He suggested that I run his water mill in a village nearby at the foot of the mountains. All I had to do was care for the mill day and night during the grinding season and collect money from the customers when the work was done. For that he was prepared to feed and clothe me and maybe give me pocket money if I worked hard. I accepted immediately. I had no choice; I had to live.

We got off the freight at a station called Devechi, which means a person who keeps a herd of camels. From there we started walking north paralleling the coast. To the west were foothills of the Caucasus, stretching up to some three thousand feet and rich with gardens and orchards. And beyond those hills I occasionally saw the snowcapped peaks of the high Caucasus, rosy with the rays of the setting sun.

As we walked I began to cool to my employer. His village was certainly not nearby, as he had said, and I wondered if his water mill existed. Also I was concerned that he had given his wife all his baggage to carry while he strolled along empty-handed as if on an evening walk. When in Baku I had heard something about such tribal habits and had thought such customs would disappear with the coming of the Soviets. Even I, accustomed to long walks, was tired. The young woman was stumbling with exhaustion. If that was the way the man treated his wife, I expected worse for myself.

We kept on and on. The sun went down, darkness covered the surface of the earth, and it was night. Only then did the man call a halt. He said since it was still some miles to the mill and all were tired, we should stop under some trees to eat and spend the night. Dropping the luggage with relief, the young wife soon built a fire and cooked us a meal. When we finished and the fire was going down, my benefactor led his wife to the shelter of a big tree where the two covered themselves with his felt cloak and were soon asleep. With nothing to cover myself with, I threw more wood on the fire and slept alongside it until wakened by rain. The rest of the night I spent under a tree trying to stay dry.

At dawn we arose. The rain had stopped, the clouds were gone, and a bright day was starting. After we had washed at a roadside irrigation ditch, the young woman loaded up to continue on the way. By then I had had enough. I thanked the man for his offer, told him I did not believe we would get along, and had decided to go my own way. He said the choice was mine, then added, "Let God make your road open." I liked that good wish of his. It was nice.

We parted at a crossroad. The man and wife continued along the coast road. I took a path that led directly to the mountains. All day I walked up and up. By noon, after crossing several ridges, I lunched under the shadow of a tree on bread, cheese, and fruit given me by an old couple working a field near the road. I had wanted to pay for the food, but had been told, "You are in the mountains, where hospitality is the law, and any stranger sent here is sent here by God." The old people also told me that I would find work in hamlets higher in the hills.

As evening came, I trudged into a little mountain settlement. The houses were made of dried earth. They all looked alike and clung to rocks and cliffs like birds' nests. They were stacked one above the other on ledges and it seemed as if one could jump from roof to roof. Atop them all, high up on a cliff, was a big, two-story house, built of stone and with a sheet metal roof.

Tired and remembering that a stranger was sent by God in those mountains, I entered the first house at the bottom of the village. Within were an old man, an old woman, and a pretty girl of about sixteen years. "Salaam Aleikum," I said. "Va Aleikum Salaam, Hosh geldiniz," I was welcomed. First I was seated near the fireplace. Next the girl brought me soap and water to wash. After that, all three—man, woman, and girl—said, "Merhaba," the greeting of the Middle East and the Caucasus.

I had been welcomed as a guest. I was not asked who I was or why I had come to their village and entered their house. All they knew was that I had the heavy accent of a Tatar and was a stranger. Formalities over with, they brought me food, meat, greens, and cheese; simple food, but much more healthful than what I had had in my wanderings.

After many, many months I was in a home with a peaceful family. I sat at their fire, eating their bread. My heart warmed. I became filled with emotion and had to make an effort to keep calm. I was only nineteen, but in that short life of mine I had learned something of my fellow man. I was sure I was in the house of good people. So, I told them of my troubles and my mistakes that had brought me to their door.

It was about midnight when I finished my tale. The family introduced themselves to me. The old man was Suleyman Effendi. His wife was called Perikhan. Their daughter was Zuleykha. Their only son had been killed fighting the Soviets. Suleyman Effendi said that if I wanted I could stay with them as long as I wished and help graze the sheep. I accepted. I became one of them, a shepherd, a sort of Caucasian cowboy.

The next morning I was taken to the sheep. I was given a bolt-action rifle, a big dagger, and the clothes which had been worn by the only son. Then I met the dogs that were going to be my companions in the mountains.

So I settled in with those kind and friendly Azerbaidzhan Turks who profess the Sunni branch of Islam. With my sheep and dogs I roamed the lofty mountains, valleys, and gorges. As well as a native, I got to know the best of the almost treeless alpine pastures, the proper watering places, and the big, lonely trees to gather my herd under during the heat of noon. My dogs were faithful, smart, and eager, and no wolf ever stole a sheep or lost lamb from my herd.

The dogs were not my only companions. Often I shared pastures with other shepherds, some of them youths my age, others older men and few of them little boys, no more than twelve. Those little fellows fascinated me, caring for their sheep or cattle as well as the older shepherds and like them, armed with rifles and pistols, girded with bandoliers, and all that always topped off with big daggers hanging in front from the belt. Those daggers terrified me. Masters of hand-to-hand fighting, those mountaineers were expert at use of the dagger and I thank God I never had to use one.

Those long days and nights under sun, moon, and stars were wonderful for me. Soon my health not only returned but improved. The fresh mountain air, the constant physical exercise in the outdoors, the simple, healthy food made me strong and full of energy. I felt there was nothing I could not do. Other shepherds gladly taught me their skill, all the fine points of caring for the animals, even what to do with newborn lambs.

Every second day, Zuleykha would find me in some upland

pasture to bring me baskets of food prepared by herself, and changes of clothes washed by her mother. On those visits she would usually tarry a while with me and tell of the life and habits of her people and sometimes sing their songs. Zuleykha was typical of those fine mountain women. Like my mother, their faces were ʌncovered. They often worked in the fields and with the animals. They rode horses and carried firearms which they could use ably, if necessary. They also had a very high regard for their honor and were very careful about love affairs.

I came to look forward to those visits from Zuleykha for her companionship, but I was never truly lonely. Since the chief occupation of the mountaineers was sheep and cattle raising, a shepherd was an important member of the community. People passing shepherds in pastures would stop to spend a few moments with them to talk about the weather or the herds. All the passersby were very friendly to me. They knew I was a stranger and so would go out of their way to greet me with encouragement and kind words.

Those attentions given me kept me from becoming unhappy, but I did become somewhat restless as week followed week and month followed month. I certainly appreciated the fact that in the mountains there were no police, no Soviet authorities, no poor jobless devils on park benches or in lodging houses, no trains, no labor exchange, no Communists. And I admired the mountain people. They were fine, brave, honest. They loved their families, their traditions, their way of living, their hard-earned property, and their mountains and valleys. They were devout, too. With an unlimited respect for their faith, all performed their religious duties wherever they happened to be, whether in the fields, at home, or in a public place. But the good people, the fine outdoor life, were not enough for me. I could not see myself settling there forever, getting married, and raising a family. Some strange force began nagging me to think of the future and plan my next step.

One morning in late summer, while I was brooding about what to do, my attention was drawn to a man riding not far from my herd along a road leading higher into the mountains. The man and horse were handsome figures. He wore a bright Circassian coat, call *Chrkeska* by the Russians, had a small, gold-plated curved dagger, and a pistol at his belt. His saddle was beautifully ornamented with silver and behind it was strapped a fine felt cloak. The horse was a high-stepping, spirited thoroughbred.

Noticing me, the lone rider wheeled in my direction to join me. Dismounting gracefully he greeted me with the customary *Salaam Aleykum*. He then asked in a kindly fashion, "Well, stranger, how are you doing? Do you like living here in our land? Is life too hard for you?"

Charmed by his appearance and his manner, I replied that I had no cause to complain, that all was fine, and thanked him for his kind words.

"Yes," he replied, "I had heard that you were doing well and that the people here liked you very much. That is why I came to visit you here. As you may know, we have no school, no teacher for the children of our village. We know from what you have told our people about yourself that you have had enough education to teach our children. Please accept our invitation to become their teacher. We would pay you. You could live in my house and its first floor is big enough for a schoolroom. I am the son of Khamidulla Effendiev. My name is Zabikhshah Effendi."

I had heard much of the father of the man standing before me. He was a chieftain famed throughout the mountains for his resistance to the Soviets. Before my arrival in that area, for two years he had led his people in battle against the Reds. He had not ordered arms put down until Mir Dzhafar Abbasovich Bagirov, chief of the Azerbaidzhan Cheka, came in person to make peace with those proud people by promising the Soviets would not interfere with their way of life. (This was the same Bagirov who later became chairman of the All Union Executive Committee, and was finally shot after the execution of Beria.) Nor was the wife of Khamidulla Effendiev unknown to me. By origin a Tatar from my own region, she was honored for her charity and for her care of the mountain children. And I knew the house of that family, too. It was the big, beautiful one of two stories overlooking the village of Suleyman Effendi.

Zabikhshah Effendi was the firstborn son of that mountain chieftain's family. I thanked him for his proposal, said I would think it over carefully and give my answer on the next day. Later that morning, Zuleykha came to the pasture with her basket of food and clothes for me and I told her I wanted to see her father. Suleyman Effendi arrived in the late afternoon. I told him of the offer of Zabikhshah Effendi, and since I respected that old man as I did my own father, I needed his approval before I could accept. Suleyman Effendi not only approved the idea but urged me to agree to it.

So, instead of a shepherd I became a teacher, a teacher not appointed by the Soviet government but chosen by the people. I swore to myself that there would be no political indoctrination, no propaganda in that little village of Kalgagyah, but just pure teaching. I would teach the children how to read and write, how to

count, and how to make pictures. I would tell them about the
world, about other people, about nature. I would teach them to do
good things and to avoid bad things.

As autumn started, I started my lessons for about twenty-five
children gathered on the first floor of the house of Khamidulla
Effendiev. Those little boys and girls were so eager to learn. How I
liked them and how they seemed to like me. I was given a living
room above the schoolroom and a good horse to use as my own.
People respected me as the teacher of their children and invited
me to their houses for pleasant evenings. What a contrast was
that work in the mountains to the so-called teaching I had done in
Chardzhou. Among those hill people I came to like teaching and
to feel that I was doing something useful, something really important. That winter of 1923-1924 was almost the best winter of my
life.

What kept me from being truly happy then was a letter I
received toward the end of the old year. Somehow that good
neighbor of Orsk, the bookdealer married to the two sisters, who
once visited me in sadness in Chardzhou, had traced me again.
Again in sadness, he wrote that my entire family, Father, Mother,
my two brothers, my two sisters, had perished in the great famine
and typhus epidemic that swept the Orsk region at about the
same time I started teaching in Kalgagyah. Before the end, the
old neighbor added, things had become so bad that Father had to
sell the house to buy food, a sale which had brought him only
twenty pounds of grain.

That was terrible news. There I was, fat and happy, while my
family starved to death. Even my pleasure with my school work
did not help my depression until the winter ended and the warm
winds began to blow again, bringing new life to the earth.

But with the coming of that spring new troubles came as well.
All new life is not necessarily good. Like a poisonous growth,
Bolshevism bloomed too and began its slow creep into those
mountains. We soon heard that a Communist cell had been organized in the village of Devechi, not too far from us. A few lazy
persons made up that group, but they had the ear of Baku.

Then in late spring communism reached our village. The
elders received notification from the district soviet that a teacher
would be sent us to instruct the children "properly" in accordance
with programs approved by Soviet education authorities. I knew
better than the villagers what "properly" instructed and
"approved" programs meant. I told them that much as I hated to
leave them and their wonderful mountains I had to look for work
somewhere else and before the new teacher came.

Zabikhshah Effendi agreed that I was wise to go and did his best to help me on a new start. At that time in Azerbaidzhan there was still some private trade and peasants could sell their extra produce in the city markets. My sponsor suggested that I might be successful in buying and selling excess grain, rice, and other agricultural products. He therefore arranged that parents of my students gave me wheat, rice, and barley for my fees rather than cash. In short order before my door there stood ten bags of grain. Since each bag weighed approximately 160 pounds, that was indeed a good reward for my teaching. That bounty was sent ahead of me by cart to the railway station while I said goodbye to those mountain people who had been so kind to me, before departing for Baku to become some kind of merchant.

In Baku I sold the grain for a good price in the market, enough to give me a tidy sum to start a small business of my own. The sales completed, and dreaming of what my next step should be, I searched out a cheap hotel for the night. I started to register and then suddenly found myself penniless except for a few kopeks. My pockets had been picked at the market. Ah, accursed Baku. That wretched city never brought me luck.

I wept in anger and shame when I found the money gone. All that I had earned so earnestly and honestly had disappeared in a few careless seconds. Without it, what was I to do? Live in Baku? By what means? Find a job? How? Thousands of jobless were still waiting at the doors of the labor exchange. Should I become a volunteer porter again? No, that was impossible. Nor could I consider going back to the mountains, awaiting the coming of the Soviet teacher confessing to people who had loved and admired me that I was a failure.

However, since I had come to know that area and reckoned that there would be work of some sort there, I ended up with the decision to go to Kuba, the district center. My mind made up, I left Baku forthwith, so as not to spend even a single night more in that luckless city. I left from the same station where I had arrived less than a dozen hours earlier with such sweet dreams. I boarded a passenger train, and with a ticket, which cost almost all the change I possessed.

I got off at Khachmaz, a little railway town some twenty miles east of Kuba. There was no rail connection between the two towns, only a road. At a small restaurant in Khachmaz I was told that working hands were needed at large orchards, famous for their apples, near Kuba. Late at night I started walking to Kuba, and by dawn I reached an area of big houses surrounded with apple orchards. At almost the very first house I knocked and asked for work. I was taken on with hardly a question. My principal work was cultivating the trees and caring for three horses. From time to time I was also sent up into the mountains to check on the shepherds and the owner's sheep.

It was good work and I was treated well, but my boss was a very odd man. He was the most superstitious person I have ever seen in eighty years of travel over half the known world. In his early thirties and strong in build, he was obsessed by *periis*, *djinns*, *shaytans*, by ghosts, by forces out of this world, and by every spirit with which the lore of the Caucasian tribes is so rich. He hated doctors and did not believe in them. But he did believe in all kinds of magic, in witches, in mysterious things. He had dozens of strange and unreasonable rules. He took great care to enter places with his right foot first and to leave them left foot first.

Once, in very serious mien, he told me that in the evenings he was accustomed to seeing a black cat with very fiery eyes just in front of him, which would suddenly disappear into space as he approached. Or he would tell me in whispers—so the evil spirits would not hear—about a big ball of fire that followed him one night when he was returning from pasture. "It followed me," he said, "until I recited a *sura* from the Koran thirty-three times."

Never would he put on a freshly washed shirt. He would ask me or one of his brothers to put it on first for a few hours and then return it to him, but usually I performed that strange ritual. He would never ride a white horse and he was very peculiar with the rest of his mounts. When one of then had bladder trouble and could not urinate, he saddled the poor beast and galloped around a nearby cemetery. When I asked what that was all about, he replied, "Why you silly Tatar. Don't you know that some of those dead people are crying loudly in their graves for their wrongdoings when they were alive? We can't hear that, but horses do hear it, become afraid and then urinate. Your stupid doctors don't know that."

That queer man never allowed work on Tuesdays, considering that would bring some misfortune. On Saturdays he forbade his household to do laundry. He believed that if clothes were washed on that day some member of the family would die.

He regarded blue eyes as very bad—although his own were blue—believed that blue-eyed people affected others with some evil. I am blue-eyed and shortly after I arrived, he called the household together and demanded a piece of lead and a cup of water. As he melted the lead in a pan over a fire, he touched in turn the foreheads of the household with the cup of water and pronounced some strange words. When the lead melted, he threw it into the water and carefully examined the cooled globules which took various forms like a heart or some animal form. These shapes must have passed inspection because he looked up at me and pronounced, "All right, boy." The household was protected from my eyes, but what preventative they had for his was beyond me.

At the start of every new venture whether business, travel, or trading, he would make sacrifices and vows. When the new thing was of small concern he would kill a cock. If it were something big and important he would kill a sheep as an offering and distribute the meat to poor neighbors. When he hired me he killed a cock. I was not too important.

That boss had a pretty young wife whom he adored. She was in poor health—I believe she had TB—when I arrived there in the spring and got worse all through the summer. I tried with no success to persuade her husband to send her to a hospital or sanatorium. He would grant the poor creature her every wish but medical aid.

Therefore there was little surprise one rainy autumn evening when nature ran its course and the young wife was on her deathbed. The boss was distraught. Neighbors had come in an effort to get a doctor, but the husband pulled out his pistol and said he would shoot the first who went to get one. His idea was that the only way to save his wife was to sacrifice an absolutely white goat as soon as possible and give the meat to the needy. I was given the job to get the beast from herds that were far away in mountain pastures. A saddled horse was brought me and I galloped high into the hills through the rain and dark.

Needless to say, it took some time for the round trip through gorges and across swollen streams, let alone to find an absolutely white goat in the dark. When I got back all was over. The young woman was dead. On seeing me with the goat, the husband gave me a powerful punch in the face. I fell down. He picked me up with his strong hands and then hit me again and again. I passed out.

When I came to some time later, I found myself tied to a pole in the stable. The husband stood beside me and the moment I opened my eyes he started to shout that his wife had died because of my blue eyes and because I was late with the goat. Between shouts he struck at my head repeatedly until he had knocked me out again.

The next time I came to it was morning. I was still in the stable, but I had been untied, probably by some more sane member of the family. My face was bloody, both eyes were swollen almost shut, and I ached all over.

It took almost all my strength just to stand up. I leaned against the stable wall until the dizziness and the nausea passed, then walked across the yard, through the orchards, and to the road to the sea and Khachmaz, the way by which I had come to that strange house. At first as I stumbled along I fumed at the brutal treatment given me without my having done anything wrong. But as I thought about it, I could not really hate that poor fellow despite what he had done to me. His beloved wife was dead. He was a victim of superstitions passed down to him by his forefathers, from pagan times. His religion was confused with pagan rituals. That was it. I forgave him. Peace be with him, I thought. One day he would recognize the terrible injustice done me.

After I had gone a few miles a cart overtook me and the driver offered me a ride. On his way to his village near the coast, he was startled by my battered face but relaxed when I told him I had been in a little fight. I asked about work in his area and he offered me the job of miller at his water mill and agreed to pay in cash. He also said I could live at the mill and that he would supply my food.

And so thus I became a miller. The mill was near the seashore and in the middle of a dense forest. It was a very lonely place. The nearest house was at least seven miles away, although there were two old Moslem cemeteries about one hundred yards distant. By night, even for me, accustomed to sleeping out in the open, it was more than a little frightening. The customers who left their grain to my care would always get away to their homes before nightfall and leave me alone with my thoughts and my imagination. I would sit there and try to concentrate on the dull, hollow sound of the millstones and try not to hear the mournful howling of jackals, the hoot of a lonely owl perched on some tombstone, or dozens of strange rustles. Under the moonlight those stooping tombstones were particularly unattractive, seeming to take on the postures and attitudes of human beings.

My chief distraction was to think about my future. Was I going to spend all my life changing from one job to another? Was I never to settle anywhere? And what about my education? I wanted so much to study and learn. In that reflection, I recalled how I had once visited the telegraphist's room in a small, lonely railway station in the deep of night. From a strange device there came a tik-tak tik-tak, taa-taa, ta-tatat, and from it rolled a tape with definite combinations of dots and dashes, having great significance. It was at the end of wires that stretched for miles and miles over hills, flat lands, deserts, gorges, mountains, over little streams and big rivers, through towns and cities, from station to station, by day and night, to carry messages of importance. I knew from my elementary schooling that the strange device was a telegraph apparatus. And I also knew how little I understood about how it ran and the electricity that powered it. I wanted to learn so many things about that electricity.

Meanwhile, November arrived. Before another winter set in, I decided I must get out of that solitary mill, back to towns and to people, and, if possible, to try once more to enter a school. The mill owner was sorry to see me go, but he was a good man and paid my earnings in cash as he had promised.

My destination again was Kuba, again for the same reason: it was the district center. To get there I had to walk to Yalama, the nearest station, to take a train back to Khachmaz, and then hike up that road that passed the apple orchards of my strange former boss.

That plan, as had others of mine, never worked out. When I got to Yalama I found it bustling with scores of young men who had gone there for profitable woodcutting work in nearby forests. The winter and its rains were not far off and the contractors had to get the timber in before that time. They hired me, too, without a question and early the next morning I joined the group in the forest. We cut wood steadily from dawn until dark with the only letup a short time out for lunch. The job paid very well, but it was tiring and after the evening meal I would sleep like a dead man.

In December the timber was felled and we were discharged. With the money earned there and my earlier work at the mill, I could afford to be idle for a while to look for another and a better job. It was by then too late to enter a school for that term, but I had to make a start somewhere, get to know somebody who might help. I was already twenty and time was running out to acquire those technical skills I needed.

Those were my thoughts as I arrived in little Khachmaz. I went immediately to the local soviet to find out about job openings in Kuba. It was the lunch hour when I rapped on the door and the office was deserted except for a smiling, blue-eyed Russian girl, with her bright, blonde hair braided on the back of her head. She was not only pretty, but kind and courteous as well, invited me into the office, and gave me a chair.

Within a few moments we were calling each other by first names. She, Dasha, was a telephone operator whose father was the baggage master at the railway station. When I told her I was looking for work, she herself offered me a job. She was the chief

and sole operator of a service supported by well-to-do apple grow-
ers of the region for their export business to Russia. (That was in
1924, when under NEP—New Economic Policy—limited private
commerce was permitted.) Dasha had been looking for an
assistant, and I qualified because I knew Russian as well as the
local tongues.

Very grateful as well as charmed by the pretty girl, I volunteered to take the night shift so that Dasha could have the evenings with her family. There were few formalities. Khachmaz was
not Baku or Moscow. All I had to do was fill out an application
blank—but why I had to address it to the local soviet when the
service was run by the apple merchants was a puzzle I did not
bother to unravel. Once the form was completed, Dasha took me
to her house near the tracks, introduced me to her mother, and
commandeered blankets and sheets for me for the bed in a corner
of the telephone office.

That very same night I settled into the most pleasant and
easiest work I ever had. All I had to do was sit and wait, sometimes hours, for incoming and outgoing long distance calls. And
since there were only a score or so of the apple exporters, there
were not too many calls. Sometimes I had a trifling bit of other
duty, to make connections between offices of the local soviets of
the area.

One evening late that winter, a pleasant-looking man came to
the switchboard and very courteously asked me to connect him
with the Kuba district soviet. After the call was completed, the
man said he had noticed my accent and asked if I were a Kazan
Tatar and about what I was doing in Khachmaz and about my
work. His questions came from kindness, not inquisitiveness, and
I welcomed his interest. Before long I told him much about myself.
He identified himself as Janbulat, whom I later learned was a
high Soviet official in the Kuba district. He was in his mid-
thirties, very well educated, well dressed, and had courtly manners. Before leaving the office he gave me his home address
and invited me to come to Kuba and spend a weekend when
possible.

A month later, with Dasha manning the switchboard in my
absence, I went to Kuba, straight to the house of Janbulat. I was
welcomed warmly and introduced to all the family, including my
host's very cultured father and mother. It was a fine house, tastefully furnished, and with valuable carpets on the floors and walls.
All were sympathetic to me and tried to make me feel at home.
Janbulat's parents were especially attentive to me, and I found
out that they were deeply religious, strictly performing all their

duties before God. I also discovered that they knew Khamidulla Effendiev, my sponsor in the mountains, very well and had deep respect for him. At the end of that wonderful weekend as I was about to leave, Janbulat called me aside. He told me that he would soon find me a good job in the Kuba district soviet.

He kept his word. In April the secretary of the Kuba district sent me an invitation to come there as assistant manager of the Kuba district soviet. Sad as it was to part from Dasha, it took almost no time to wind up my work as an operator, pack my few things in a little bag, and get a ride in a cart going to Kuba. At the office door I kissed Dasha goodbye, thanked her for all her kindness and for bringing me luck, and was off.

The work in the Kuba soviet office was easy. Through Janbulat I also made some other friends there as well. However, accustomed to working outdoors in the fresh air, I soon found the work confining and pretty monotonous. I also could see my chances of entering a technical school fading unless I moved soon and before I was much older. I told my worries to Janbulat and he agreed to help.

The weeks dragged on and on. Spring went, summer came, finally July. Then one hot morning, Janbulat called me to his room. On his desk he had a letter, a short one, which he gave me. it read:

"The Central Committee of the Azerbaidzhan Communist Party suggests that you recommend to the Department of Personnel of the C.C. a young man of your choice to send to the Leningrad Military Signal School for training. Report immediately the name of the candidate.

S. M. Kirov."

Janbulat was smiling as I handed the paper back to him. "How would that be, Ismail," he asked, "to become an officer in the signal troops?"

To me that represented an opportunity beyond my wildest dream, but I wanted to appear mature and responsible to my older friend. I said I would like to sleep on the suggestion. He laughed but agreed.

Sleep, of course, was impossible that night. I dreamed and dreamed, but with eyes wide open. Petrograd, now Leningrad. Military school. To become an officer. Signal troops. To be sent to any part of Russia after graduation. Secure future. Promotions. The possibility of further training. To learn about electricity and communications devices. Perhaps one day to be made a military attaché in some foreign country.

The security of the opportunity attracted me just as much as its more romantic aspects. From my own brief but bitter experience in the private field, I had learned that the chance to survive was very limited and certainly guaranteed by no law. Janbulat, who had a very good understanding of communism, had frequently told me in discussing my future that the only way to survive and get somewhere under the Soviets was to graduate from some educational institution and that the best education offered then was in military colleges.

To enter a military college at that time, one had to be a graduate of some military school and to have had at least two years' service in the field. The civil war was over. The army was being reorganized, needed new and trained officers.

What would I gain by staying in Kuba? Become some sort of clerk in a Soviet office, get married, and then drift step by step into decline? Not for me.

I would become a military engineer. That is what I told Janbulat the very first thing the next morning. He was pleased, gave me good references, and in two days I left Kuba for Baku. (Years later I made a special trip to Kuba to thank Janbulat once more in person for his help and kindness. He was no longer there. He had been purged from the Party for opposition to collectivization and for nationalism, and sent as a petty official to some remote district in the Far East. In other words, he was sent into exile.)

The chief of the personnel department himself welcomed me at the Central Committee offices in Baku. His staff had all my papers ready and signed. Before I left I told them that three years earlier, in that very same office, my Party membership card had been taken from me because I could not prove I had undergone the 1922 purge in Central Asia. The official who had grabbed the card from me back then put on a studied act of recognizing me again with difficulty, and then asked where I had been all those years. He said that about eight months after my card had been taken from me, notification was received from the Chardzhou that my purge status was in order. Ever since, he claimed, he had looked for me without success. I had been reconfirmed as a full Party member, dating from the start, May 1921. The Party Control Commission of the Leningrad Military District would be notified of that and would have the new form of membership card ready for me.

At the door I told that official a bit of what had happened to me since he grabbed my old card. He laughed nervously, told me to have a good trip, try to be a good commander, and maybe one day I would have time to write a good book about my wanderings.

I did not find him, either, on my next trip to the area. In the 1932 purges he was classed an "enemy of the people" and shot.

That evening I went to the station. It was the same station where so many times I had been a volunteer porter to get something to eat, where I had boarded trains without tickets or documents, without definite destination, without definite plan.

That time—and ever since—I had a real destination, a real plan. I was going to Leningrad and I was to be an officer in the Red Army. And I had more. I had travel and living expenses and in my pocket this paper:

"To the Commanding Officer of the Leningrad Military Signal School; Smol'ny, Leningrad.

"The bearer of this pass, Comrade Ismail Gusseynovich Akhmedov, is sent by the Central Committee of the Azerbaidzhan Communist Party to the city of Leningrad to enroll in the Leningrad Military Signal School."

That was the pass to my future. Through the Northern Caucasus, through the Don, the Ukraine, through Moscow, I finally arrived in the middle of August 1925 at Leningrad, which was to become my residence for quite a number of years.

# Part Two

# 4

## Survival, I

March forward, Take the field,
   Red Hussars;
Dashing sound calls us to the
   battle,
Fill the cups.

The autumn morning was crisp, sunny, and invigorating. It was one of those days when it was wonderful just to be alive and healthy.

We the *kursants* or cadets of the Leningrad Military School of Radio Communications sang our best as we swung along Suvorov Avenue, making our daily march in battalion formation. We also tried hard to be as precise and smart as possible, because we imagined that behind the curtained windows of the buildings standing at attention on each side of the avenue were sweet girls with dark eyes admiring our march. At least it said the girls were there in other lines of the old, pre-Revolutionary marching song, originally called "Black Hussars," and changed to "Red" to fit with Marxism. An old Imperial Russian Army air, it was our school's favorite song and much preferred to such Communist music as, "Sergey Pop, Sergey Pop," an atheistic attack on an Orthodox priest, or the banal, "We Blacksmiths, We Blacksmiths, We Build the Happiness for the People," dedicated to the builders of communism.

Alas, much as we blared out "Red Hussars," there were no more dark-eyed beauties left behind the curtains to watch our brave performance. The Revolution had ousted all of them from their handsome homes, scattering them to all four corners of the former Empire, or to lands beyond its borders. In fact many of those windows not only lacked girls but curtains as well. A curtain, like a necktie, or a bird cage, was a sign of capitalist degeneracy, the symbol of the petty bourgeoisie. Instead most windows were covered with sheets of old newspapers.

The girls who did stay behind were either at schools or working at local factories such as the Khalturin Textile Mills, which had been named the workers' patron of our signal school. And the truth was that few of the girls who were left had any time for us. For them we were a dull mass of country boys, parasites in gray coats, not the builders and creators. Their eyes were turned to engineers, technicians, the new breed of university students, the future builders of the new world of promise and challenge. "Nothing can be expected from those poor cadets," was a frequent remark during those days of the New Economic Policy of the mid-twenties.

Our imaginations and sighs to the contrary, those daily marches were not for the girls at all. Their object was to get us in top shape for that year's major event, the eighth anniversary of the October Revolution.

The great day came November 7, 1925. From the four corners of Urizkiy Square silver trumpets blared to sound the beginning of the parade.

A strong but modulated voice roared the command, "Parade, Attention." Massed military bands struck up the *International*.

Hurrah, Hurrah. Thunderous Hurrahs rolled from one end of the square to the other and echoes crashed back in successive waves from the surrounding buildings.

Formations of students of military academies, of the Political Academy, the Artillery Academy, the Engineers, the Naval Academy, the Electrotechnical Academy, of the cadets of the military schools such as mine, of regular units of infantry, cavalry, artillery, armor, signals, all stood rigid as stone, at attention, shouting Hurrah.

The commanding officer of the parade, inspecting the troops, arrived at our unit.

Almost with one voice we cadets bellowed, "I swear to defend the first country of socialism to the last drop of my blood.

"I swear to devote myself to the last breath to my people, to the Soviet Motherland and to the Soviet Government.

"I swear to carry out unquestioningly the orders of my superiors.

"I swear. . . ."

For me and most of my comrades that was the first military parade. We stood almost dumbfounded, exalted, hypnotized, ready for sacrifices. Some of the weaker fainted and were taken away silently on stretchers.

What a magnificent setting! There I stood in the very center of that historic square, the square that had been the scene of oath-taking ceremonies of the past, the square that had witnessed the tears and suffering of the people and the shedding of their blood. In the middle, high on a marble column, was the statue of the Angel looking down on us with sorrowful eyes, with cross in hand, seeming to bless the army of those who had rejected all angels with the same sincerity she once bestowed on other armies that fought in her name.

To the right of us the rows and rows of the windows of the Hermitage reflected the northern sky. To the left of us, like sentries at attention and glinting in the rays of the sun, were the colonnades of the former Tsarist General Staff building, taken over as headquarters of the Leningrad military district. And in front of us the spire of the Admiralty pointed straight up into space, a bold symbol of Russian expansion to new frontiers.

Yes, you, Leningrad, I dreamed as I stood there. You are really one of the most beautiful and fascinating cities in the world, with your Neva River and its granite embankments; with your Winter Palace, the Hermitage; with your Cathedral of St. Isaac's; with Mednyy Vsadnik, the statue of Peter the Great; with your broad and straight avenues; with your parks; with your *nuit blanches*; and the Petropavlovskiy Fortress. For me you were not only the former capital of the Russian Empire, not only the birthplace of the Revolution, you were also the first heart of Russian culture. Pushkin, Lermontov, Gogol, Dostoyevsky, Lev Tolstoy, walked your streets, loved you, and wrote about you. I too would investigate all your corners, enjoy your sights, become intimate with you, visit your rich libraries, enjoy your ballet, your operas, enrich my mind, deepen my culture, love your sweet girls, and the devil take my troubles of the past. Salute to you, Leningrad!

My reveries snapped to a halt as the strong voice again commanded, "Parade, Attention."

It was the ceremonial march in battalion formation at the distance of a guidon bearer. The Military Political Academy, "Forward." The others, "Right Face. Shoulder Arms. Eyes Right. March." Pacing in step past the platforms, saluting the generals and Party bosses, shouting in unison one more great Hurrah, then back to quarters and reality.

What a naive bumpkin I was in those days. But I was far from alone. I was only one of hundreds of thousands, no, of millions of the sons of enigmatic Russia, clad in gray uniforms, armed to the teeth, to march in precise formation on the eighth anniversary, in uncounted towns, cities, and garrisons, from Leningrad to Baku, from Kiev to Vladivostok, to participate in the ritual of carrying out the orders of our masters unquestioningly. The Bolsheviks called the armies of other nations cannon fodder. What were we then? And could I have known then that little more than a decade later the majority of officers who took part in that mighty parade would be arrested, tortured, sent to Siberian concentration camps, executed without trial by firing squads, disgraced forever as "enemies of the people," their wives and children forced to denounce them as traitors, and their families left to the mercy of the fates? No, to have thought that could happen would have been beyond my wildest imagination.

Instead, when I returned from the parade I was actually very happy. I was overjoyed to be in Leningrad, the city of my dreams, the center of my world, in those days of NEP, rich with private shops and windows full of merchandise, with nightclubs, bars, movie houses, and, of course, first-class ballet and opera theaters.

I was also tremendously pleased to be in the school. Our classrooms, laboratories, and motor vehicle park were on Suvorov Avenue in the buildings of the former Tsarist General Staff Academy, on whose marble walls the names of former graduates were still written in gold. Our living quarters were at Smol'ny in a former institute for young women of noble birth. Next to us was the main section of Smol'ny, Lenin's headquarters during the Revolution, and later the offices of the Leningrad Party organization. From time to time, in rotation, the cadets of our school were posted on guard there, a duty which was considered an honor and a sign of trust.

The Leningrad Military School of Radio Communications and Signals—its full name—was an outgrowth or successor of the Petrograd Officers Electrotechnical School, a fine military educational establishment founded in Tsarist days of recognition of Marconi and Tesla. In contrast to accelerated short courses then the fashion in many other institutions, my school offered a solid four-year program. The emphasis was on mathematics, physics, electro techniques, radio, and tactics and signal service organization in the armed forces. Additional subjects were history and foreign languages, as well, of course, as political indoctrination.

Our teachers were mainly officers, but there were also some civilians. In the main the military instructors were ex-officers of the Imperial Army, retained by the Soviets as specialists. Most were very able. All were seasoned soldiers, some brilliant, some cynical. They were most precise in their drill, and their uniforms fit them like gloves. One could recognize them from a distance. Like Prussian officers they had their own peculiar military bearing, their own way of speaking Russian, and their own manners.

I remember with pleasure the tall, handsome, eternally young-looking Voskressenskiy, a former Senior Signal Officer of the Supreme Military Headquarters of the Imperial Army. With his clean-shaven face, with his graying hair parted most exactly, with his superbly fitting uniform, his large golden ring, and his polished speech, he seemed to me the very personification of an officer. He taught us signal service.

And there was a former colonel, a certain Eristov, once a Georgian prince. His subject was tactics and his philosophy was to take it easy and joke. "All a real man needs," he would say, "is the shadow of a tree, a girl, and a bottle of good wine." When a new cadet got up courage to ask him about his native Georgia and the city Tbilisi, he would tell this yarn:

Once, a Russian on a train bound from Moscow to Tbilisi met a friendly Georgian returning to his capital city. The Russian asked about Tbilisi and how big it was. The Georgian answered that Tbilisi was almost as big as Moscow and that the only real difference was that Moscow had one more streetlight than Tbilisi did. Annoyed, the Russian reacted by asking if there were many fools in Tbilisi. None at all, replied the Georgian, and he then told the Russian he would have the honor of being the first one.

The moral of the Georgian's tale was that Russians were not too welcome in Georgia. And although the majority of cadets to whom the Georgian spun that tale were Russians, they swallowed it peacefully, remembering that Stalin, too, was a Georgian.

Then there was an old man, Zagorskiy, a former general, who commanded an Imperial division during World War I on the Rumanian front. His troops were badly mauled by Austrian and Hungarian units there. His thinking was beyond our understanding, but because of the defeat he hated not Austrians and Hungarians, but Rumanians. He would tell us that the Rumanians were the world's poorest soldiers, and claim that if the Soviet government gave him a brigade of cavalry and the marching orders, he could subdue Rumania within a week. His opinions about a nation's soldiers varied. Usually he held that the Turks made the world's best soldiers, followed by the Japanese and the Germans. But when asked about the Russians, he would put them in the number one position. At that we would tease him by quoting Stalin to the effect that Russians had a long history of defeat by such invaders as Poles, Swedes, Tatars, Germans, Turks, and Japanese. Not daring to contradict Stalin, the poor old man would splutter and go silent.

In contrast to the ex-officers, the majority of our civilian instructors and political officers were dull and uninteresting.

Their main handicap was that their educational and historical backgrounds were poor and they were incapable, therefore, of making interesting presentations of political subjects. But of course there were some exceptions.

One was our social science teacher, who would fascinate us with hours-long discussions of Kant, Huxley, and Hegel. He was a peculiar kind of Communist, less dogmatic, a free thinker, a revolutionary, a man still looking for the answer. On the one hand he would hold that choice of action was not free, then scan various degrees of determinism and even assume the existence of some freedom of human will. He paid for that thinking and was expelled from the Party as a Menshevik sympathizer.

Another civilian exception was a Party official, a young man with the double family name of Kiselev-Gusev, the secretary of the school's Party organization. He fought hard for expansion of democratic action within the Party, and was transferred to some wilderness for his pains.

The student body in those days was about evenly split between raw youngsters like myself and aging but poorly educated combat veterans of the Revolutionary struggles. Those oldsters already had officers' rank, or *Komandirskiye Zvaniya*— commanders' titles—since the use of specific grades had not yet been reinstituted in the armed forces. They wore commanders' uniforms, were paid salaries commensurate with their titles, and were permitted to leave the school grounds whenever free. They were the rich and privileged category. Many had been decorated for gallantry, but that helped them little at school. Most were approaching middle age. For them to fight was relatively simple, but to think in abstract terms and appreciate theories was next to impossible. When they arrived many of them did not even know how to draw a simple map.

Although they had more freedom and material advantages they naturally envied the youth and freer brains of the younger students. We, for our part, were pretty cocky about things. We believed that the future was in our hands alone. We realized that knowledge in the military, technical, or political fields was our only weapon, and we made a full assault on the fortresses of learning. For all that, we youngsters lived in our own world, a world isolated from the outside by many barriers. We dreamed about uniforms, new, smart, and splendid, like those once worn by Tsarist officers. We dreamed about officer ranks and titles, about becoming the elite.

Unfortunately for all my early hopes about enjoying Leningrad and getting to know its every nook and cranny, as a student I had little chance to see much of the city and its people. First, we were not permitted off the premises whenever we wished, even if classes were over and we were off duty. We had to have approval from a superior and a pass. But the main drawback was lack of funds. Our monthly allowance was not adequate for even a single meal and drink in a moderately priced restaurant, so we always returned to school for meals even when on pass.

A few months after my arrival at the school I got a letter from Dasha, the jolly telephone operator at Khachmaz, asking about Leningrad and how I was getting along. Since I had no family that was my only correspondence and I treasured it, and answered that kind girl's letters lengthily and frequently. In time, however, she started writing of love and marriage. That frightened me off, not that I did not like her and admire her, but because I felt I could not allow romance to interfere with my career at that stage. Somewhat brusquely, I am afraid, I cut off those exchanges. Later, I learned to my pleasure, she married a nice Russian young man and the marriage was a happy one.

The fact that I had meanwhile found a nice Russian girlfriend in Leningrad also contributed to my not getting serious with Dasha. That other girl, Maria, had hair as shining black as Dasha's was blonde, big black eyes like ripe cherries, a Hellenic nose, and high cheekbones. She was well developed to plump for her age, and probably became a pretty fat old woman. About the only real bond between us, besides my liking for her gaiety, was that she was the daughter of a division commander. As such, Maria was more ready to accept me for my company only and could understand that I had little to no pocket money to spend on her. Relations between Maria and me never got to the serious stage, but we had much happiness in walks in the parks and exploring the city.

Besides, I was too interested in school to have much time for girls. We had just started to learn basic tactics, to grasp the concepts of actions of platoons, companies, battalions, and regiments, to learn what offense and defense were as applied to such units. Those basics were eye openers to me, making me realize how scant was my knowledge of military art and how much study in that field lay ahead of me. That and our laboratories and workshops, spotless and shining with tools, radio components, electric and combustion motors, were my real loves at that time.

In the summer of 1927, because I had been above the average in grades and deportment, I was given a month's leave at the end of my second year. Cadets so rewarded were also given free railroad warrants to places of their choice, usually their homes. With my family dead I had no real home to go to, but I got a warrant for Orsk because it was my duty to at least honor the graves of my people.

As it turned out, I spent only a week in that town of my happy childhood, and quite a sad one. I asked everywhere, but nobody could tell me where my family had been buried or even what had happened to their bodies. The only relatives I had at all who were still there were an aunt, who had not been in Orsk during the troubles and was unhappily married to a local policeman, and one of my prospector uncles from Aydyrlinsky. Neither of those two gave me any welcome, and the uncle disgusted me. Once a Socialist, he had become a minor Communist functionary, and a drunken one at that, who argued that he was a better Party member than I because he was a worker while I was a soldier. There was also much discontent and grumbling among the other people I still knew there because they objected to collectivization of the land, which was just beginning in the Orsk area. I returned to Leningrad with two weeks of my leave unused and never again went back to Orsk. The whole visit there had depressed me greatly.

Perhaps it was my first contact with the outside world after two years of isolation in the school that was the chief cause of my gloom. Our work and position as students who would be the administrators did shield us from the rough and tumble of politics and economics outside the walls, but not completely. At the end of 1927 Stalin won final victory over Trotsky and his followers when the Fifteenth Congress condemned the Trotskyites as deviationists and ordered them purged. Trotskyites in the army were discharged from military service and expelled from the Party. Our school was not an exception in that respect. Several score students, mainly the oldsters, disappeared from classes and drill, as well as a handful of instructors.

But that purge—a really trifling one as later events proved—was only a temporary distraction. It caused no break at all in my studies and my fascination with them. My interest deepened immensely as I learned more about electronics, so much so that I had little time for basic military matters, let alone politics.

As my horizon expanded to vector analysis, partial differential equations, the theory of numbers, the functions of complex variables, the Fourier integral, I grew greedier. I knew that to learn more I had to qualify for the Electrotechnical Academy and that to do that I needed good marks in my four years at school, plus satisfactory service in the field as a junior officer after commission. As one of the preliminary steps I enrolled in extra, optional courses. I became somewhat of a grind. When out of classes on guard duty, I started taking technical books with me to the guard room. I developed quite a flair for electrical oscillations, and since the Germans were then expert on that subject, I took night courses in German to learn that language. In the same way I also studied Turkish, not because that language contributed to my studies, but because of my interest, as a Tatar, in the Turks, a fellow people.

Toward the end of my senior year I was given the assignment to deliver a lecture on the international situation to our patron workers' group, the textile mill. It was not an assignment that I welcomed or felt capable of doing well, but I had to do it as part of our required course in politics. Without any great enthusiasm I went to a public library to do the research I badly needed.

In the stacks a pretty blonde girl asked me for a cigarette, then wanted to know what I was doing there. I told her my problem and she was not only sympathetic but offered to help. She was a pedagogical student at the university and said she would gladly prepare the paper for me. I accepted immediately.

After I had read the thesis, which was quite a success at the workers' gathering, I called at the girl's home to thank her. She introduced me to her father, a medical professor at the university, and made me feel at home. I liked her name, Natalia. I also liked her blonde hair, braided round her head, her slim figure, her shy, quiet smile. She evidently liked me too. Not only had she done the thesis for me, but that first evening at her home she decided to wash her hair and in order to better show it off, asked me to help her rinse it. It was beautiful and when unbraided cascaded to the middle of her back.

By that time in 1929 I had long since given up Maria. Although she was gay and amusing, I just found her too flighty, too little interested in serious things, especially my studies and hopes. But I had regretted not having a girl for company on pass, as most of my fellow cadets did.

Natalia stepped easily and quickly into that gap. I not only liked her for her good looks and a serious approach to her own studies, I also soon came to love her. It was fumbling, awkward, youthful love, but it was really love, my first love. She loved me too and we spent all of my passes and many a *nuit blanche* in each other's company.

Unfortunately for that love, it came too late in the lives of both of us. Just scant weeks after I met Natalia, we both graduated. A lieutenant, my orders were to report to Tbilisi in Georgia as platoon commander in a radio battalion. Natalia was to go to what to us seemed the opposite end of the world, to Pskov, near Leningrad, to teach. With graduation I was given a week's leave and we spent it all together in Leningrad. At the end I had to take the train south. I will never forget her coming to the station to see me off. For the first time she gave me the kiss that a woman gives a man. Tears were in her eyes and in mine, too. As the train pulled out she called, "Ismail, I love you. Never forget me." I never did, but I lost her. I could not ask her to join me in Tbilisi because I was a very junior officer, supplied with no quarters nor enough money to pay for private lodging. Instead we wrote each other constantly for several months. Then suddenly her letters stopped. I tried to find her; I could not, ever.

Thank goodness I was young. My heartbreak, although terrible, was not perpetual, nor was love my only interest in life. Even before I lost Natalia, I had distractions as the train rolled south. It was my first trip on a really first-class train. The seats were plush. I had a fine compartment with a bed all for myself. There was a dining car. One evening as I was sitting in the diner with dinner and wine before me, the train halted briefly in a little station in the foothills of the Caucasus. Through the window I saw the telegraphist's office and an old Morse apparatus receiving messages. Years earlier as a hungry, homeless boy, I had first seen that kind of equipment and wondered at it. School had explained those mysteries and many more to me. It had also given me a job and a future. I was thankful to God.

My first command, the platoon, was part of the Eleventh Radio Battalion of the Caucasian Red Banner Army, and was deployed in the outskirts of Tbilisi. The troops lived in barracks there, but I was assigned quarters in town, a single room in the old part of the city near Metekhi Castle, a venerable fortress long used for political prisoners by the Tsars as well as the Communists.

Once the newness of having my own command had worn off—and that did not take long—I began to find that kind of army life monotonous and boring. Days were spent in the barracks or field instructing and drilling soldiers. The evenings were passed either at the officers' club or reading in my little room. The first Sundays and other free days after arrival, I had much pleasure in exploring Tbilisi, found it most picturesque and interesting. Although small as compared to Leningrad, it makes up for that with fine vistas encircled by hills and mountains and its division by the swift-rushing, almost wild mountain river, the Kura. It has a number of very old churches and cathedrals, and because of the Russian influence a few broad avenues, its own theaters of opera and ballet, and, of course, a university. Nevertheless, it lacked the cosmopolitanism of Leningrad and I soon exhausted its tourist possibilities.

Therefore with time on my hands—I did not care much for the officers' club with its heavy drinking and crude stories, often repetitious, and felt cramped in my room—I enrolled in evening classes at the Institute of Foreign Languages to improve my German. I wanted a goodly knowledge of that language not only for future technical studies, but also because the army gave additional pay to those proficient in foreign languages, and my lieutenant's salary was very small.

In the spring of 1930 I got my last letter from Natalia. My unhappiness and disappointment were great, but it was spring and I was a normal young man. There were about fifteen students in the German class, some of them young girls. For some time, one of those girls had attracted me in particular. A brunette, she sat in the front row ahead of me. Her rich brown hair was naturally curly. Her dark brown eyes were brilliant and seemed to me to be full of fun and mischief. Her neck was graceful and slim, her forehead was high and noble. There was no makeup on her clear skin although her nails were manicured. Her clothes were modest and in good taste. A bit boyish, she was also provocative, very delicate and feminine, had an extremely shapely figure, and a fine carriage. She was also the best student in the German class and had an even better command of French.

One evening during recess I got up the courage to introduce myself. She was kind about my shyness, put me at ease with a big smile—that also showed off her lovely lips and perfect teeth to advantage—and chatted. She was Tamara Yefimovna Perskaya, a Jewess.

At the end of class I escorted Tamara to the doors of her apartment—small, too. Slowly we became good friends as we discovered we had much in common. She liked hiking, so did I. She liked opera, theater, good books, art; so did I. She played the piano well. I did not play at all, but I enjoyed listening to her play.

Tamara's family came from Poltava in the Ukraine and had had much trouble. Because of pogroms at the end of the last century, they fled to Berlin. Tamara was born there in 1906 and the family returned to Poltava after the Revolution, hoping that oppression of Jews in Russia would be ended. Her father was an antiquarian of repute. Before the family fled to Berlin he had hidden the late short story writer Vladimir Korolenko, who, although an anti-Bolshevik, also was sought by the Tsarist regime.

Her family had sent Tamara to Tbilisi to go to the university there, primarily because Poltava did not offer the same educational opportunities, but also because she had two uncles in the Georgian capital who could act as her guardians. After graduation Tamara got a job as a civilian secretary for the chief of the medical service of the Caucasian Red Banner Army, and that was what she was doing when I met her. Her pay was the same as mine was at that time.

During that spring that we met, my fascination with Tamara increased as we got to know each other better. At first I was surprised, later captivated, by her liking for American clothes. They really were American, too, albeit secondhand. She got them in the market where they were sold by people who had received them from relatives or sympathizers in the U.S., people who were either afraid to wear foreign styles or who needed the money more than the clothing. Another of her idiosyncrasies was vegetarianism. She took me to several of her favorite no-meat restaurants. I enjoyed her company at those places, but being brought up a Tatar, I found the fare not quite to my taste. She also took me to meet her uncles, one a physician, the other a very capable tailor who had learned his trade in Paris.

At the end of spring I got a pair of low-priced tickets to the opera. It was *Romeo and Juliet* and while taking her home after it, I proposed to Tamara. Of course, the story of the two Italians had affected me, but by then I was also deeply in love with that wonderful girl. To my relief and joy, she was not coy about my proposal. She heard me out, then said, "Ismail, I love you, too. I also know you will be a good husband and I will try to be a good wife." How happy I was!

However, getting married immediately was out of the question. The problem—as it is with most young people in Communist countries—was where to live. My tiny room was too small; so was hers. So, we had to wait. And during that waiting, the army added difficulties to our romance. In summer my battalion was moved out of Tbilisi to the Vaziani area in the mountains some twenty miles distant for a period of field training. Every day out there without Tamara seemed to last a month. Each weekend, however, I would see her. On Sunday mornings I galloped to Tbilisi and spent the day and most of the night with my love. I would arrive back at camp at dawn on Mondays in time to go out in the field again, sleepless, but so happy.

At the end of summer 1930, a year after my arrival in Tbilisi, I completed my course at the language institute and applied to the army for examinations in both German and Turkish. I thought that if I passed in both languages, my salary increase would be enough for me to pay for better quarters so that Tamara and I could be married and live together. I also wanted language proficiency on my record to help me to further studies. Although I had not the slightest idea of it at the time, when I applied for examination I also triggered some decisive changes in my life.

A week after I had made application I was ordered to report to a board for examination. The chairman was introduced to me as General Minzakir Absalyamov. His name remains etched in my memory because he had a profound effect on my career—although I never saw him again in later years—and also because he was a fellow Tatar. After brief questions about my army status the general turned me over to a pleasant and smiling officer, a Colonel Kuzyuberdin. By his manners and looks, by the way he talked and behaved, the colonel was a much more educated and cultured officer than the field commanders I knew in the battalion. He took me to his office and gave me a Turkish paper on field regulations of the Turkish army and a German technical text on oscillations—by chance one of my favorite subjects—to translate into Russian within a specified time. After checking my work, he then examined me orally by posing as a prisoner of war and directing me to interrogate him. Next I was given a pair of military situation reports in both languages to translate. That done, the colonel smiled, said the examination was over, and that I would be notified of the result shortly.

A few days later I was given a copy of Army Orders. On it was a paragraph stating that I had qualified as military translator, second rank, in both languages, as result of which my salary had been increased by twenty percent. As soon as I was off duty I rushed with the copy to Tamara, and we talked of marriage as soon as we could find a place. She, we agreed, was to look for it.

That planning and Tamara's looking soon proved completely unneccesary. The very next day my battalion commander called me to his office and told me that I was to report immediately to the Fourth, or Intelligence, Department of the Caucasian Red Banner Army.

At Army headquarters I was escorted to the office of the chief of the Fourth Department. There behind a large desk in a tastefully well-furnished, spacious room, was none other than the chairman of my language board, General Absalyamov. I literally gaped with surprise, and that seemed to please the general and amuse him as well. He motioned me to a chair and as I gazed around the room with walls lined with big maps of the Transcaucasus, Iran, and Turkey; with bookcases of British, French, and

German encyclopedias; and with tables piled with foreign publications, even the Russian emigree papers, all forbidden to average Soviet citizens, most Red Army officers included; I realized that I faced a far from average situation. For a few minutes, to put me at ease, the general chatted about my Party and military background. Then, standing up and walking toward me, he came to the point. His department, he told me, was in charge of operational intelligence and was in need of qualified personnel. I, he said, was qualified. I was young, I already knew two languages, I had professional radio training. A transfer from my battalion to his department, he went on, would benefit both the army and myself. My character and background had been thoroughly checked and clearance had been obtained for me. Had I any objections to transfer?

How nice! How could I have objected? Nor could I stall and ask for time to sleep on it or think it over. I knew I had no choice. It had already been made for me. If I refused I would rot there in Tbilisi; I would never get further technical training. Besides, these thoughts raced through my head: the battalion work was monotonous, intelligence might be interesting, and maybe I would even be sent abroad.

"Yes, Comrade General, I agree with your opinions. I have no objection to the transfer."

The general shook my hand in agreement and while he was smiling with pleasure, I put in my oar about my future hopes of entering the Electro-Technical Academy. He responded by clapping me on the shoulder and saying that after service in his department I could go to any academy I wished.

Then he led me to an adjoining office where he left me with the chief of operations, the same Colonel Kuzyuberdin who had tested my knowledge of German and Turkish. The colonel congratulated me on my decision, said my transfer orders would be completed soon, and dismissed me for the day.

The orders came through in less than a week and with them my promotion to the rank equivalent to senior lieutenant. And that was not all. I was also given new quarters, fine ones: two rooms, kitchen and a bath. That was the accommodation for at least a captain. In regular service I would have had only one room, normally. The second room was allowed me as an intelligence officer. From it I was to operate my radio transmitter and receiver.

That day I was waiting outside the door of Tamara's office to tell her the good news as she left work. And how wonderful it made things for us! The next day we would be married—and we were. My new office was close to Tamara's. At lunch hour, with a few friends from my old battalion and from Tamara's office, we went to the civil registry office and declared our wish to be husband and wife.

After my second and serious meeting with General Absalyamov, I had done much imaginative bragging to Tamara about the romantics attached to intelligence work, its secrecy, its danger. Never a Party member, always not interested in politics, she held my hand and listened attentively. When I had finished, she said she was glad I was interested in my new work and hoped even more than I did that eventually I would be able to go to the Leningrad Academy. Education, she said then, and always said, was what really counted. I must, she urged, acquire some real skill, some technical knowledge, not be just an ordinary, thoughtless army officer sitting it out until a war.

For all my tall talk to Tamara about intelligence, I really knew nothing at all about it when that transfer came through. That was made very plain to me when I started work in Colonel Kuzyuberdin's office. For general theory I was assigned a pair of volumes, *Strategic Intelligence*, by Colonel Walther Nicolai, World War I chief of intelligence and counterintelligence of the German general staff. When I had digested that, my colonel examined my reactions to it, then told me what I have never forgotten, so basic is it to the operations of Soviet intelligence:

"Ismail, what you have read is just the beginning. We Communists are different. Our intelligence must be different. It must be more active, stronger. Nicholai is, so to speak, a technician. We are revolutionaries.

"Our revolutionary ethics and Communist tactics are the foundations upon which we must build our intelligence. Following the rules laid down by Nicolai, by the Tsarist Okhranka, and by many others is okay, provided we do not stop there. Instead of *razvedka* [intelligence] we must use the term *podpol'naya rabota* [underground work] because we are the secret army of our Party.

"We do not just collect and disseminate intelligence data. We must do that, of course, but we must also do much more. We must know the plans and intentions of not only our enemies, but also those who are now our friends. We must know the roads in our countries of interest, the terrain, the deployment of troops, their tables of organizations, and dispositions and types of armaments. We must recruit and train agents, dispatch them across borders, establish agent *residenturas* abroad.

"But such tasks were and are being carried out by other countries as well. Ours is much greater. The most important thing to remember is that our purpose is to destroy the world as it now is and build a new one. We do not shout, 'Long live the world revolution,' for nothing. We mean it.

"Therefore, our whole intelligence system is not limited to classic espionage as described in these foreign publications you see in this room, but it also comprises the sum total of active clandestine actions directed toward the destruction of the capitalistic world. For us that means not just classic espionage, but also sabotage, terror, kidnappings, assassinations, penetrations into foreign governments and political parties in order to manipulate them from within, the organization of small and big disorders, strikes and protests, the conduct of psychological warfare, provocations, and disinformation. Those are the normal weapons in our arsenal. That is why we enjoy special position and power within our own armed forces."

For practical knowledge I was given the department's agent files to read and absorb, to learn of the successes of some, the failures and errors of others, and the reasons for those outcomes. Most of what I read was a study of techniques, but some of it shocked me terribly.

One awful find of mine was a lengthy report on the suppression of "unrests"—really uprisings—in those mountains of Azerbaidzhan where as a youth I had been so kindly welcomed as a shepherd and teacher of little children. Those friends of mine had resisted the Sovietization from which I had fled before the Communist teacher arrived. They and many others of the same mind had gone high into the mountains in a fruitless effort to survive. Against them the Communists had organized a so-called Azerbaidzhan Rifle Division, actually made up not of local peole, but of such non-Turkic elements as Ukrainians, Russian draftees from Siberia, some cavalry units of the Red Banner Army, and, of course, the border troop reserves, the field soldiers of the OGPU (a precursor of the KGB). As a sort of summer exercise, an "expedition" had been conducted against my friends. Despite all their bravery, they were caught and eliminated. I read page after page of how little children were bayonetted, young girls and mothers were raped, men machine-gunned, settlements shelled and burned. Oh, those poor people, who had only wanted to live in accordance with their own customs, as the Communists had promised them in order to get their support in the days of the Revolution!

I read on. My friends were not the only people so liquidated. Down near the Iranian border, it appeared, others had resisted Sovietization and collectivization, too. Those people also had taken up arms and revolted. Against them were dispatched regular Red Army units as well as the border guards. In my hands were the daily situation reports sent by those punitive forces to my department. One I remember indelibly said: "Whole villages are offering desperate resistance. Our units were forced to burn the villages, to put to the sword not only men, but also the women and children. When the men were killed fighting our forces, their women, instead of surrendering, threw themselves to death on the bayonets of the Red soldiers." Some of those people, other reports said, had managed to escape across the border to Iran, but to no avail. The Soviet troops reported that they crossed the border in pursuit and wiped them out.

In further reading, I came across a long account from the chief of our unit at Leninakan in Armenia, near the Turkish border. Colonel Shakir Al'Kayev had the task of infiltrating a recently recruited and trained agent back into Turkey. He wrote, ". . . as reported earlier, I was looking for a proper occasion to dispatch X. Our 'neighbors' [the Soviet military intelligence term for internal security] advised me that I could use an operation of their own as cover for getting X across. They had learned from informers that a group of about eighty local men, women, and children intended to cross the Soviet border illegally and flee to Turkey. The 'neighbors' were taking measures to intercept that group at the border and liquidate it. They suggested that X join the group—not too great a problem since he had once been a teacher of their children—and act as if he were accompanying them in flight. They promised not to shoot him during the firing that was to come, provided he would stay in a prearranged place and would identify himself in some manner. I agreed to the offer, for the idea of sending X across the border among people running away from the Soviets was sound operationally. Therefore at the appointed time I joined the 'neighbors' *opergruppa* [the liquidation unit]. When we approached the place of ambush it was almost midnight. Clouds occasionally obscured the moon. Everything was quiet and it was warm, even for a summer night. Finally we heard the movements and muted voices of people approaching. Then, from our hiding place behind rocks, we saw them. Some of the men were armed, some not. Some were walking; some were on horses. The women and children were on donkeys. At that moment the 'neighbors' were given the command to attack. There was much firing, much shouting, many cries and curses, women asking for mercy, children crying. Few survived the skirmish. Among those who escaped to Turkey was our agent X."

More reading brought up a report of an operation in the opposite direction that had occurred in that same frontier area, just a few months earlier, at the time I was courting Tamara. The file gave details of a great rising of the Kurds in Turkey, not far from the junction of the Turkish, Iranian, and Soviet borders. My department had helped numbers of those Kurds to flee from Turkey into Soviet Armenia. All of the escapees were being organized into special military units, skilled in guerrilla warfare, for possible use in Turkey in the future.

I was terribly distressed about what I had been reading, especially about what had been done to my friends in Azerbaidzhan, and said so in one of my daily discussions with Colonel Kuzyuberdin. He listened to me almost open-mouthed before giving me a direct order to stop talking. Then he stepped from behind his desk, shook an index finger at me and said very quietly but most seriously, "You know, Comrade Akhmedov, if I were to call the OO [Osoby Otdel, the counterintelligence section of the OGPU in the armed forces], they would have done with you very quickly. Let me hear no more of that nonsense, ever. You are dismissed."

That night I unburdened myself to Tamara. That was in violation of security regulations and also in violation of my own decision not to bother my wife with my affairs. But I was deeply troubled, not only about what I had learned of the organization of which I was a member, but also at the colonel's reaction. For a moment she held my hand, stroked it, said nothing. Then she admitted that she, too, was shocked and troubled by what I had told her, but could see no way out except for me to hold my tongue, be patient, work hard, and become an expert in other fields so that I could make my living in an honest way.

I accepted her advice with gratitude. There truly was no other way. From that moment on I kept my thoughts to myself. In the colonel's office I applied myself with all intensity, recognizing that hard work there was the only route to the academy the general had promised. For his part, the colonel never made further mention of my lapse.

Within a few more weeks I completed the book work part of my training and started to learn how to cipher and decipher incoming and outgoing cables, telegrams, and letters of the department. There were interchanges between the Tbilisi headquarters and Teheran and Tabriz, Ankara, Erzurum, and Kars and, of course, with Moscow. That communications work not only gave me deeper insight into the local intelligence operations, but also often had an amusing side, even though betrayal accompanied the laughter.

One day the general sent over a message to be ciphered and wired immediately to the chief of intelligence in Batumi. It read something like this: "Burn this message after reading. A Turkish general staff officer is travelling from Moscow to Ankara via Batumi [and here the exact time, the number of the train and the number of the compartment in the international sleeping car were given]. Pass to him an expensive Bukhara rug as a token of the Director's appreciation." I knew enough by then to interpret that rug deal to mean that somewhere in Moscow, some time ago, some case officer of the Directorate of military intelligence had succeeded in recruiting that Turkish staff officer who was on his way back home to work for the Red Army.

But the Turks were not the only ones in our net. Later I got another ciphering and transmission task of similar import addressed to our chief at Djul'fa on the Iranian border. That one I recall as: "The governor of Tabriz is returning from Baku to Tabriz via Djul'fa. Render military honors and make the border crossing pleasant." Another big bird recruited, I thought, and mused that governors, staff officers, teachers, Kurds, Armenians, Azerbaidzhanians, high-level agents, low-level agents, each had his own place in the designs of our intelligence.

Once my cipher work had become proficient—and that did not take long—I was put to studying the organization of our department. It consisted of three sections: espionage operations (mine), information, and tactical (combat) intelligence. My section's centers of activity were the *Pogranichnye Razvedyvatelnye Punkti* (frontier intelligence points), or as we called them, PRPs. Leninakan, where the agent was infiltrated at the cost of the lives of scores of would-be escapees, was one; Djul'fa, where the governor of Tabriz was buttered up, was another of several such points in our sector. The PRPs were our closest contacts with more than a dozen spy centers across the border in Turkey, and with nearly half that number the other side of the Iranian frontier. At the PRPs our units masked their presence by posing as frontier guards of the internal security, even wore the uniforms of border guards of the OGPU.

At the same time that I was taught as a junior officer about the cooperation between the organs of internal security and of military intelligence, I was also carefully advised about the conflict between the two groups. The OGPU boasted—as the KGB still does—that they are the trusted ones, the elite, and as such have the right to supervise and control everything. My organization boasted that they were the military professionals and as such knew the business. I was told that the competition and struggle between the two was constant and often very bitter and I found that to be absolutely correct.

In that respect, the military intelligence, or GRU as it was later named, was having a big laugh at that time at the OGPU. Just before my joining the organization, Grigory Bessedovsky, the Soviet chargé d'affaires in Paris, and Georges Agabekov, the OGPU chief in Iran, and later in Turkey, had defected to the West. Both had published their memoirs while I was there in Tbilisi. Those revelations were among the foreign literature banned to almost all Soviet citizens that we as intelligence officers were not only allowed to read but had to study. I found them thrilling as pure accounts, and also very interesting as eye openers on the modus operandi of every Russian citizen's watchdog, the Soviet secret police. Those memoirs, coupled with my training in ciphered messages, the reading of secret and top-secret files, the emigré newspapers and foreign magazines, were also rapidly expanding my horizon, not necessarily to cynicism but to the beginning of an understanding of the world as it really was.

My basic training was completed toward the end of 1930. With that, I was assigned to very serious study of Turkish and Iranian Kurdistan. That involved obtaining intimate and detailed knowledge of the character and background of chieftains of Kurdish tribes, of routes and paths, of sources of water, of local history and folklore, of the origins and current reasons of the hatreds separating the many tribes and people of the Middle East, of the struggle between the various political parties. The smallest detail was not neglected. For example, exact methods were determined, and then put in writing as secret regulations, on how to conceal small detachments of insurgents in the mountains or in the deserts, how to cook meat under the soil, how to maintain communications, how Soviet advisors should appeal to and play on the national and religious feelings and customs of individual local populations.

I was deep in that work in January of 1931 when the colonel told me that I was being sent to school again. In 1931 the organization was turning to radio as the primary means of communication in operational intelligence. I was to take a course in Moscow at the top-secret Radio School of the Intelligence Directorate (that is, the Fourth Directorate or *Chetvortoye Upravleniye*) of the General Staff of the Red Army.

Tamara was pleased because she hoped that advanced study would give me the specialization I needed. I did not take her to Moscow with me. I could not. The course was only four months long. Besides, her days were occupied because she was still working at the army medical headquarters. Also, in addition to her uncles, she had a large circle of friends and acquaintances in Tbilisi. Nevertheless, leaving her troubled me. It was our first parting and was to prove our only separation of any length until the final one.

The radio school was located in the Lenin Hills district, then on the very outskirts of Moscow. The grounds, surrounded with barbed wire, were patrolled day and night by special OGPU troops. Much of the space within was allocated to complex antenna systems, the heart of the worldwide radio network of the intelligence directorate. At that time the administration and operational buildings, as well as quarters, were sparsely spread about the compound. However, a number of other large buildings and laboratories were under construction, since radio was taking its place as a weapon of intelligence.

The director of this huge compound was a brilliant former Austrian signal officer named Lyamberg. He had been taken prisoner during World War I. During the October Revolution he joined both the Communist party and the Red Army voluntarily, and eventually was appointed to military intelligence. To me, most of the rest of the staff of consultants, engineers, and technicians were just as foreign. Russian was rarely heard at the school, although German, English, French, and Italian were common. Clothing and manners, as well as language, also showed those people as foreigners. Their suits were better cut, their ties more tasteful, their shoes better made than those of the Russians, and they laughed more and were generally more pleasant than the local staff. The reason for the foreigners' different aspect and attitude was that most were visitors, being the Red Army's most valuable illegal agents, foreign Communists, or Comintern operatives.

Basics of the school's course for me were radio communication as it served espionage plus the ever-present political indoctrination, handled there by commissars from the political division of military intelligence headquarters. The strictly technical work was on the properties and propagation of short waves and the miniaturization of radio sets for the use of agents.

In the course of that I also got my introduction to the communications wonders of those times: two-way radio sets ranging from midgets to be carried in pockets to big ones assembled in innocent-looking leather suitcases. Some of the larger models of those special sets were packed at the school in special water- and dust-proofed packages to be secretly buried abroad, usually in solitary places. Exact topographical drawings of the selected sites of the buried sets were prepared and kept on file in Moscow against the day they might be needed in uprisings or guerrilla warfare.

The chief item of the commissars' indoctrination, of course, was world revolution, the ultimate goal of the Party. We were told that the most hated enemy of the U.S.S.R., "the base of world revolution," was the U.S.A., "the base of world capitalism." And even in those times it was drilled into us that one of the most important objectives in the fight against "Anglo-American imperialism" was control (the word *liberation* was never used) of the Middle East, because of its oil wealth, as well as because of its strategic position as a bridge of continents. In closed-door meetings we were advised that Litvinov's harping on peace, his theme then at Geneva and elsewhere in the West, was no more than so much diplomatic eyewash, an expediency of the moment. Disregard all that, they said; our duty to the Party as intelligence officers requires preparation of uprisings and civil wars in neighboring countries as a prelude to a Communist offensive on a global scale.

Upon completion of the course in April 1931, I was sent back to Tbilisi, back to the Fourth Department of General Absalyamov. I was accompanied by special couriers who carried what looked like three fine pieces of leather luggage, but which were actually a trio of transceivers, each with its individual power unit. The latest achievements of Lyamberg's technicians, those sets became our chief radio communications with Moscow as well as with Teheran, Ankara, and Istanbul.

One of those magnificent pieces of equipment was given to me to install in that extra room I had been given as part of my fancy quarters when I transferred to the department. Tamara, although of course happy to have me back, was a bit disappointed at having to give up part of the apartment to my set. When I had hushed her complaints she gave me an odd little bit of news. While I was gone we had gotten a new occupant of the apartment building, one of the finest dwellings in the city. The new tenant, known better to Tamara than me, was the elder Oystvakh, the violinist. Rather odd, we thought, to quarter an artist with agents; in any case, we also gained an appreciation that nothing was too good for intelligence.

On return I was given new duty which I found very pleasant work, indeed. It only lasted six months, but for me it was a very good half year. I was ordered to become a short-wave ham, and spent long days and nights at home, talking with other hams in all parts of the world. My amateur call sign was AU7CS. I joined the local short-wave club and participated in much harmless discussion about low-power transmission, especially on the new and sophisticated wave lengths. I was allowed to wear civilian clothes, all supplied by our agents in Turkey. I felt and looked like a foreigner.

The purpose of that masquerading was not innocent. My real job was to recruit operators for our radio nets from the local hams. My first find of many was probably the best. He was a young Georgian of good standing in the Komsomol. Not only was he very capable technically and in love with short-wave experimenting, but he was also quite simple to win over to the department. I trained him in cipher techniques and agent communication, and then we sent him to Teheran, making him a member of a trade delegation for cover purposes.

After my trainee had settled himself in the Iranian capital he started regular clandestine transmission with me in Tbilisi. Earlier we had moved another good operator into Turkey, again under trade delegation cover. Through diplomatic channels, we sent that one another of Lyamberg's sets to put him on the air to me from Erzurum. The Iranian and Turkish communications, plus routine contacts with our PRPs along the borders, comprised the rest of my serious duty in that pleasant half year.

That good time ended in November 1931, when the general of my department was transferred to field duty. His replacement was also a Tatar, but one who believed in frequent shifts of his personnel. He ordered the chief of the Leninakan PRP, Colonel Al'Kayev, whose report of getting an agent into Turkey had once so troubled me, to Moscow for further intelligence training. I was sent to the Armenian border to take over the PRP from Al'Kayev.

At first that transfer made me nervous. I, then only a senior lieutenant, was to take over for a colonel, although I found later that was not too unusual in our service. Nor did the move please me personally much, either. It meant that I had to give up our fine apartment in Tbilisi. It also meant that Tamara and I would be parted, for there were no married quarters at the PRPs. A good wife as always, she made the best of things, reminded me that I had to have field work if I wanted to get ahead, particularly if I wanted further technical training. She was right, of course, but the move was not to my liking.

Despite our differences in rank, the colonel received me kindly and with courtesy. His orders were to stay on a few weeks after my arrival until I had learned the ropes. Before he left he showed me how our agents were passed back and forth across the border, one of the prime tasks at a PRP.

My first agent handling involved a Kurd expected over the border by night with information about the political situation of the tribes in the Lake Van area.

The colonel and I set out for the border rendezvous point a day before the agent was expected. Although in early winter, it was quite warm the afternoon we left Leninakan. Even though we rode leisurely, we and our mounts were soon sweating because of the warmth and the difficulty our horses were having picking their way over rocks and around cliffs. I also felt a bit uncomfortable in my new uniform, that of the OGPU border guards, the regulation attire for military intelligence officers at PRPs. And to further hide our operations we also carried identity cards of OGPU border guard case officers.

Behind us, deeper within the northwestern corner of Soviet Armenia, towered volcanic Mount Alaguz (Alagez in Russian), its 13,435-foot peak shining with snow. Far to the south, occasionally we could see still higher mountains in Turkey, grouped around the 16,873-foot-high snowcapped cone of Mount Great Ararat, allegedly Noah's flood-time landing place. We were making our way through a terribly barren area, especially so to me, since en route from Tbilisi to Leninakan I had found northern Armenia lush with vegetation. Everywhere in the south, however, there was nothing but bare rock, and I could understand why some called Armenia the land of stones. It looked like the surface of a dead planet. We saw nothing but stones. Large boulders the size of huge buildings, smaller ones the size of houses, still smaller ones like paving cobbles, countless numbers of them scattered everywhere, as if a crazed giant had smashed some of the mountains to bits. Adding to the atmosphere of desolation was the almost complete solitude. Since we were in a border zone, the entire area was restricted. In that whole afternoon's ride, we met not a single person except a lone border partrolman.

Just before nightfall we heard the barking of dogs and the sound of water rushing through a canyon. We were approaching our destination. We rounded a final cliff and looked down. There at the very bottom of a gorge was the *zastava*, the border guard post, one of the loneliest, most forbidding of the hundreds that ring the Soviet Union. It was a small stone house clinging to the edge of a lesser cliff just a few yards above the wild waters of the Arpachay, there tumbling madly to the south to join the Araks on its course to the Caspian. The Arpachay formed the border there, and on a bluff on its opposite side was the post of the Turkish frontier guards.

After a not too comfortable night at the OGPU post, we were up early the next morning so that I could familiarize myself with the area for use in future agent border crossings. As the colonel pointed out to me, there were many fords across the Arpachay in that region, making it ideal for our work. Finally the night came, the night of the rendezvous. It was dark, moonless, cloudy, very good for agent reception. Strong winds howled across from Turkey. With glasses we watched the Turkish post and saw the guards there retreat to their quarters to play cards as the weather worsened.

On vigil with us was the chief of the *zastava*. He was authorized to "open" the frontier for us. That meant that at the time of agent reception or dispatch he withdrew the border guards from a selected short stretch of the frontier for a specified time for military intelligence. Although not allowed on the scene while we were doing the debriefing or instructing of an agent, the *zastava* chief had to be present during the arrivals and departures of our operators to make sure who was doing the border crossing.

On that occasion the border was opened toward midnight. A few minutes later we made out the silhouette of someone fording the river several yards below us. We went down to the bank, identified the crosser as our Kurd. That done, the *zastava* chief left us, to return as arranged within an hour to certify the departure of our man from the Soviet Union.

Tall and dark-skinned, that Kurd was a rather fierce looking character. But he was able. He had had plenty of trouble with the Turks, and knew that part of the border down to the last rock. His information, however, was not exceptional. We could have debriefed him in less than the assigned hour before sending him back into the dark to Turkey.

The next day we returned to Leninakan, Al'Kayev to leave for Moscow and me to take over the PRP command, one that I held for almost a year. In the beginning I found the work interesting and exciting but it soon palled.

I also found it difficult to adjust to working with the OGPU, as was necessary in almost every instance. There was always an element of danger, too, in meeting agents alone, usually by night in lonely places, but it was the OGPU that I really could not stand, especially the border guard units.

Border guard troops were established by Lenin in 1918 and made the main component of the state security organization. Under the Lenin decree, it was charged with preventing unauthorized entry and exit of persons, defending border areas against armed attacks, combatting contraband, controlling offshore waters, maintaining public order in border areas, and, in case of need, establishing quarantine. Accordingly it should have been not much different from border guard units of other countries. After 1923, however, it was vastly expanded into a force of many thousands of men equipped with its own tanks, airplanes, and artillery. All that expansion was to carry out primarily one duty—preventing unauthorized exit of persons—in other words, the prevention of escapes from the Soviet Union, escapes of the so-called free Soviet people. Particularly nauseating to me was what went on every May 28, the anniversary of Lenin's establishment of the border guards. On those occasions, newspapers ran headlines such as "Standing [a number] years on guard at our borders," and average "free" citizens would be called upon to contribute individual words of praise. It was like prisoners congratulating their wardens.

It was with that kind of people that my PRP—and all the others—had to do business. We not only wore their uniforms and insignia and carried their identity cards for cover, but we worked as well under their aegis. Nor was a PRP too lily white itself. In my files among other top-secret regulations was this combination of cynicism and naiveté: "The PRP chief is entrusted to keep the foreign currency for his operations, the dollars, tumans, liras, marks, krones. He is entrusted to have a typewriter to type his confidential correspondence. He is entrusted to maintain safehouses to house and train his agents. He is entrusted to support his prostitutes to entertain his spies. . . ."

Despite that kind of working milieu and atmosphere, one very nice thing happened at Leninakan in the spring of 1932. I had been several days at the border on another agent-crossing problem, and returned quite tired and fed up to my quarters, a rather mean and monastic single room. When I entered it, I thought I had gone to the wrong room. There was a curtain at the window, a small but pretty rug on the floor, several cushions piled about, and a good-smelling soup simmering on the primus stove. As I gaped, Tamara stepped out from behind the curtain and threw her arms around me. She had come from Tbilisi for the weekend to give her husband a bit of home. She had also come to tell him the wonderful news that she was pregnant and expected the baby in the summer.

Tamara's brief presence and her news were boosters I had badly needed. For weeks, in fact for several months thereafter, my morale was high. Then everything crashed to bits. I got more news from Tamara—actually from a friend. She was very, very ill in a hospital in Tbilisi. She had had a miscarriage. And as if that were not bad enough, she also had to be sterilized. Our family would never be more than just us two.

Long before that terrible blow to us, I had formally put in my application to enter the Electro-Technical Academy in Leningrad. After Tamara lost the baby, I pressed the general of my department, told him that because of a family tragedy I wanted a transfer from the area, preferably to the academy. I did not tell him that I had also had all I could take of dispatching and receiving low-level agents; garnering trifling and meager information on local troop dispositions, the moods of Kurdish chieftains, about routes, terrain, and petty politicans; plus playing hand in glove with the OGPU.

In September of 1932 orders came through for me to proceed to Leningrad. Farewell Transcaucasus. I hoped forever.

# 5

## Survival, II

At Moscow I had to break the trip to Leningrad. When my train pulled into the capital I was feeling very weak and wobbly and had a high temperature. I went to a military clinic and was sent from there to hospital. I had pneumonia and the doctors declared it a pretty bad case.

Exactly what had made me sick I do not know. Normally my constitution was excellent. I admit, though, that depression may have played a part. I was terribly sad at the loss of the baby and the knowledge we could never have children. I was very worried about Tamara's health and having to leave her.

The train trip from the south had done much to lower my morale, too. Everywhere, in the northern Caucasus, in the Ukraine, the stations swarmed with thousands and thousands of unfortunates. There were scenes that reminded me of the line-ups at the Baku labor office, except for the fact they were much worse.

The cause of that misery at the stations was collectivization plus the displacement and starvation that accompanied that program. At the time I passed through those stations in September 1932, more than 50 percent of the peasantry had been forcibly collectivized.

I had read something about that tragedy in the *svodkas* or summaries of the intelligence departments of various armies, not only of my units, but also of those elsewhere in the Caucasus, in Central Asia, in Kazakhstan, in the area around my hometown, in the Ukraine. Every *svodka* referred to those poor devils who resisted collectivization as "bandits" and told of military action to overcome them.

I sensed some of the horror inflicted on the peasants and tribesmen in the *svodkas*, but I never even guessed the true awfulness of it until I saw some of the results with my own eyes in those stations. There on the platforms were not only local people, but

Bashkirs, Kazakhs, Kirghiz, Turkmen, Uzbeks, Tatars—men, women and children—all forlorn, unkempt, lost, hungry, begging for scraps of food or a little money. Particularly afflicted were the Kirghiz—who had been so good to me when I was a boy—and other nomads. Denomadization was incorporated in collectiviza- tion, and that was an impossible change of life for that generation of people accustomed to wandering freely from pasture to pasture for centuries.

Rather than submit, those of the nomads and peasants who had not resisted with arms had abandoned their lands, slaught- ered their flocks and herds. The famine and the deaths of millions that followed in the next two years was not an act of God, but a deliberate evil deed of Stalin.

It is of important note that it was the minorities of the Soviet Union, the non-Russians, who suffered under collectivization, and not the hereditary colonizers of that vast land. Freed from serfdom only several score years earlier, the peasants of the Great Russian heartland—except for the Cossacks—had never pro- gressed beyond a crude form of communal life. To them collectivi- zation meant practically no change. The non-Russians, however, had always been free, owners of their land and livestock. There- fore collectivization was truly a catastrophe of biblical proportion for the minorities.

On my train trip north through that deeply troubled area, I also saw the beginnings of the mass deportations that went along with collectivization. At several stations, armed soldiers were forcing hundreds and hundreds of despairing people into long trains of freight cars headed nobody knew where. It has always been my opinion that deportations and famine were dismissed by the Communist leadership as mere penalties exacted upon people regarded as handicaps better off dead because they refused to comply with the system. Ah, what a terrible condemnation of a system that blossomed in the bloody land of Ivan the Terrible and Catherine the Great.

With awful impressions like that on my mind, with much on my conscience because I was an elite part of that system, it took me more than two months to recover at the Moscow military hospital. I was also distressed at the possibility that the delay might keep me from entering the Leningrad academy.

The bright spot in that bad period was Tamara. We had planned that she join me in Leningrad after I had settled in, but the moment she heard I was sick she quit her job and came to Moscow. I had been in the hospital less than a week when there was my love at my bedside with smiles, cheering words, flowers, and books to read to me.

Fortunately for my limited income, Tamara had several relatives in Moscow. During my hospitalization she stayed with her sister, Anna, married to Zinaid—to us, Zyama—Gural'nik, a brilliant professor of economics at the Plekhanov Institute. He was Jewish, too. That was a very happy couple, very much in love. When they were engaged they had very little money and Zyama worked at night for months painting signs and placards for enterprises to earn enough for a small apartment. An ardent Party member, he had an awful lot of energy for a man of his wee size, four feet six inches at the most.

I had first met that pair when I was at Lenin Hills earlier in the year. Their Party membership was being put to severe strain at the time of my visit, which coincided with the trial of the so-called Counter-Revolutionary Menshevik Organization. That was a preliminary to the great purges of the mid-thirties and after, and was aimed at intellectuals, primarily writers and key economists. In protest the poet Vladimir Mayakovsky in 1930 had hanged himself in his apartment just below that of Anna and Zyama.

Naturally the two of them were very upset when I arrived. Zyama was pacing up and down the floor muttering to himself and Anna was crying. Awkwardly, I asked if I could do anything for them.

"Help," shouted Zyama, "how can you help? This Georgian, not satisfied with making himself dictator, is now going to wipe out all the intelligentsia. He is going to purge the writers. He is going to purge the economists. You are a soldier with little concern for politics or economics. But I tell you Stalin is going to ruin the economy. The ignorant members of the Party, and they are the majority, are supporting him. We are in for trouble, bad trouble." That outburst shocked me, and was a sample of how worried the two poor things were.

When I next visited them with Tamara after being released from the hospital on convalescence, the excitement of that little purge had passed and they were more their true, delightful selves. They introduced us to their writer and artist friends, and Tamara had a wonderful time talking with them all and going to concerts and the opera.

My concerns were more serious. I went out to Lenin Hills several times before I could see the director, Lyamberg, for his advice on entering the Leningrad academy two months late. He made light of my fears and gave me a memo to the chief of Leningrad military intelligence, explaining my difficulty.

A few days later, almost literally clutching that note from Lyamberg, Tamara and I took the train to Leningrad. She also had relatives there. A pair of them who were in the publishing business and pretty well-off for quarters put us up on arrival. Then I started knocking on the door of the Military Electro-Technical Academy.

For a whole month I made a daily effort to see the commandant of the academy or someone who could process my entrance, with no success at all. I was too late for that term, I was told.

Pretty desperate by that time, I finally used Lyamberg's note and called at the intelligence office. The general in charge put me in his staff car and whisked me to the academy. Why, he asked me en route, had I waited so long to ask his help. Because, I told him, I wanted to enter without special help. He said something like "stubborn Tatar," but that did not stop him from giving me a handsome recommendation for admission when we met the commandant.

With that intercession, my troubles ended as if by magic. I had to take examinations, of course, but I had studied hard for them in dull periods as the Leninakan PRP and passed with good marks.

Once I had qualified, I was given quarters in an old apartment building assigned to other students and their families in the Smol'ny district. Poor Tamara. Those quarters were some comedown from our fine setup in Tbilisi. Our entire four years at the academy were spent in that cramped red brick building. It was a four-storied structure. A long corridor ran down the length of each floor and on each side of the corridor were five rooms, all identical, all no bigger than ten by twelve feet. At one end of the corridor was the stairway, at the other were a community kitchen and two washrooms that had half a dozen toilets and wash basins each.

Our room had one window and one door, the one onto the corridor. There was no room for a closet or a wardrobe. We kept the clothes we were not wearing in a trunk, but being childless we were not as confined as some of the other tenants, several of whom had two or three youngsters. The walls were paper thin, and we overheard every argument and family fight on our floor. We not only slept and ate in that little room, but I often studied until late at night there as well. During those long night sessions, Tamara, bless her, would always sit up reading to keep me company and to show that my light did not annoy her.

It was in that community kitchen that I felt really sorry for

Tamara and also for the other nine wives on our floor. At each meal there were the ten women pumping at their primus stoves, putting pots and pans over each one by one, rushing to the rooms to serve, and then back later with the dirty dishes to wash up. And the adjoining community washrooms were the only place the women had to do the laundry. The drying, when weather permitted, was on lines in the yard below; otherwise, the wet laundry had to be hung in the rooms.

Shopping was also a chore for the wives. We did better than the civilians. We had the comparative luxury of a military commissary, which, unlike civilian shops, never ran out of essentials, but still the women had to queue for hours for the weekly rations. While in those lines they also were the recipients of acid comments from civilians passing by, all of whom envied what was given the military. We also got nasty cracks from the civilians at the public bathhouses. With no bathing except cat washes possible in quarters, we had to use the public baths. At them there were special lines for the military, an arrangement greatly resented by the civilians. Even with those special lines, however, it took at least four hours standing in nothing more than bathrobes, and often shivering, to get a bath. As result we bathed only every ten days, and, at that, we were considered as exceptionally clean by others.

My particular daily grind was getting to and from the academy, a streetcar trip that took one hour and twenty minutes, and often more. But I gladly accepted that as well as the inconveniences to hardships Tamara was undergoing with all sweetness on her part. I was out of intelligence; I hoped forever. I was once more studying, and had the chance to improve my skill and knowledge in my chosen field of communications, even though at a military academy. And again I thank Tamara for doing the daily menial work that so helped me in my work. She put up with that drudgery for three years. In the final year of my course she got a job as a cataloguer at the public library and used her earnings to pay for a part-time servant.

For me those four years opened new vistas. Scholastically and technically, the academy was a fine institution. The first year was chiefly analysis and higher math, and specialized subjects in the fields of electricity and radio. The second year concentrated on advanced math and physics, and on integral and differential equations; the third on vector analysis, matrices, and the theory of relativity. The fourth year specialized in advanced chemistry and physics, including study of the structure of the atom. In the final months of the course, before graduation as an engineer captain, I was sent to a radio factory for practical experience in the workshops. Of course, throughout we also studied electrical currents, electric motors, radio techniques, radio control, as well as design of radio equipment. At the factory, for my final paper, I had to design radio equipment that could be used by the infantry.

That work plus much study after hours so occupied me that I had practically no time for outside interests. As during my first four years in Leningrad I was pretty much isolated behind the walls of the academy. But that does not mean that I was completely cut off, just that there was no special concern and almost no participation in affairs of the outside world. Fellow students from many parts of the country learned in letters from home of further suffering caused by collectivization, and some local details of the great famine of 1932-1933. We discussed that information among ourselves and at Party gatherings, but with considerable reserve.

Late in 1934, however, we were jolted from our almost monastic seclusion and briefly forced into a form of particpation in a major political affair. On December 1, Leningrad, in fact the whole Soviet Union, was shocked to the core by the assassination of one of the country's most powerful men, a member of the Politburo, Sergei M. Kirov, first secretary of the Leningrad Party, a favorite and trusted lieutenant of Stalin, a really good Communist and a talented man on whom great hopes had been pinned for industrial development.

Although a minor army officer, a nobody in the Party, I, too, was deeply shocked. Amost a decade earlier, it was Kirov, then first secretary of the Azerbaidzhan Communist Party, who had made it possible, through my friend Janbulat, for me to attend the Leningrad Signal School, and who had thus been responsible for starting me on my military career. And just a few months before his death I had seen him again in Leningrad and he had had a kind word of recognition for me. We met at an exhibit of paintings of the Red Army, where I had been assigned as one of the guides to conduct Party dignitaries.

Officially the assassin was said to be one Leonid Nikolayev, whose wife had been Kirov's secretary. In Party meetings, however, we were told that the real blame rested on Trotskyites. The chief perpetrator was said to have been a veteran Bolshevik and Politburo member, Grigoryi Zinoviev, who earlier, as virtual dictator of Lenigrad, had terrorized the city with arbitrary and mass executions of his opponents. Because of that bloody record, as well as his close association with Trotsky before the latter had fled the country, Stalin had replaced Zinoviev with Kirov.

Stalin reacted very brutally to the killing of his favorite. Scores of old regime survivors, who certainly had nothing at all to do with the assassination, were summarily executed in Leningrad. At the same time, of course, Zinoviev and his associates were rounded up and imprisoned. None knew it then, to be sure, but the Kirov killing triggered the really great purges of the mid-thirties and later. Zinoviev was one of the first prominent old Bolsheviks to be arrested. Two years later he was also one of the first of them to be executed after the start of the mass show trials.

Stalin left little doubt about the importance he attached to the assassination. He himself went to Leningrad to participate in Kirov's funeral honors, an observance in which I and thousands of other military officers and students took part on orders.

The day after Kirov had been shot dead in his office, his body lay in state, and members of my academy, in fact the rank and file of almost all other military and civilian organizations in Leningrad, spent hours filing past the bier.

The next day Stalin came to Leningrad to escort Kirov's body back to Moscow for burial at the Kremlin walls. More than five hours before his arrival my academy had been marched out to its place on the funeral route, a stretch of almost eight miles, leading from the former Duma (parliament) building, where Kirov lay in state, into Volodarsky Prospect, then into Nevsky Prospect, and to the railroad station. My academy was only a small part of the thousands of military and civilians who lined those streets, a massed Soviet turnout matched only by the annual observance of the October Revolution. Troops and cadets from every academy and school, the entire Leningrad garrison, infantry, artillery, armor, air, navy, units from every factory and administrative section, had been assembled.

We and other officers carried sidearms, the soldiers their rifles. However, before leaving for the route, every one of the massed military there, officers as well as men, had been individually examined by political officers to make sure none carried any ammunition. The military was formed in front of the civilians, but in front of the military, lining both sides of the long prospects, were the internal security troops of the NKVD (another predecessor of the KGB). In front of them were crack detachments of the NKVD border guards. They alone were trusted enough to carry ammunition as well as weapons.

Since winter days are short in Leningrad, darkness fell shortly after we had assembled. Usually streetlights and those in buildings would have been turned on. On that occasion, however, the entire route was kept blacked out. The only illumination came from red and green searchlights that were mounted on top of buildings and cast eerie swatches of light and shadow as they swept up and down the prospects. Occasionally those lights made background silhouettes of other NKVD border guards, on top of the buildings with machine guns, again with live ammunition showing.

Finally, with those searchlights playing on it, the cortege passed by. Kirov's coffin, covered with the red flag of the Soviet Union, was on a gun carriage drawn by black horses. Next, a few paces behind, walked Stalin bareheaded, his moustache drooping more than in official photographs, wearing a brown military greatcoat and black boots. His appearance was that of a mourner, certainly not that of a man who had deliberately murdered his favorite as an excuse to wipe out his opposition, as charged later in Party congresses that followed his death. The rest in the funeral procession, walking slightly behind Stalin, were members of the Politburo, selected members of the central committee, and high-ranking officers of the military and security services.

Shortly after that great funeral procession, purges started in earnest. At first NKVD men themselves were arrested, then Party members, then military commanders in a long, awful process affecting thousands and thousands of mostly innocent people, a vast upheaval of personnel that did not really end until the eve of World War II. Forced labor camps were expanded. Torture of suspects was made legal. The death penalty was also relegalized, although plenty of prisoners had already died in Moscow's Lubyanka and other jails without that formality. Many deaths were called suicides, such as those of Mikhail Tomski, the trade union leader, and of Vsevolod Meyerhold, the theatrical director. There were others who just "died," like Maxim Gorky, believed poisoned, and Sergei Kuybyschev, reported murdered. And with that terror there was developed a veritable mania about "spies," "enemies of the people," and any and all foreigners. The claque responsible for it all was organized and orchestrated for Party demonstrations—a re-emergence of those terrible Russian mobs, descendants of those used in the pogroms, with their inhuman shouts of "finish them" for the innocents brought to trial.

It was a most awful period. I tried my best to bury myself in books and laboratories, but everybody was forced to play a part if he wanted to survive. The system of the purges was most pernicious and encompassing. Death was the only escape. Detesting myself as a Party member, I had to take part.

Here is the way it worked: somewhere in the Party top echelon, it was decided that the purge should affect 50 percent of the membership. Quotas of denunciations and eliminations were then ordered produced by the lower echelons, down to the smallest Party cell, in all organizations, military as well as civilian. On receipt of the orders, the individual Party units would meet to try to determine the proper charges to be made against the candidates for expulsion.

My knowledge of that terrible area extends only to the purge operation of a military unit. Ours posed certain primary questions. Did the candidate discharge his duties inefficiently? Had he ever been out of the country on some mission? What was his family background? Was his wife or another relative connected in the past with the old regime? With the clergy? With merchants? With the intelligentsia? Had he ever criticized the general line of the Party? Had he taken sides with Trotsky, with Zinoviev, with Buhkarin? Had he criticized Stalin? Had he any record of drunkeness, of sexual abnormality?

Everything about the candidates was examined in great detail, because usually they were top personnel. Then they were called to closed sessions, put on the rostrum, and asked, "You did this, you did that, you did the other thing?" The poor devils would deny some of the charges, maybe all of those made, but admit others. That was enough. Their files were turned over to the NKVD and they were arrested, one by one. Usually, the NKVD picked them up at about midnight in black cars at their quarters or homes. Then the next day brief announcements were made that this engineer or that commander had been arrested as an "enemy of the people" or a "spy." Sometimes, however, they were just called "traitors." Many were executed immediately. Others were sent to labor camps where death, coming more slowly, finally caught up with them. All had their personal property—even though very little—seized; their families were expelled from homes and quarters, and their names were disgraced.

In that way at my academy, the Party unit of which I was a member purged the commandant, the four-star General Polishchuk; my classmates Klinger, Meyer and Shulman (a trio with names of foreign origin); and many, many others long ago sent to oblivion.

I thank God that Tamara was with me in that terrible time. Otherwise I feel sure I would have lost control of myself. When I could not stand myself after having been a party to one of those dreadful meetings of denunciation, she would hold my hands until I had calmed down. Only then would she speak. She would say, so gently, "Ismail, I am terribly, terribly sorry for you. We live in brutal times among brutal people. My people once died in the pogroms of these people. You and I are not going to die. We are going to survive. Things cannot always be this bad, even here." Thank you, Tamara, thank you.

So, life went on. In 1936, in my final year at the academy, I applied for graduate work at the electro-technical and radio control research division of the Signal Corps Central Scientific Institute in Moscow. My aim was to become a topnotch research engineer, to spend my time in the laboratory and in the field, to read, think, design, test, and try to find solutions for the many new problems in the field of military communications.

My application was granted, I trust not because of my acquiescence to the purge, although that must have been taken into consideration. Tamara and I had hoped that association with that terror had ended when we left for Moscow in August of 1936.

For a while that hope proved true. We were assigned a comfortable two-room apartment with kitchen and bath. Tamara picked up the threads with her sister and other relatives and friends again. She found her world of music, theater, and opera once more, and was at her happiest. She did not work, either, except to keep the apartment in order. My pay was enough.

I, too, was very happy at the institute, delighted at having what I believed would be two years of pure research ahead of me. There was so much to be done. Current models of mobile radio stations of the Soviet Army were not up to date, their sizes huge, their weights terrible, their range limited, their frequencies on the long side, their aerial systems awkward, their tubes and component parts in need of modernization. That was the moment to re-evaluate the whole field of military radio communications, to rebuild the whole network of army radio stations, from those of headquarters of fronts and armies down to the equipment of battalions, companies, and individual tanks. Time was short. Germany was getting stronger and stronger. Hitler had already concluded the pact with Japan, a pact directed against the Soviet Union. Only the most naive believed that confrontation with Germany was not far off.

I was just as naive in thinking that the mere move from the Leningrad academy to the Moscow institute had removed me from the activities of the purge. Within a few short months after arrival at the institute I was suddenly made acting chief of my division. Me, a relatively young and inexperienced engineer captain, to be given a post normally held by a colonel.

The reason for my being skyrocketed to that position I had not earned and did not deserve was simple. The purge, even though late as compared to Leningrad, had started its sweep through the institute.

When I arrived in Moscow the first of the great show trials, that of Zinoviev and of more than a dozen others, charged at that time with having tried to kill Stalin, was in progress. When that lot was convicted and executed, I deluded myself with the belief that the pressure was off the military and on the politicians. I could not have been more wrong.

The first to go at the institute was the deputy director, an engineer general. Next on the list were chiefs of divisions, including a colonel who had been head of the radio faculty at the Leningrad academy. Eventually Engineer Colonel Kuznetsov, the chief of my division, joined the victims. That was how I "achieved" my promotion.

Upon being made chief of division I was assigned new quarters, a handsome three-room apartment, again with kitchen and bath, the latter two being amenities very rare indeed in the Soviet Union in those days.

There were, however, some drawbacks to those accommodations, despite their quality. The chief was that it had been the apartment of the chief of the institute up until the time he was purged. As a result, one of the three rooms was still occupied by his wife and their two small children, a boy and a girl. The poor things, they had no place else to go. The wife of the ex-chief was embarrassed. So were we. Unlike many others in her position, she was a true wife who did not join in denouncing her husband, but defended him, repeatedly assured us and others, although quietly, that he was not guilty. She worked long hours as a sales clerk in a state-run store to keep her family fed and clothed. The children went to school but were ostracized by their classmates. Tamara was a good woman, too. Instead of objecting to the presence of those unfortunates, or trying to get them thrown out as many others did, she made them feel as welcome as possible. For her, their being there meant not only the loss of a room, but sharing the kitchen and bathroom as well.

But wonderful as she was, Tamara was not a paragon of perfection. She had her failings, too, albeit small ones. She was always jealous of my attention to others, and in Moscow that caused a bit of trouble between us. The cause of it was my affection for Lucia, the delightful six-year-old daughter of Anna and Zyama. Whenever I patted Lucia on the head, took her some candy, or spoke of her fondly, Tamara would snap at me. At first I could not understand what she had against my liking for her own niece. Slowly, however, it finally dawned upon me that the root of it was sadness at not being able to have children of her own. Tamara was my true love, so I tempered my show of affection for the little girl, no matter much I cared for her.

Meanwhile, at the institute, I had plenty to do. The civil war had started in Spain, and bad troubles were reported with the antennas of the tanks we had sent the Loyalists. The same bad reports also came from the Manchurian border, from units involved in clashes with the Japanese.

Soviet tanks of that time were equipped with a ring antenna, a copper band that girded the turret. In battle conditions—the first the Red Army armor had experienced—not only was that type of antenna found to be weak in transmission and reception, but it also proved to be very vulnerable to enemy fire.

My task was to correct the failure, modify the equipment. Within a few months, after scores of simulated battle trials, we found the answer. We replaced the rings with whip antennas, the spring-mounted type eventually used by all nations involved in World War II.

Spain and the Far East also showed deficiencies in our infantry radio equipment. My colleagues and I had always known of those weaknesses, but it took battle conditions to establish them as facts to the upper echelons, so that changes could be made.

That was much more complex work than the tank antenna, involving a wholesale switch over from long waves to the high frequencies and, thereby, considerable replacement of equipment and manufacturing installations. The basic problem was what our specialists had long appreciated: miniaturization. We had to develop sets small enough, light enough, and rugged enough, not only for use of divisions, regiments, and battalions, but right down to company level.

For me that meant months and months of negotiations with industrial plants, the developing and testing of pilot models to go into eventual serial production. At the same time I had to spend much time and a lot of disputing on determination and allocation of the correct short-wave lengths as well as the proper power assigments for individual sets for units of the entire army, from supreme headquarters down to companies.

In the course of my work at the institute I became painfully aware of some shortcomings of my own. It was all very good to be a first-rate specialist, a competent technician. But I was an officer, and my services were for the armed forces. Therefore I needed to really know about the army, exactly what its needs and problems were on all levels. The one place to really learn that in the Red Army was at its number one academy, the War College of the General Staff in Moscow. Well before the end of my two-year course at the institute I applied for entry to that top school.

As at the Leningrad Military Electro-Technical Academy, all I wanted to do at the research institute was to wrap myself in my work, the only device available to me to keep my mind off the purges, then at full pitch. To completely divorce oneself from politics there proved, however, not only difficult but impossible. Our political commissar was none other than a former fellow student in Leningrad, as was his assistant. I had known both of them in the north as very, very poor students. That, though, made not the slightest difference to their careers. They were arch supporters of every word of Stalin, and of the purges. To enlist the support of myself and my decent colleagues, they told us that we were the elite, the cream of the nation, that the army depended upon us and that the purges were only temporary.

It was most nauseating to have to accept that combination of flattery and falsehood with the purge in full swing. Old Bolsheviks, other Party veterans with fine records, brilliant engineers, economists, agriculturists, army officers, industrialists, intellectuals, the whole gamut of society, were going to death, dishonor, and forced labor en masse. Even the simplest fool knew that all those thousands were not "traitors," "enemies of the people," or "spies."

We junior officers knew that personally we ran no hazards. We had been as much as told that we were exempt, that we were being groomed for commands of the future. Had not I already been boosted to a post way beyond my rank? Nevertheless, those arbitrary eliminations of our superiors were devastating to morale. Might not we, too, just as innocent, one day be similarly denounced and slaughtered? To survive, however—and I blush to say this—we became hardened to the horror; waves of arrests became as ordinary as orders of the day.

A particular blow to us younger officers at that time was the 1937 closed session trial by the highest military court of Marshal Mikhail Nikolayevich Tukhachevski, our great hero of the Revolution, and seven other top commanders of the Red Army. Tukhachevski's portrait had hung in honor in the halls of my cadet school, in the halls of the Leningrad academy. It was given similar honor in the institute until the day after the trial. It was a portrait that charmed us youngsters, showing him not in panoply of military rank, but playing a violin, at which he was a near virtuoso. He had been our idol. We would have fought to the death under him. Yet there he was befouled, so reported *Izvestia,* charged with high treason, with having dealings with the Germans, then condemned, and shot.

Later, we noted with some pleasure, several members of that same high court were themselves convicted of similar charges and executed. One of those, I saw with personal interest, was N.D. Kashirin, the one-time commander of the Red cavalry, who years before had chased General Dutov, my family, and me out of Orsk.

In 1938, just after I had been accepted as a student at the War College, there came the greatest trial of all, the process against the "Anti-Soviet, Rightist, Trotskyst Bloc." Principal defendants of the nine in court were Nikolai Bukharin, once editor of *Pravda*, and Genrikh Grigovgevich Yagoda, one of the most bestial chiefs of state security. By then I had become even more hardened to those affairs. My only interest in that one was that the defendants had been induced to confess before they were convicted and shot.

Study at the War College was interesting, challenging, and very demanding. The subjects were basic but all-encompassing—tactics, operational art, strategy, and general staff work. There was much reading to be done of great battles of the past down to small but important engagements, of great possible battles of the future. There were thousands of maps to study and scores upon scores of lectures to attend. I threw myself into the work almost fanatically, feeling that I had found myself and my true field at last. And with Hitler swallowing Austria, then moving against Czechoslovakia, patriotism colored my thinking and efforts, too. I felt in my bones that Nazi Germany would strike against us in time, and I wanted to be fully capable of serving my country well.

I grant that attitude may have been an escape mechanism as well. Dedication like that could overcome my revulsion to the purges, I must have subconsciously felt. However, the horror was too widespread for me to be able to avoid it completely.

Toward the end of 1938 while going down Gorky Street, I crossed paths with a tall man whom I thought I vaguely recognized. He was terrible to see. His cheeks were ashen and sunken. His eyes stared piercingly and almost blankly. He was as thin as a starving man. He hobbled as he walked, and one arm seemed deformed. He spoke first. "Hello, Comrade Akhmedov," he croaked, "don't you remember me?" Yes, I knew that voice, even with the croak. It belonged to Colonel Gaberman, a bemedalled hero of the Civil War, once the secretary of the Party bureau at the Leningrad academy.

He drew me close to him, told me, as if in a hurry, that he had been arrested, beaten, tortured, then sent to a forced labor camp, later freed and "rehabilitated."

"And what now?" he asked. "I am good for nothing, not even for my wife. Curse them, curse them eternally." Then he added, "But I must leave you. I am dangerous. I am like a virus," and shuffled away. That was my last and most awful connection with the purge. The effect was to make me work even harder at the War College, almost in a sort of desperation. A year later, however, with World War II started and after Hitler had crushed Poland, my theoretical studies ended abruptly.

In mid-November 1939 the War College suspended operations. I, all my fellow students, all my instructors, were ordered to report immediately to Leningrad headquarters. We were given no further instructions, knew only that the Soviet Union had been objecting to Finnish frontier fortifications near Leningrad. Our orders were field orders, and Tamara and all other wives and families were left at home.

# 6

# War

There probably was a deliberate element of drama imposed on that mid-November suspension of the War College. It was early afternoon and we were at map class. Without knocking, an orderly entered and whispered to our instructor. Class was halted immediately and we were ordered to report to the conference hall on the double. At the doors, armed sentries checked our names off lists before allowing us to enter. After other classes had been checked in, the chief of the academy entered and went to the platform, flanked by his commissar and chief of staff. Quickly and sharply our chief told us that on a top-secret order of the chief of the General Staff of the Red Army, we were to report immediately to headquarters of the Leningrad Military District, "to perform special tasks of our Party and government." He then gave us four hours to clear our affairs and board a special train for Leningrad.

The next morning we arrived in the former capital and were billeted in an officers' hotel run by the provost marshal of the city. We were not confined to quarters, but no passes were for longer than six hours and there were none for overnight.

For ten days we waited there. We used the passes to renew acquaintance with the city, stroll along the Neva, and visit old friends.

Among our group as a fellow student was a dashing, almost swashbuckling, colonel who had been in the operations section of the Leningrad Military District before attending the War College. He was a professional, had been decorated with the Order of the Red Banner for gallantry in the Civil War, and was a graduate of the Frunze Military Academy. Although a Communist, he was very outspoken and could get away with that because of his ability. He used to regale us with scandals about distinguished Soviet generals. Among those was an account that Marshal

? Semeon Dudenny had killed his wife, a beautiful ballet dancer, after accusing her of being a German spy.

On the afternoon of November 26, 1939, that colonel returned to the billets after a visit with old friends at the military district. Quite excited, he came up to me and several other students in the lobby and said, "Well, comrades, acting on orders from Moscow, our own artillery shelled our own troops on the Karelian Isthmus. Tomorrow the war is starting and this evening we all will leave to join the troops. A 'protest' has already been delivered to the Finns, accusing them of the shelling. Isn't it funny?"

His information about our departure was very correct, indeed. That night we all received orders to report to our respective units and moved out immediately. Later I saw secret reports that confirmed that the Soviets and not the Finns had done the shelling. The incident happened near the highway to Viipuri in the Soviet village of Mainila, separated by the little Sestra River from the Finnish settlement of Tamisspeni. In a quick flurry that stopped as suddenly as it had started, seven Soviet artillery rounds were fired. Four Red Army soldiers were killed, nine were wounded.

In the early hours of the next morning I reported to headquarters of the Seventh Army north of Lake Ladoga and some two hundred miles north of Leningrad. Promoted temporarily to the rank of major, I was to be the army signal officer.

Only after I had seen maps at headquarters did I realize how extensive, how massive, the Red Army preparations had been. Sending us from the War College was just a trifling last-minute addition. Hundreds of thousands of men, thousands of tanks and artillery pieces, great dumps of materiel, had been in position all along the Finnish frontier for weeks before our arrival.

The Seventh Army was just a part of the entire plan, and not a major one at that. To its north were three other armies, the Eighth, Ninth, and Tenth, and to the far north, opposite the Finnish Barents Sea port of Petsamo, was a special army corps. Despite that array, it was to the south, south of Lake Ladoga and up the Karelian Isthmus toward Viipuri, that the main effort was to be made. Concentrated there—and later reinforced—were twelve rifle divisions, a tank corps, and two separate tank brigades and special ski battalions, supported by the air force and the heavy artillery of the fortress island of Kronstadt, as well as by fire from the Red Navy. The task of that aggregation of forces in the south was to break through the redoubtable steel and concrete fortifications of the Mannerheim Line, a little more than a score of miles north of Leningrad. These southern troops formed the Leningrad Military District and were under the personal command of Stalin.

On November 29, two days after I had arrived at Seventh Army, we heard Molotov declare on the radio that relations had been broken with Finland as a result of the Mainila incident. The next day the war started, and the Red Army attacked all along the Finnish frontier, meeting able and determined resistance.

I saw practically none of the fighting in the Seventh Army sector because I was transferred almost immediately after hostilities started. That army was under command of General Stern (later purged), made a hero of the Soviet Union for his conduct of the campaign against the Japanese on the Manchurian border a year earlier. His chief of staff was the officer responsible for my transfer. He had been one of my instructors at the War College and several times had praised me for my work there. Practically the moment he laid eyes on me at Seventh Army he said I should be doing staff, not signal, work.

The next day I was sent north to Ninth Army headquarters at Kem, on the White Sea coast, to be the assistant G-1 officer. The Ninth comprised two corps, the northern one consisting of the Forty-fourth and One Hundred and Sixty-third Divisions, the southern one of the Fifty-fourth Division and a Siberian Ski Brigade; both were supported by artillery and tank units. The commanding general of that army was Vasily Chuykov—then a three-star general. His commissar, whose party connections made him the real chief of the army, was Lev Mekhlis, once an editor of *Pravda* and a former chief of the Political Department of the Red Army. Mekhlis was a four-star officer.

The mission of the Ninth Army was to advance across the border in the general direction of the town of Suomussalmi and across the waist of Finland to the port of Oulu (Uleaborg) on the Gulf of Bothnia and occupy that city, destroying Finnish forces and defenses en route. The border was 175 miles east of Oulu. Between the two points lay difficult terrain, heavily forested, with few roads, and spotted with scores of Finland's thousands of lakes. The original battle order of the Ninth, signed by Stalin, specified that Oulu be taken on the "eighteenth day" of the offensive. Even Chuykov laughed at the optimism of that order.

My first three days at Kem were spent on map work, an attempt to coordinate the positions of the various units. It was particularly difficult because the maps of Finland supplied to us by military intelligence were extremely poor, an indication of sloppy work, indeed, by the PRPs responsible for that area.

At midnight of the third day I was awakened and summoned to the chief of staff's office. There I was ordered to proceed immediately to the most advanced battalion of the Forty-fourth Division, then just east of the town of Suomussalmi some twenty miles into Finland, observe its situation and operations, and report back. More than 18,000 men strong, the Forty-fourth Ukrainian Rifles was made up not only of Ukrainians but also of Kazakhs, Azerbaidzhanians, even troops from Turkistan. It was regarded as a crack outfit, although, trained in the steppes, it was not familiar with operations in forested areas nor accustomed to the severe cold of the north. Its mission was to push beyond Suomussalmi on the shore of Kianta Jarvi (lake), already thickly encrusted with ice, so as to relieve the inadequately equipped and poorly trained One Hundred Sixty-third Division on the right flank, in bad trouble.

After I had been given my orders I was introduced to a Major Nikolayev, a political school graduate. Nikolayev, who had had practically no military training, was to accompany me as my commissar. For the trip we were given a staff car and soldier driver. For arms we carried light machine guns, machine pistols, and grenades.

Our starting point, Kem, was some 140 miles east of the frontier, although later army headquarters was advanced to Ukhta, less than a third of that distance from Finland. Ironically, we soon found that the maps of that part of the Soviet Union were just as poor as those we had for Finland. As result, we had to rely upon our own ingenuity and what advice we could get from advancing units of the Ninth that we passed over the snow-covered route. The longest stretch was west to Ukhta, from whence we paralleled the frontier in a southerly direction until we reached the headquarters of the Forty-fourth at the small town of Raate, right on the frontier.

When we left Kem that night, some of our fellow officers had shaken hands with us as if they never expected to see us again. The weather we faced was no more cheerful. It was mid-December, the temperature about twenty degrees below zero Fahrenheit, snow loomed four to eight feet high on either side of the icy ruts we bounced and skidded over, and a sharp, cutting wind blew from the north. There was only one advantage to that cold. It had formed such heavy ice on lakes and marshes, so common to that territory, that tanks and artillery could travel without trouble. That was the reason the offensive had started when it did.

North of Raate we overtook elements of the Forty-fourth moving toward headquarters and the front. Some were resting, others were on the march. I checked the schedule of each unit we passed, and whenever possible I talked to individual officers and men. Some of those we passed were pretty young girls, part of the medical and signal units. None of those hundreds seemed in the least bit enthusiastic about the campaign, as Party papers we read at headquarters had reported. Their faces were sullen, their bodies tired, their spirits low. Men, machines, artillery, tanks, horses, all moving to their final destination, Suomussalmi; most of them, it proved, to destruction and death.

At one stop among those troops, a soldier, a simple Ukrainian peasant from the Poltava area, asked me a question. "Comrade Commander," he said, "tell me, why do we fight this war? Did not Comrade Voroshilov declare at the Party congress that we don't want an inch of other people's land and we will not surrender an inch of ours? Now, we are going to fight. For what? I do not understand." Nikolayev gave me no chance to reply, butted in to tell the soldier about the Finnish danger to Leningrad.

At another halt my attention was drawn to a middle-aged soldier, a horse driver who was having trouble with one of his pack animals. The horse was very obstinate and did not want to go on one step further. Yet the driver did not beat or curse the stubborn beast as a *Muzhik* would have done. Instead, the man looked as if he were ashamed for not understanding the horse and was trying his best to convince him into going on. The soldier was clean-shaven and his face was that of a man from a different world. Puzzled, I asked his name and background. He explained that before being drafted he had been a professor of physics at Leningrad University, that by some bureaucratic error he had been made a horse driver. He smiled and said he had no objection, but I made a note to do something about his case. When I did, however, it was far too late for him.

Near Raate our car broke down and the driver said it would take at least two days to repair it. We walked a few miles to the nearest service unit and commandeered the car of that outfit's commissar. He protested loudly, but that did him no good. We had army orders.

Just before nightfall we arrived at the Raate headquarters. There we passed the night in the only quarters available, a small house filled with about one hundred officers trying to keep warm. Only a few lucky ones could sit. The others had to rest standing. Everybody was drunk. Vodka—250 grams daily for officers and men alike—was a chief item in our rations. And those who liked to drink could get more from those who did not.

By evening the stench of the smoke of cheap cigarettes, as well as that of too many bodies in too small a place, sickened me. I went out to get some air, not caring if I lost my standing place.

I had only barely cleared my lungs when I heard someone approaching in the dark slip, curse, and fall. Upon impact, there came the cracks of two sharp explosions, a scream, then silence. I went forward with my flashlight. There on the ground dead, his guts torn out, was a lieutenant. The fall had tripped his grenades somehow. He was only a boy.

Sicker than when I had left the house, I wandered around until a sentry stopped me. Ahead of us, a few yards away, were the houses of the Finnish town. They were dark, abandoned, but first the Finns had stripped them of everything. All the people were gone, all the livestock. The streets and roads leading out of the town were mined. It was a hostile land, dead, too. Nearer by was the building of the Finnish border post, likewise abandoned. By the light of the stars I could see several figures on the ground at the door of the building. They were Russian soldiers and they were dead, very dead. The sentry told me that those men had tried to loot the border post of a radio, a record player, and a bicycle left behind by the Finns. All three of those prizes had been booby trapped. The soldiers' bodies had been left there as a warning to others.

At dawn the following morning, the three of us left Raate in our quest for the isolated advanced—or vanguard as we called it—battalion of the Forty-fourth. From the moment of crossing the frontier we went slowly and very cautiously. Our slow speed was due to the fact that we were not traveling a real road, only a dirt path beneath packed snow and ice. Our caution came from the knowledge that until we reached the battalion, some twenty miles to the west, we were alone in enemy territory. Often we halted and prodded at suspicious looking humps in the road, wary of mines. At other times, through the darkness of the forests to either side of us, we saw—out of the corners of our eyes rather than full on—flitting figures all in white. We had no ski troops in the area. Those were Finns, but they evidently thought our single vehicle was not worth their trouble.

Every once in a while we came across the single body or groups of bodies of Soviet soldiers killed in the advance of the battalion. There had been no chance to recover and bury the dead. There never was any chance to bury our men in that short but terrible war.

The eyes of some of the dead were wide open. All were in exactly the same positions as when they had met their deaths.

**Manisa, Turkey, 1944. A political refugee.**

**Manisa, Turkey, 1946. With friend N. Barlass, then the public prosecutor, and his son Jem.**

**Manisa, Turkey, 1948. Working as assistant to the chief soil specialist of an agricultural project from the United States.**

**West Germany, 1952. Working for the U.S. Army in Frankfurt.**

**Washington, DC, 1954. At home.**

**Washington, DC, 1961. Near home.**

**Filip Ivanovich Golikov. Director of the GRU in the early 1940s. Appointed chief of the Soviet Navy and Army, 1958. Photo taken 1958.** *Wide World Photos.*

**Lev Zakharovich Meklis. Chief of the Political Department of the Red Army during the Finnish War; renamed to that post in 1941. Photo taken in 1941.** *Wide World Photos.*

The cold had frozen them to stony hardness, and they looked like figures in some museum of horror. One corpse stood stark upright in deep snow beside the road, both arms stretched upward toward something. Another was half crouched, his bayonet rifle still in firing position. Most, however, were lying face down, bodies covered with frozen blood.

Everywhere, except for the sound of our motor and the noise of the tires crunching in the snow, the silence was absolute. Occasionally that deathly stillness would be broken suddenly by explosions, some like rifle shots, others sounding like high velocity artillery shells. At first we flinched until we learned that the lesser sounds were ice cracking on some unseen lake or stream nearby, and the bigger ones were frozen sap bursting in some unfortunate tree.

All was terribly unreal. I thought of the haunted forests of the fairy tales of boyhood. I was very nervous, but tried not to appear so. I looked at the faces of Nikolayev and the driver. They were ashen. I guess mine must have been the same color.

That first ordeal of fear ended a little after noon when we caught up with the vanguard battalion. The entire outfit was dug in behind snow pits on either side of the road. The earth was too frozen for real defense positions to be made. Nor could the men be deployed off the edges of the road as they should have been. The snow was too deep. They had no skis or snowshoes.

At the battalion command post—also right on the road—the commander told me that his outfit had undergone heavy harassment from Finnish ski troops the day before. That accounted for some of the bodies we had seen on the road up. In a combination of three raids—from both flanks, the rear, and forward—the enemy had tried to slice the battalion into pieces, like a salami. The battalion had been kept together, but at the cost of heavy losses.

The commander said he had orders to attack the following morning. But where, where, he asked, were the Finns? Where was the front? Where were the Finnish fortifications? The Finns were everywhere and nowhere. From ambush up in the trees, they attacked with machine guns, then disappeared into the forests on skis and in uniforms of the same whiteness as the snow. They were gone before counterfire could be brought into position. That was a very harassed commander. His orders were to get through to Suomussalmi, dig in there, and await the rest of the division. Where was the division, he asked, and who was securing the road behind him? I felt very sorry for him. The Finns had sucked him in and he was getting none of the support promised from the rear.

Evening came and then darkness. Outposts were doubled

and orders were given that there would be no fires. Two nights before the battalion had been badly punished when the men had lit fires to warm themselves and heat food. From treetops the Finns had machine-gunned every fire, easily picking out the dark silhouettes of the men against the snow.

The men had learned their lesson about fires, but they were miserable with the cold as I walked among them. Some were terrified, too, so afraid that they did not leave positions where they were dug in to relieve themselves. Whole units stank with the smell of offal and the sharp odor of men long in the same uniforms and too long unwashed. That was a sorry sample of the glorious Red Army, I mused. Good soldiers reduced to that condition because higher echelons, currying political favor, had sent them into battle without proper equipment, without adequate maps, with no knowledge of the terrain, with no information about the enemy's tactics and defenses. It was criminal. And it was certainly no occupation, as ordered from on high, no destruction of the Finns and their defenses. Except for that one piece of road, the Finns had control of everything else, were free to move practically everywhere. Unlike our men, they knew where they were, what they were doing. My conclusion was that it would take the Ninth Army not eighteen days but at least eighty to reach Oulu.

The next morning the battalion was put into attack position at dawn. Then the commander held a briefing. At it were company commanders, artillery officers, commanders of supporting units. Also there were all the political officers, the battalion commissar, the Party organizers, even the editor of the battalion newspaper, *Bulletin Board.*

Under the critical eyes of those political troops the commander started to give the battle order. As I watched, I felt very sorry for the battalion officer. If the attack were a success, the politicos would get the credit for it, would get medals for bravery in action. Those types carried weapons but actually were very poor soldiers and only by mistake got into dangerous areas. If the attack were a failure the commander would get the blame, with politicos describing that he had done wrong in great detail. That system was later changed, but at that time troop commanders had no freedom of action. The purges were still going on. Political zealots had the real control.

"Comrades, commanders, and political instructors," said the battalion commander, "the enemy is entrenched in front of us. The battalion must advance to Suomussalmi and dig in there in preparation for the arrival of the main forces of our glorious division which will be concentrated in this area. Company A must attack from the right, Company B from the left. Battalion artillery, after preliminary shelling of surrounding trees, will support the companies. . . ."

The shelling started. Not only were some trees hit from which the Finns had earlier fired a few machine gun rounds, but all the trees in sight. It was a senseless and terrible harvesting of timber, but the commander knew—as did every other officer of that division—that his troops, accustomed to the open plains, were afraid of the forest. The soldiers thought that every tree in sight was a deadly trap, that every treetop was a machine gun nest. Boom, boom, boom, went the guns on and on, but not a single Finn fell from the trees.

Only after that artillery display did the infantry start to move forward down the road. That, too, was a great noise. Forward, to both flanks, to the rear, went the staccato of machine gun fire, the single shots of many rifles, the bangs of grenades and the whumps of mortars, all directed at imaginary but completely nonexistent Finns in imaginary foxholes or in treetops.

Not a Finn was hit, not a Finn was seen, not a Finn was taken prisoner. Prisoners were badly wanted for information. But in the whole campaign, even after sending out the Siberian ski troops to get some, the Ninth Army never took a single Finn. Only one man was caught in Finnish uniform. A great prize, he was taken all the way back to headquarters, stuffed with food, and almost drowned in vodka. Then, when it came time to really interrogate him, we found out that he was not a Finn, but a very recent Swedish volunteer, and knew absolutely nothing at all.

That noisy attack continued throughout the morning. Really, it was not an attack at all, but a slow move westward with much waste of ammunition. From time to time, from the flanks and from the rear, a few machine gun shots, a few rounds from light mortars coming from treetops, hit the column. Seconds later the Finns up there would drop out of the trees and disappear into the forest as if by magic. At noon a halt was called to that "attack." The troops again began the sorry process of digging in along the roadside. They had moved up a few more miles toward Suomussalmi.

That evening Nikolayev, the driver, and I started on the road back to Raate. The battalion had both signal line and radio contact with division headquarters, but that was not adequate to send my report to army. First, my findings had been lengthy; second, they had to be sent in cipher. Division had teleprinter connection with the Ninth. We were nervous, of course, on that trip back, but we had no trouble at all, never saw a Finn. It was as uneventful as a visit to the corner store.

We found Raate humming with activity. The main elements of the Forty-fourth were pulling in, in addition to supporting tanks and a great amount of artillery and service units. All were preparing to move forward down that same little road to the west. The easy trip back to division headquarters had made me very uneasy because of its very simplicity. That and the relatively light harassment taken by the vanguard battalion gave me a feeling in my bones that the Finns were just waiting for the main forces of the division.

The morning after I had filed my report to army, I got orders from the chief of staff to stay with the Forty-fourth. We were told that further information was wanted on the advance of the main elements. That meant another trip up that road.

Before leaving division headquarters I saw special orders just issued to regimental commanders. The division emphasized that better efforts must be made to secure the flanks and rears, and that service units should get special protection. Those orders were correct, but I did not see how they could be carried out. They were in accord with standard field regulations: reconnaissance troops and other patrols should be deployed forward and on the flanks, rear guards should bring up the tail of each column. That was what it said in the manuals, but that was a procedure impossible to follow. There was only that one road west, not a single flanking path within miles. Also, with no skis or other equipment to negotiate the snow, reconnaissance or deploying in depth was impossible with the snow shoulder high in the forests. The Siberians should have been used for that task, but they all had been assigned to the southern corps.

Again the three of us traveled the road to Suomossalmi without incident. By midafternoon we reached the CP [command post] of the most advanced, or vanguard, regiment. Within moments of our arrival pandemonium broke loose. Eerie silence was suddenly replaced by the chatter of machine guns from treetops; the crunch of mortar; and, even more distant, artillery shells into our position. At first the confusion was terrible. Some of our men shouted, some threw themselves flat, some were hit, some had been killed instantly. Near me a big Ukrainian fell, crying like a baby from the pain of his wound. He had been hit in the stomach. There was blood, cursing, and agony.

Then our troops recovered from the surprise and started to return the fire. Everyone fired everything. But it was not effective, just a lot of noise and another waste of ammunition. Nobody knew what to fire at. It was a textbook situation. The Finns were in control of the area.

A message came from the rear. The Finns had cut the column in half and were chopping up the rear echelon. It was a sausage-cutting operation. Moments later we lost communications with the rear. The signal line had been cut and the radio units knocked out.

Darkness was falling and the Finnish firing becoming heavier. Our casualties were mounting so rapidly the medics could care for only the most seriously wounded. The dead, of course, were left where they fell. (After the war, a special corps was sent into those forests to collect and bury 60,000 Red Army dead, well decomposed by then because the spring thaws had set in.) The situation was clearly becoming critical.

Fortunately, that twilight onslaught proved to be the final major attack on us of the day. With dark the firing slackened off, except for sporadic shots. The survivors around me were badly shaken and many doubted they would see the dawn of another day.

At 10 p.m. I was handed a radio message from army. We were ordered to return to the Ninth, then at Ukhta, immediately. Nikolayev protested, said he wanted to stay with the regiment and distinguish himself. A T-34 tank and two platoons of infantry in two trucks were assigned to us for the trip to Raate.

When it came time to go Nikolayev could not be found. He must have been very frightened to have disobeyed that order. Certainly I was nervous, too, but not to that extent.

I left regiment a quarter of an hour after getting my orders. The tank was in the lead of our little convoy, with the two trucks of soldiers following. I rode in the turret of the tank at the machine gun.

As we left, a thin sliver of a moon was just rising in the east. By that and the light of the stars, we could see about 100 yards ahead of us. Our parting site of the regiment was a grim one. Strewn all about, making our passage difficult, were the dead men and burnt out vehicles of the rear echelon chopped up late that afternoon.

We had made it safely about half of the some twenty miles back to Raate when the tank driver called that he thought he saw mines in the road ahead. Sure enough, scattered across our path, I made out a half dozen or so little humps. As I fired into them ahead with the machine gun, they exploded one by one. With the first of my shots, several men in white, Finns, jumped from the side of the road and into the forest. I tried but could not hit them, too.

Then we went on. The tank rolled over the mined strip safely. The first truck following was not so lucky. Its wheelbase narrower than our tracks, it hit a mine I had missed. With a crashing roar and cries of pain, pieces of the truck and bodies of soldiers flew into the air. I got out of the tank and did the little I could to help—order the dead and wounded crowded into the second truck before starting on again.

Several miles farther on we met another regiment, halted for the night in its march up the road. I left the truckload of troops—wounded and dead—with them and continued to Raate in the tank without further trouble. From there on a staff car took me to Ukhta, where I reported to army in full on the troubles and deficiences of the Forty-fourth.

Some two weeks later, in early January of 1940, the chief of staff ordered me to accompany him to headquarters of our northern corps, the one to which the Forty-fourth and One Hundred Sixty-third divisions were assigned. Our destination was the corps CP on the eastern shore of Kianta Jarvi, a few miles north of Suomussalmi. The mission was to get the corps and the One Hundred Sixty-third to beef up their operations in support of the Forty-fourth.

We never got to the CP, and that mission was never accomplished. As we approached the area where the CP was supposed to have been, we found everything in great disorder. The CP had been abandoned. The corps was in full retreat up the lake, to the north and east. So was the One Hundred Sixty-third, but for that division it was more of a rout than a withdrawal. I, a lowly junior officer, was amazed that the chief of staff of army had been unaware such a mess was imminent.

That senior officer and I went into retreat, too.

We finally located corps headquarters on the move and joined them on the retreat up the lake that followed the luckless attempt of the One Hundred Sixty-third to take Suomussalmi. Never had I dreamed of such disorderly retreat: horses, artillery, men, running in every direction, trying to get back across the frontier. To make matters worse, Finnish planes attacked the fleeing units. Big holes were blasted in the lake ice, over which we were moving. Scores of men and much materiel vanished into the cold waters opened up by the bombs.

On the bad trek back I personally met Mekhlis for the first time. He had been with the corps headquarters, perhaps in search of battle honors just like the lesser commissars. What else he could have been doing there was beyond me. He was the real boss of the army. He alone had the connections to get it the equipment, the supplies, the troops it needed. He should have been back at Ukhta. There, and only there, he could have done something about the bad trouble facing the army.

During the retreat Mekhlis asked me about the Forty-fourth. Since our days, if not hours, might be numbered, I told him quite bluntly. I told him how fine were the soldiers in that division, but how inadequately trained they were for fighting in that terrain. I told him of the dearth of proper maps and intelligence about the enemy. I told him of the lack of ski troops in the right places at the right times.

Mekhlis did not regard that as an impertinent outburst but heard me out. And I regarded him highly as a man. A fine type of Jewish intellectual, he was broad and high of forehead and his eyes were large, deep set, and extremely intelligent. His manner was urbane, his voice usually low and modulated.

Most of that routed corps and division made it back across the border without further serious trouble, although all corps artillery, about half of the troops of the One Hundred Sixty-third, and almost all of its equipment had been lost.

Four days after that rout on the lake and two days after the return to Ukhta, we got the very bad word that the Forty-fourth had been annihilated, or, as the official report said, "more than seven hundred men overcame all difficulties" and made it back to Raate.

Mekhlis named a commission to investigate the disaster. He had to. It was his army and he had already lost almost all of one of his two corps.

I, no doubt because I had talked so frankly on the lake, was made head of the commission. There were two other members, the routed army corps' chief of counterintelligence and the representative of the NKVD with the troops; and a commissar under Mekhlis. As a War College student, I was supposed to have the technical knowledge for the inquiry, while the presence of the other two men was to give weight to the commission.

We went to the staff of the northern corps. We went to the staff of the One Hundred Sixty-third, and finally to the remnants of the Forty-fourth at Raate. Among those survivors were the division commander, General Vinogradov, and his commissar, Gusev.

After interviewing scores of men from the three units, we composed our report. We listed as principal reasons for the disaster: faulty coordination with the One Hundred Sixty-third on the right flank; poor organization by army staff; the lack of sufficient machine guns and other automatic weapons; and the lack of ski troop support. Other causes we gave were scanty intelligence about the terrain and enemy techniques, poor maps, inadequate training—in fact, almost everything we had learned, down to the smallest detail.

Mekhlis turned our report over to a military tribunal with orders for severe consideration of Vinogradov and Gusev, who should never have returned. The trial was held almost on receipt of our report. The two men were found guilty of treason and ordered executed.

The day after that, as chief of the investigating commission, I had to go to Raate to be present at the executions. The general and the commissar were put before a counterintelligence (NKVD) firing squad and shot. Also present at the execution—in fact it was staged in front of them—were the seven hundred remnants of the Forty-fourth.

In with those survivors was none other than my former commissar, Nikolayev. He had become a physical and mental wreck. He cried steadily, babbled incoherently, shot blindly at anybody, was soon sent to an asylum. Nikolayev was one of many commissars, too many commissars in proportion, that had made it back to Raate. Our report had mentioned how those types had torn their insignias from their uniforms fearing capture, and then had run like beasts madly through the forests. Our report had also mentioned how the line soldiers had stayed and fought almost to the last man, fighting from behind the stacked bodies of their fallen comrades.

That report proved to be almost too much for my career, almost, even, for my life. Mekhlis had instructed me to make the report in an original and one copy, with both the original and copy to be delivered to him only.

A week after I had completed it and Vinogradov and Gusev were well underground, orders came for me to report to Mekhlis's office posthaste. I found him in a terrible rage, stuttering, and hardly able to control himself.

"You idiot," he screamed at me, "I'm going to have you hauled before a tribunal. I'm going to have you shot. Illegally, and probably intentionally, you let the NKVD have a copy of that inquiry. It's probably in Moscow, in Beria's hands by now."

Ai, ai! Me, a simple Tatar, a mere temporary major caught up in a mess like that! I was literally shaking all over. I could hardly speak, but I did manage to mumble a denial. I had not done what I had been accused of, but neither was I too simple a Tatar not to understand the weapon against Mekhlis that report could be in high NKVD hands, especially with purges continuing.

Also in the office during that awful session were the two corps commanders and Chuykov. The army general had looked on quietly while Mekhlis yelled and I mumbled in reply.

As I stood there waiting for the axe to fall, Chuykov interceded. He turned to Mekhlis and said "I believe Akhmedov is telling the truth. After all, the NKVD took part in the inquiry. It would have been no trouble to them to make not just one copy, but as many as they pleased."

Maybe Mekhlis recalled that he should have been at Ukhta and not with the corps at the time of the rout. Maybe it was that he was the decent man I had thought. I do not know the reason, but as Chuykov spoke he cooled down. In the end he said he understood what had happened, apologized for yelling at me, and excused me.

Some days later in a letter from Tamara, clippings from Moscow newspapers were enclosed. They said that I—among many others—had been cited for gallantry in combat on the Finnish front. Only Mekhlis could have been responsible for that. And if only Tamara had known at what level that combat had been.

After that very near thing, I spent almost a month quietly keeping my maps in order and carrying out my other duties at G-1. Work was not too strenuous with everything static in the northern sector after the Forty-fourth had been wiped out, the One Hundred Sixty-third mauled, and that corps lost its artillery. Nor were things too busy with the southern corps and its Fifty-fourth Division and ski troops. In that sector they were not advancing, but at least they were not retreating.

The lull for me ended early in March. Mekhlis again called me to his office. That time he did not bawl me out, but was smiling. Maybe he liked me. He had decided to visit the Fifty-fourth Division—probably on another try for a medal—and I was to accompany him.

On March 8 we went on Mekhlis's special plane to the CP of the Fifty-fourth. Aboard were also about fifty high-ranking officers from army headquarters. I was the most junior person among them.

Except for Mekhlis's whim, plus the fact he did not like my chief, the head of G-1, there was really no purpose in my going on that trip. With the Fifty-fourth I just wandered around, doing nothing of real importance.

On the night of March 12—exactly at midnight it was—I was

in the headquarters teleprinter room, rather idly watching incoming and outgoing traffic. At the zero hour the bell for an urgent message sounded. On the machine I read that a truce had been arranged and would become effective at noon the next day, March 13. The message was preceded and followed by the warning that the information was secret and was for distribution for staff officers only. The last sentence of the text was startling. It read: until the truce hour, "spare not a single bullet."

My first reaction, since I had been mixed with Mekhlis's affairs whether I liked it or not, and since I had been taken to the Fifty-fourth by him, was to wonder what he was doing there at a time like that. I would not have thought that a man of his authority would not have had an inkling of the truce arrangements being under way. Also, it was strange for him to be away from his headquarters at such a time.

I got the answer to the last question very soon. The next morning he and his plane had returned to Ukhta. And the next few days, before I made my way back to the Ninth by staff car, I found Mekhlis gone from there, too, and already in Moscow.

Early on the last day of the war, I went to a regimental CP to see it out. The commander was a fellow Tatar, a Colonel Ibragimov. He, not being a staff officer of the army, had not the slightest idea that the truce was only hours away.

That poor man's outfit was involved in a very sharp fire fight all over its sector when I arrived. It was the Finns rather than the Russians who were not sparing bullets.

Shortly before noon the Finns charged, and our forward lines collapsed. At five minutes to noon they had driven to within a handful of yards of our CP.

At that very moment the CP came under direct fire. The colonel fell, shot through the head. I held him in my arms, and before he died I told him how narrowly he had missed the end of the war.

At noon exactly, messengers ran everywhere calling the cease-fire, and announcements came repeatedly over the radio. Finns, Russians alike threw down their arms. All embraced.

The war was over. Only later did we learn what had been lost: sixty thousand killed; two hundred thousand wounded; ten thousand of those with feet or legs amputated because of frostbite; the respect of much of the civilized world for fighting so small a neighbor, and so poorly, as well. Gained was the town of Viipuri, some fortifications, a few thousand square miles of forests, lakes and marshes; the downgrading of the commissars and the establishment of real rather than simulated grades and ranks in the

Russian armed forces. The last was all that counted, but it was gained at terrible cost.

That disastrous war over, I was returned to Moscow to resume my studies at the War College, but not for very long. That period, the spring of 1940, was when Stalin had his eyes on other small border states, hoping to grab some territory while Germany and the West were involved in World War II. His first of several of those efforts was a nibble at Rumania, a demand that she cede him her border provinces of Northern Bukovina and Bessarabia. Historically he had some claim to Bessarabia, which Russia annexed early in the nineteenth century in war with the Ottoman Empire, but he had no clear right at all to Northern Bukovina.

In mid-June, when pressure on Bucharest was reaching its height, the War College was once more closed down. Again students and instructors were put aboard a special train. Our destination that time was Kamenets Podol'skiy, in the extreme southwestern corner of the Ukraine near the Rumanian border.

I do not mean to be critical of Rumania, but as happened in so many affairs involving that nation, my brief role in that operation was comic opera as compared to my work on the Finnish front.

On June 26, 1940, I was summoned to the high command at Kamenets Podol'skiy. There I was handed top-secret orders for attack, in the event Rumania rejected a Soviet ultimatum, to deliver in person to the commander of the Twelfth Army. A small observation plane and pilot were put at my disposal.

Our destination was Kolomyya—Polish before that nation's collapse—a small city on the river Prut, just north of Bukovina. It was good weather when we left, but by the time we approached Kolomyya, in the foothills of the Carpathian Mountains, we were plagued by very thick and low-lying cloud cover.

Around and around we flew for several hours looking for an opening. We found none at all and the clouds, instead of thinning as we had hoped, became ever thicker. The pilot seemed unconcerned, but I had seen some pretty impressive peaks on the map and just prayed we were nowhere near them.

Finally, when the time came that we had just enough gas to get back to Kamenets Podol'skiy, the pilot jokingly suggested I use my parachute and jump. I had thought of that, not with any pleasure at all, but as a dutiful officer. However, my map reading showed me that in those clouds we might have been over Bukovina or the eastern tip of Czechoslovakia that the Soviet Union had grabbed at the end of the war. I was not going to run the chance of being taken prisoner or interned, especially with those orders on me.

In the end I returned a bit shamefacedly to Kamenets Podol'skiy. There I was given a staff car for the trip. Then, shortly after midnight June 27, while winding through tortuous roads paralleling the Bukovina frontier, I was advised by radio that my mission was over. The Rumanians, I was told, had agreed to Soviet demands.

For several days after that capitulation I was with our troops as Bukovina was "liberated." Our radio broadcasts were making much of that occupation. They spoke about the "great joy of the liberated people," of the "great joy" with which they welcomed the Red Army. What I saw were sullen and frightened people and Soviet troops wide-eyed at the wealth of consumer goods in stores.

As Bukovina, and Bessarabia as well, were duly "liberated," we were all sent back to Moscow and at the War College started again. I was glad to get back. I was behind on a lot of reading—although I well knew the value of the field work that had caused the interruptions—and the course was ending in August.

To be graduated we had to acquit ourselves of two prime tasks, a thesis and an oral presentation on military subjects. Many of my fellow students took the easy way out with their final papers. They selected "The Achievements of Stalin in the Civil War," and were, of course, commended. I preferred the "Battle of the Marne" of World War I. That was work, not sycophancy, but I was commended, too.

I must admit, however, that my oral presentation played the Party line and was also very well timed. It was made before the chief of staff of the Red Army and many other high-ranking officers. The commissar of the college had just made a poor speech on electrification because it happened to be the very anniversary of a boring book by Lenin, entitled, *Electrification Plus Cooperation Is Equal to Socialism*. The speech was poor because its subject matter was limited to such mundane matters as supplying power to factories and cooperatives, forgetting the advances made since Lenin's death.

I was called to the rostrum to discuss the speech and was told: "Comrade Akhmedov, you have specialized in electrical subjects, let us hear your views." So I did for five minutes. I supported the views of the new breed of officers who envisaged the increasing sophistication of electricity and power. I spoke about research with magnetrons (from which radar eventually was developed), about remote control of tanks, about military applications of television, about the role the atom might play someday, and about possible push-button wars of the future, running the gamut of new developments that force modification of military doctrine. In closing, I said, ". . . and all that, plus cooperation, will make socialism. Long live our Lenin." The generals called "bravo," they clapped, they cheered.

Primarily on the basis of those remarks, but also with consideration of my decoration and my other work during the course, I graduated high in my class in August 1940 and was promoted to engineer major.

# Part Three

# 7

## Committed

I had several weeks' leave after gradution from the War College. Instead of going to the seaside or some other resort, I spent it at home, getting reacquainted with Tamara—of whom I had seen too little even when in Moscow—and otherwise just lolling around and thinking.

Our quarters of that time were so comfortable that rather than go away from them on vacation, I wanted to relax in them and enjoy them. They had been assigned me by the research institute, to which I had requested to be returned, and were at Mytishshi, a little town north of Moscow. We were in an apartment building, to be sure, but from the balcony I could rest my eyes on pleasant woods in the distance.

Inwardly I was pleased with myself. In the fifteen years since I had left Kuba, I had accomplished pretty much what I had wanted. I had not soared to the rank of colonel or even general or commissar as had some of my classmates of those years. But I had not sold out my instructors, friends, and associates as my classmates had done to claw their way to a never very secure top. Nor was I in the position of others I had known in the army, others who had no interest in study or the grind at academies and who were still lieutenants, or captains at the most, somewhere in the field. Granted I was only a major, but that was high enough in the structure for me to observe and get along without becoming too involved or committed. Or so I thought.

On a fine September afternoon toward the end of my leave, I was on my balcony, lazy and contented after lunch, drinking tea, smoking, and musing. Gazing into the woods I fell into a doze, remembering the good times I had had in the open with Father, the mixed bag of trouble and adventure that had followed.

A crashing of thunder awakened me. The fine day had succumbed to a storm. Dark clouds zigzagged with lightning hung low over Moscow on the horizon. Lesser clouds above me began to spit and I went in.

As I did, there was a steady knocking at the apartment door. Tamara had gone out after lunch. I was alone. Perhaps that rapping, not the thunder, had awakened me. Not too graciously I let in the caller, a colonel of the Red Army, a man completely unknown to me. With no more than a grunt for a greeting, he said he was under orders to take me with him immediately to the chief of the Intelligence Directorate of the General Staff, Lieutenant General Ivan Filippovich Golikov.

So there it was. My research, my staff work, had been of no use. The long arm of the GRU had caught up with me.

A military sedan and driver were waiting at the door of my building. Once under way, the colonel said that he was chief of the GRU personnel division and that three of my classmates at the War College had also been appointed to the Intelligence Directorate, known also as "Metro," sometimes the "Center," to GRU men abroad.

Through a heavy downpour, through thunder and lightning, we were driven to the heart of Moscow and past armed sentries through the gates of one of the Soviet Union's most closely guarded buildings, Znamensky 19, the headquarters of the Directorate.

Once within, we were escorted to the third floor to the office of the Director. Returning my salute from behind a big desk, General Golikov invited me to be seated.

Although resplendent in the full uniform of a lieutenant general of the Red Army, he did not cut much of a figure. He was short, no more than five feet, two inches. He was stocky. He was completely bald. His face was rather unpleasantly flushed. The power of the man was quickly apparent, however, in his eyes. They were not remarkable for size, but they were steely blue and terribly penetrating when directed at another person.

He was a newcomer to the post, even to GRU. Previously he had commanded troops at L'vov during the division of Poland. At the Directorate he had succeeded one of those many former favorites of Stalin, General Proskurov, a hero of the Soviet Union for his combat missions flown in the Spanish Civil War, before being purged into the unknown. As Director, Golikov had also become second deputy chief of the General Staff and was personally responsible to Stalin for all military intelligence.

Golikov's office was as severe as he was. On his desk were only a few papers in good order, and several telephones. Except for portraits of Lenin and Stalin, the walls were given over to strategic maps of the world. In one corner of the room was a large globe. In another was the latest and largest model of a good German radio receiver.

Only in subsequent meetings did I gain so full an impression of my new chief and his office. I had little time for that on my first visit on that stormy evening. Then, before dismissing me, Golikov spared me only enough time to tell me I had been made acting chief of the Fourth Division—technological espionage—and to order me to report for duty the following morning.

Tamara had retured from a visit to friends by the time I got back home that night. We spent much of it talking over the sudden change in my plans, fortunes, and future. She was disappointed—as I was, too—that the chance of getting into a completely technical field, as apolitical as possible, seemed ruled out, probably forever. But remembering the fairly nice life we had had at Tbilisi before I was sent to the PRP, she was somewhat pleased with my return to intelligence work. More than that, she—like every other Soviet citizen—regarded intelligence as highly honorable, as something done, even though secretly, in the highest service to Party and government. Again like every other Soviet citizen, she had scorn to hatred for internal security (NKVD), as compared to respect and admiration for military intelligence. Only the West degrades its intelligence officers by referring to them as "spies" and "agents." Tamara finished her thoughts by saying she was proud of me and kissing me. Knowing a bit more than she did about what might be involved, I was not exactly proud; rather, I was relieved. I still shook whenever I recalled that close shave I had with Mekhlis on the Finnish front, a mess I might have avoided had I been under the aegis of GRU. It was comforting, I admit, in that mad world of Stalin's time to be part of a powerful organization that usually took care of its own, at least its underlings.

After appointment it took me weeks, in fact several months, to get settled in. I had an awful lot of reading to do, an awful lot of people to see and get to know, before feeling sure of myself. I also had to become accustomed to the very strangeness of the Directorate Building itself, to become used to some of its more unusual personnel.

In some respects buildings and people are alike. Careful scrutiny of either often will show their natures, sometimes even what goes on within. There are, however, a few structures and a few people that reveal nothing of themselves from the outside, that might as well be faceless, nameless. Znamensky 19, the Directorate Building, was in that latter category.

It was an ill-favored, plain, insignificant-looking, almost imperceptible, and relatively old building. It was not one of Moscow's high, modern buildings, shining with marble or granite, and equipped with fast-moving elevators. It was a slum structure in comparison with the grand house of the Council of Ministers, or the building of the Ministry of Internal Affairs. It had no name, like "Lubyanka," the headquarters of internal security (NKVD), or like "Kremlin," the traditonal seat of the autocrats. Like a spy, it had no known identity. Even its entry was hidden from the street by a gate, a garage, a one-story pass office, and finally a courtyard.

A casual stroller would pass the Directorate without a glance. At the outer gate, only a trained observer might notice that traffic in and out of the building was not of the same pattern as that at other Soviet offices. Cars using that single gate are not Soviet-made only, as elsewhere, but are also of western origin, American, British, French, German. The people passing in and out there include not only officers in standard uniforms, but also many civilians, well dressed, and usually in latest foreign fashion. Those civilians are the oddest of that traffic. Most carry themselves with a decided military bearing, step and return salutes smartly when tendered them by men in uniform. Nor would men out of uniform, plainclothes security officers, be on their tails, as usual for other well-dressed foreigners off the beaten tourist track.

I never overcame my revulsion for that odd and evil working address of mine. For me it was almost a prison. No normal friends ever called there for me, nor indeed were any allowed to do so. Its very address was better known in western countries than in the Soviet Union.

By its occupants it was not called Znamensky 19. To us it was *Razvedupr,* an abbreviated form of *Razvedyvatelnoe Upravelenie,* meaning Intelligence Directorate. It was in a complex of buildings that housed the *Pervyy DOM NKO* (the First House of the Peoples' Commisariat for Defense), which also included the General Staff and the Political Directorate of the Red Army.

Odd people not only visited *Razvedupr,* but even stranger people led strange lives and followed strange pursuits within its walls. They were of many nationalities, spoke a multitude of tongues. Most had traveled widely to the *zagranitsa,* the foreign lands forbidden to ordinary Soviet mortals, were often more familiar with the streets of New York, Tokyo, Istanbul, London, Berlin, or Paris than with those of Moscow and Leningrad.

Many of the inmates as well as the visitors had double, often triple names. Few knew who they really were. Perhaps some of them were confused themselves. All were trained not to recognize each other in case they should meet by chance outside the walls. It was also forbidden to ask any of them what they were doing, where they came from, or were going. There was just one sharp division among them: clandestine or overt. All those engaged in clandestine work were at least majors of the General Staff no matter what their cover titles, be they ambassadors, trade delegates, consular officials, or newspapermen.

That hodgepodge of personalities, nationalities, and identities was bound together by only two factors—membership in the Party and allegiance to the government of the U.S.S.R. They did have one other prime bond, an intangible one that none mentioned but none forgot. That was fear. All were exposed to western publications, travel, and contacts. That made them suspect to the very Party and government they served, often with great hardship and danger. For them peril was always double.

Those hard facts were brought home to me only by experience. The morning I reported for duty at *Razvedupr* I was a complete innocent, no matter what I thought I had learned of intelligence in my comparatively trifling work in the Transcaucasus.

I was welcomed—that is hardly the correct word—to my new office by a female assistant in the Fourth Division. An attractive woman, with large brown eyes, carefully tended brown hair and high cheekbones, she was an officer, Capt. Maria Polyakova, a Jewess. She showed me my working area, a large desk with several phones hooked into city and private master systems, connected with various defense headquarters, plus a direct line to Golikov, and a comfortable armchair, but no maps, no radio.

I had hoped she would leave quickly, but she stayed with me for a few moments longer, then blurted out this: "Comrade Nachalnik [chief], in their own time other chiefs of this division have sat behind that desk, plotting many operations, working day and night for the glory of our Party and country. They were all shot or sent to concentration camps. That was their reward. Now, some trouble must be coming for Comrade Konovalov [a colonel who had been sent to Germany and was actual head of the division of which I had been made acting chief]. I sincerely hope you will not share their unhappy fate."

That was my introduction. In my naiveté, I had envied the fact that Konovalov was abroad, while I was put in to do the routine paperwork. I found out quickly that he was on the skids. Polyakova and others in the division had liked him and admired him. They resented my arrival and Polyakova had been frank enough to say so. They must also have thought I was a little dense.

A few days later Polyakova handed me a real eye opener, a letter. To my recollection it read something like this: "Dear Comrade Stalin. During the purges I was arrested, beaten, and tortured by security investigators in the most inhuman manner. I was accused of things I did not do, crimes I did not commit. I was threatened and humiliated. I was not given the chance to defend myself. I had served this regime faithfully since the days of the Revolution. I was decorated three times with the Order of the Red Banner. Now, after months of the most dreadful interrogation, of which not even the Tsarist security could have conceived, I am being set to a concentration camp somewhere far away in Siberia. I have not been permitted to communicate with my family, friends, or associates. I have been sentenced to labor camp without due trial. In the name of the Revolution and of the Party, please intervene on my behalf and save me. Being deprived of any other channel, I am throwing this letter from the door of a freight car taking me and scores of other innocent people to Siberia."

A routing slip was pinned to that letter. The slip showed the appeal had been found along the tracks in a Moscow suburb and had, indeed, been sent to Stalin's secretariat. There it had been initialed by Georgi Malenkov, Stalin's lieutenant, who forwarded it to Golikov. Goilikov had made the notation, "For divisional circulation and files." The writer of that hopeless letter was Konovalov's predecessor, had once sat in the same armchair in which I was then ensconced.

Well before the shock of that letter had worn off, Golikov called a meeting of his six operational division chiefs. At it were the newcomers, myself, my three classmates from the War College, and two holdovers from the Proskurov regime.

During the preliminaries of that session, I reflected on the power held by that short man in the uniform of a lieutenant general. He could influence the choice of every Soviet diplomat, of every ambassador, and other appointments to overseas duties. He could send Red Army officers assigned to GRU to any place on the globe. He had millions in any kind of currency in special funds to spend on his operations. From behind the scenes he held the reins to all kinds of subversion, disruption, and terror, from organizing worldwide uprisings and strikes to arranging kidnappings and assassinations. His evaluations and intelligence estimates were the basis on which his superiors in the Politburo made policy decisions and charted war plans.

Golikov jolted me from that speculation with the statement he had just seen Malenkov and Stalin. Both, he said, had called for an intensification of intelligence and improvement of the product. Both had urged further housecleaning of the old-timers on the basis that too many had been too long abroad, had too many foreign contacts and associations, and were, therefore, "security risks." His program in the field, Golikov said, was already well under way. It was our task, as chiefs of divisions, to carry out the changeover for the rest of the organization, to get new personnel both at home and abroad.

I was somewhat shocked that the Director had expressed himself so bluntly in the presence of the two holdover chiefs, who later, of course, joined the never-ending list of the missing. I do not believe that he meant to be intentionally brutal, rather that he was just being his matter-of-fact, hard-boiled self.

I was also bothered about the meaning of the Director's instructions in plain language—not just a continuation but an increase in the pace of the purges.

For me it was an awful and dreary business. It required combing through the files of my division, picking out candidates for elimination. Sometimes I was fortunate and found some luckless souls who had actual deficiencies or slip-ups against them and would have been ousted sooner or later. In the main, however, I had to rely on the formula of too much association with the West.

With the records of those unfortunates in hand and the damnations attached to them, I would then report to the deputy director for operations, who would forward the findings to internal security. That part especially curdled my spirits: to have internal security in the guise of counterintelligence at my level, or as a deputy director for political affairs in Golikov's office at the top! GRU had nobody at Lubyanka, but NKVD had the final word at the Directorate.

Concurrent with that purge, on Malenkov's insistence and Golikov's orders, we were told that the GRU should develop "mutual understanding and cooperation" with the NKVD. So far as I was concerned, that resulted in a surprise call at my office one raw afternoon in the late autumn of 1940 by the chief of technical intelligence of the foreign department of the NKVD—my opposite number.

It was called a courtesy visit, but there actually was some business, too. That involved an apportionment of our respective agents in New York operating under cover of *Amtorg*, the Soviet trade organization there. NKVD insisted on 60 percent of the technical intelligence agents in *Amtorg* on the grounds that they were responsible for economic as well as scientific intelligence. However, we did not really fare so badly. The agents alloted to the Red Navy in New York came only from GRU, and we had some of the wives of our operatives recruited, too. That left us with more than the minority of 40 percent of the agents proposed by the NKVD.

In compliance with that enforced aura of amity between the GRU and the NKVD, I had to return that call of my counterpart. That was my one and only visit to Lubyanka. From our files I had learned quite a bit more about what went on in that frightful place that was later disclosed in *Darkness at Noon* and other revelations of defectors to the West.

On the surface, however, I found that the administrative side—not the prison, of course—was a very fancy place. With a very special pass, and after much escorting by armed guards in and out of several elevators and along many corridors, I arrived at the NKVD technical intelligence section. What a contrast to my crowded and shoddy office!

There was a reception room. Beyond that were a library and study rooms. The floors were richly carpeted. On the walls were the usual portraits of Lenin and Stalin, of course, but there were also paintings that looked of value. All the furnishings were of handsome polished wood, of foreign origin, probably Scandinavian. Every bit of the house communications system was American. The secretaries were quite an improvement over my lone, awkwardly uniformed Polykova. All were very, very attractive, some even glamorous. When closeted with my opposite number, he offered me my first American cigarette. I believe it was a Chesterfield. Then, when it had been settled that he was to get the lion's share of *Amtorg,* he pulled open a desk drawer and brought out a bottle of Scotch whiskey to celebrate. I returned to the grim Directorate in a haze, and not because of the liquor.

In mid-December of 1940 Golikov suddenly summoned a special session of his entire top staff, some twenty-five officers. I thought that the meeting would have something to do with the Battle of Britain, then at its height. It did concern that struggle, but not directly.

Golikov liked to have frequent and sudden meetings with his subordinates, but that one was unique. Top security measures were taken. At the doors of his office were armed soldiers and an officer of the day. Our names were on a list we had to sign. Looking stern, the Director was at his desk, flanked by his deputy for political affairs and his deputy for operations, a rugged former tank officer.

The little general opened the meeting with the warning that it was top-secret. He had just had a conference with Stalin, he said. Then he told us the following:

Our thinking should not be influenced by the nonaggression treaty between the Soviet Union and Germany, the Molotov-Ribbentrop Pact signed in August 1939, at the eve of World War II. We should disregard it entirely. It was a "document of temporary character." It was a "product of the dialectical genius of our Comrade Stalin." Like any other international agreement signed by the Soviet Union, it could be annulled at any time the Party and government found it expedient.

The chance of Germany making war on us was very unlikely. Hitler and his marshals "were not going to attempt suicide." They were not "maniacs or lunatics."

Britain soon would be brought to her knees by Germany. That would mean that British possessions would be divided between Germany and Japan. We would "liberate" the Balkans, "our brothers in blood," and thereby open for ourselves the Middle East, its oil resources and strategic routes. In an effort to save the British Empire from total collapse, the U.S.A., "the heartland of classic capitalism," would attack Germany and there would be a new and more terrible war.

Meanwhile, the Soviet Union would wait patiently until the time came to fulfill its historical role. Once the capitalists were bleeding and exhausted, we would "liberate" the world.

We must prepare for our hour. For us, intelligence officers, that meant new networks, new operatives, new plans, new cadres of agents, new groups of underground forces, ready to go into action on orders from our Party and government.

That being our task, continued Golikov, we must perfect two plans for mobilization of our intelligence forces, both at home, and abroad. Plan A must be based on the most logical assumption, namely that the U.S.A. would fight Germany and Japan, while the Soviet Union, at least provisionally, allied itself with Germany and Japan against the U.S.A. Plan B should be in accord with the more unlikely assumption that we would fight Germany, and the U.S.A. would be our "temporary" ally. He emphasized the adjective "temporary," and made no mention of the inclusion of Japan in Plan B.

The entire Directorate went to work feverishly on the double plan. It required alerting not only the existing legal and illegal networks abroad, but also the organization of completely new networks, communications, financial arrangements, and courier services on a worldwide basis.

Many of us—the junior officers especially—were hindered by the conviction that work on Plan A was not only a waste of time, but a criminal dispersion of our efforts and forces. To our group, Germany was just as capitalistic as the U.S.A., and the latter had no Nazis, and no common frontier with the heart of our nation. As much as it was possible for Soviet intelligence officers, we liked Americans, did not like or trust Germans.

Secretly our group set down its views on paper with a wealth of supporting facts and sent those findings directly to Malenkov, carefully avoiding Directorate channels. Several weeks after that the Directorate did an about-face, ordered Plan A dropped completely and demanded the speedy development of a real, rather than hypothetical, Plan B. But by then, as we found later, we were running out of time to halt clandestine operations against the U.S.A. and against countries fighting Germany, and certainly to set up any practical arrangements with U.S.A. intelligence.

Just as that regrouping got under way I got my first chance to go abroad, something I had hoped to do ever since being recruited by the GRU in Tbilisi ten years earlier. It was not really abroad either, only to the former Baltic states, but I was still pleased to see something other than pure Soviet Union.

In January 1941, Moscow and Berlin came to agreement about repatriation of German nationals in Esthonia, Latvia, and Lithuania. Those Germans had been caught there in June of the year before when those three little countries were "liberated" by the Soviet Union, at the same time that I was playing my small part in the "liberation" of Bukovina.

Why I was picked for that mission to the Baltic I have no idea. Perhaps my service on the Finnish front or in Bukovina had something to do with it. Probably my command of German was responsible.

My task was relatively simple. I had to recruit intended repatriates for the GRU. My only problem was beating the NKVD, which was also looking for recruits among those people. It gave me some pleasure to find that candidates were willing to work for GRU, whereas only those compromised by personal entanglements or bad marks on their record were enlisted by the NKVD, and most of them only by pressure and threat. Besides Germans returning to Germany, I also recruited several who could not go back there—Jews forced to emigrate to the U.S.A. and Britain—and I thereby got personal praise from Golikov.

I was given no narrow time limit on that mission. So, as far as reasonable, I did some ordinary touring and sightseeing. I also bought a little clothing and a watch for Tamara. On that shopping expedition in Riga, I ran into a former classmate from the Leningrad academy, Ivan Timofeyvich Peresypkin, the man who had forged his way to success at the start of the purges by turning in his fellows and instructors. He had gone a long way since then, was commissar of communications for the whole U.S.S.R. He, that arch foe of capitalism, was buying up everything he could lay his hands on in the Latvian capital. His expenditures and his activity were not pleasing to the Riga sales clerks. They looked on just as unhappily and suddenly as had the people of Bukovina when "greeting with joy" the "liberating" Red Army.

That pleasant interlude on the Baltic could not last forever; in fact it came to an end in early April. Back at the Directorate, I was once more engulfed in Plan B when Polyakova, quite excited for her normally taciturn self, handed me an urgent message she had just deciphered.

It read: "The German High Command has ordered an immediate halt in the manufacture of Soviet heavy armament at the Skoda plants. Senior German officers stationed in Czechoslovakia have told friends that German divisions were concentrating on the western borders of the U.S.S.R. It is believed that Hitler will attack the U.S.S.R. during the second half of June." The date of the message was April 17, 1941.

That brief but jarring piece of information was signed by our legal resident in Prague, whose cover was that of commercial attaché at the embassy. His source of information was well known to us: the chief engineer of the Skoda plants, a Czechoslovak who was not a Communist, but had turned to us in patriotism after the German takeover of his country.

Needless to say I rushed to Golikov's office with the cable. Carefully, he checked me and our files on its source. Everything we had on that engineer was good, was reliable. All his information, all his evaluations he had sent for months before, had proved bona fide.

That evening we prepared a very full report on the message and its source. Golikov signed the report and it was sent by special courier to Stalin, Malenkov, and the chief of staff.

That night passed, the next night. Nothing happened.

The third night I was home in the quarters the Directorate had given us, in a high apartment building overlooking the Moscow River, below the Kremlin. I was looking at the lights across the river, a drink in my hand. I had just finished reading Lawrence's *Seven Pillars of Wisdom* and was wondering about life in British intelligence.

Then the phone rang, not at regular intervals, but continuously and insistently. I raised the receiver. "Ismail," I heard, "the general wants you, immediately. A duty car should be at your door now." Speaking had been my neighbor, a major who was Golikov's personal adjutant.

There were a dozen other officers waiting at Golikov's office door when I arrived, but I was given priority. As I entered, he was seated at his desk, shuffling some papers in an annoyed way.

Without asking me to be seated, he tossed them to me. They were our report on the Prague cable to Stalin. But something had been scrawled across it in red ink. That scrawl read:

"Angleyskaya Provokatsiya Rassledovat! Stalin." ["This is a British provocation. Investigate the matter. Stalin."]

As I handed the papers back, Golikov turned those steely blue eyes on me at full power. He said, "Comrade Akhmedov. I charge you personally with the investigation demanded. I had been thinking of sending you to Germany later. You must go now and be in Berlin no later than mid-May. I have arranged that your cover will be that of manager of the *Tass* office, replacing the present manager. Complete those cover details and get your division and personal affairs in order."

I was so excited that I could hardly talk when I got back home again. I was terribly shocked at Stalin's reaction. (So compartmentalized was the Directorate that only after the war did I learn Stalin had also been advised of the Hitler attack by Richard Sorge, working for GRU, too, but far from us, in Tokyo.) I was also greatly worried about the spot I was in, being responsible to Stalin for the investigation. None of that, Stalin's reaction, nor my real task, could I tell to Tamara, of course. But I did tell her that I was to be sent to Germany and soon.

She was very distressed to hear where I was going. And so was I, for her. Technically, there was nothing to prevent her accompanying me, her husband. Actually, however, as a Jewess, she wanted nothing to do with Nazi Germany. She did not think she could comfort herself properly there, considering what they were doing to her race. She was not afraid to go, but I would have been, for her, if she had.

Our personal decision made, we went to bed in the early hours. Tamara fell asleep immediately, but I tossed, open-eyed. until it was time to start the next day. To be going abroad at last, but to what a place and what a time. Hitler, Goebbels, air raids, and conducting espionage not only in a country at war, but where they chopped the heads of Communists and spies. And there was so much preparation for my cover.

First I got myself a new name, one our records showed had never been involved in intelligence, had never been compromised abroad. Next I had to make up my *legenda* and learn it by heart. According to that fictitious biography, I was born two years later than my actual birthdate in Tbilisi, graduated from journalism institute there after honorable discharge from military service as a private, and entered the field of journalism. The rest of the story was that I had worked for some years for local papers in the Transcaucasus, later was transferred to the Moscow headquarters of *Tass*. Finally I created a list of nonexistent relatives and friends. It was a satisfactory *legenda*. I knew the Transcaucasus and Tbilisi well. *Tass* reports were highly similar to, although much less detailed than, those I had been writing for years.

That done, as a Party member, I next had to go through the formality of being cleared by the central committee to get a passport. No Party member may leave the country without that clearance, and no Party member may take his membership papers with him, but must surrender them to the committee. For me that was just a formality because the Directorate had interceded with the committee. For most other Party members, however, except for the hierarchs, clearance is not that simple. On the committee are representatives of both the GRU and the NKVD. They are present to give both arms of the intelligence the chance to recruit people going abroad—writers, artists, athletes, anybody. If the applicant refuses to work for either, he gets no clearance.

That over, I got my passport, the service type given then to *Tass* and other Soviet newspapermen. Duly signed by Vyacheslav Molotov, the foreign minister, it said the bearer was Nikolayev, Georgy Petrovich, born in 1906 in Tbilisi, and was a *Tass* correspondent, assigned to perform journalistic work in Germany.

Then it was time for me to report to *Tass*. In civilian clothes— supplied by the Directorate, of course—I reported to the Director. He had been expecting me, having been informed of my mission by Golikov. He told me I would replace a NKVD man who had not performed his cover job as Berlin manager for *Tass* well enough and had to be recalled before the Gestapo grabbed him.

So that I would not make the same mistake, the Director had arranged that I work several hours daily in the *Tass* office until departure to familiarize myself with the organization, its routines, other procedures, and personnel. Although I naturally welcomed that short course, personally I was more interested in the fact that my predecessor was NKVD than that he had failed in his cover work. I wondered, but never found out, if the replacement of a NKVD man by me of the GRU meant that some of the hierarchy might regard a German attack on the Soviet Union as possible.

In addition to my cover work, *Tass* gave me two odd additional assignments. The *Tass* director told me to forget all the propaganda about Nazis and Fascists, that our Party was interested in what made the Nazi party work, how it had trampled most of Europe underfoot. Especially, he said, was Stalin interested in Hitler's source of strength, and I should give uncolored, unbiased reports on those subjects. Also, for his own information, he wanted me to find out the facts about Rudolf Hess's defection to Britain.

My main preparatory work, however, was at the Directorate. For the GRU I had two basic tasks. The first was to reorganize and strengthen the intelligence activities of the Fourth Division, for which I would be chief legal resident in Germany, despite my *Tass* cover. I would have to coordinate that work with the chief GRU resident in Germany, the military attaché, but I was not to be completely subordinate to him and would have my own ciphers and communications channels. The second task, of course, was the really nasty one: checking the truth of the Prague cable that Stalin had condemned. On that I hoped for some help from the military attaché, but most of that would be up to me, since the source was controlled by my division. Readying myself for both those tasks required exhaustive reviews of many files at the Directorate and a great number of conferences with specialists.

I also had considerable research to do to back up my cover. Since I had never stepped foot in Germany before, I decided I could not be handicapped after arrival by lack of knowledge of the country. To fill in those blanks I studied, almost memorized, street plans, especially those of Berlin. In addition, I looked at so many photographs of the German capital, read so much descriptive literature about it, that when finished I felt I knew Berlin almost as well as a native.

In the midst of my preparations May Day came. Because of my impending departure abroad, for the first time in my army life I did not have to be an active participant in the observance of that date. Instead I was given a pass to watch the parade from beside the Lenin mausoleum. For the occasion Red Square had been scrubbed spotless, the air was warm and balmy, and the skies were blue. In addition, I had Tamara with me.

I like parades, the blaring bands, the smartly marching soldiers, but my main purpose in being at that march by was to get a look at Vladimir G. Dekanozov, the Soviet ambassador to Germany, with whom I had an appointment the following day on

Golikov's orders. I had been told that Dekanozov would be on the reviewing stand atop the mausoleum.

The ambassador certainly was there, could not have been missed. A tiny man, five feet tall at the most, he stood in the front rank, alone there except for his fellow Georgian, Stalin, to his right. True, Dekanozov was an old and close associate of Stalin, but that unusual honor shown him must have been for the benefit of the Germans.

I was cautious at the meeting with that little man. He was a veteran underground activist, having started well before the Revolution. He was also high in the NKVD, having been chief of its foreign intelligence operations before being sent to Germany. I had been required to call on him because of top-secret orders Stalin issued after the outbreak of World War II, requiring that GRU and NKVD operations abroad be coordinated and be under the control of the respective ambassadors. The object of that was to prevent interservice rivalry, but the practical effect was to put the GRU under NKVD control abroad as well as at home, since most ambassadors were NKVD men.

Although I had been warned at the Directorate that Dekanozov was frequently despotic and used insulting and dirty language in dealing with his subordinates, he was pleasant enough to me. He asked my background, checked my command of German, and welcomed my joining the Soviet colony in Berlin. Only one thing troubled me. He was convinced that Germany would not attack us and said that I had plenty of time to get settled in and do my work.

On my return from the foreign ministry session with the ambassador, Golikov complimented me on my comportment there; he had just received a phone call from Dekanozov after my departure. The Director said I had passed my first diplomatic examination.

My last official briefing was given me by Golikov's deputy, the rough and hearty former tank commander. Mostly it was encouraging talk about my tasks, coupled with repeated warnings to avoid trouble with the NKVD. He was glad that I was replacing a NKVD man, Tarasov, who had failed by being unable to maintain his cover. At the close, however, his sendoff bothered me extremely. His final words were: "Comrade Akhmedov, don't be afraid of those NKVD men. We will protect you. The man you are replacing in Berlin is not only a NKVD man, he is a Jew. Their days will soon be over. We are glad that you are a Tatar." I could not tell whether that high-ranking officer was expressing personal opinion, or was telling me that anti-Semitism was about to be revived in Russia.

For many reasons that left a bad taste in my mouth, not the least being that my own dear wife was a Jewess. I gradually forgot it, however, as I turned to the last bit of getting ready to leave, the most pleasant part of the process: getting a new wardrobe, and all civilian. For several hours at the Directorate's special store, where just about everything in women's as well as men's apparel was available, I tried on things. In the end I selected three fine suits, a dozen dress shirts, several pairs of shoes, overcoat, hat, underwear, stockings, and handerchiefs, the clothing all a perfect fit, and all British made. For luggage I picked out an expensive leather suitcase. Whether capable or not, at least I would look like a successful newspaperman.

When I got home from that shopping spree for a couple of days' leave before departure, Tamara hardly recognized me. She turned me round and round admiring me and made me stand in front of a mirror while she adjusted my hat to her idea of the correct position.

That was the only gay part of our last days together. Everything else was quite serious and sad with that lovely person, who had never complained about the little money and the simple life of being the wife of an army officer, with whom I had never had a real quarrel or misunderstanding in almost eleven years of marriage.

We had no farewell party, nor did anybody give us one. Soviet intelligence officers sent abroad could not let that be known to any but the closest relatives. Then when they have gone, wives and mothers cannot say where they went, only that they were on a "mission."

Our last hours together we spent devising little codes to include in our letters to let each other know of anything serious happening to either of us. During that, I asked her if she would reconsider and join me after all.

She took my hand, as was her custom when deeply moved, and said, "Ismail, of course I want to be with you. But this time you go alone. It is your job and you must go. Anyway, you will be able to see Europe, not only Germany, but maybe other countries like Switzerland, Italy. It is good to see the world. I would love to go with you and enjoy the sights, the other people, the cities we dreamed to see together one day. But I can't go now to Germany. I couldn't stand to see the Nazi beasts torturing Jewish people. I do not have the nerve for that, so please understand me and excuse me. Go alone; I'll manage here. When and if you will be transferred to another country, say England or France, I will come gladly. Nazi Germany—never."

A few hours later, after dark on that day in the last week of May, she went with me to the Byelorussky Terminal, from where the trains leave for the West. On that platform I held her in my arms. She was crying quietly and there were tears in my eyes, too. We parted as the train started to move. As I leaned from the window, she called, "Darling, God protect you and bless you. Don't worry about me. I'll be waiting for you." Farewell, my darling. . . .

Two days later, in the afternoon, I arrived in Berlin after an uneventful trip. The NKVD man I was to replace and his wife were at the station to meet me. It took them a bit of time to find me, even though I had had only a dozen or so fellow Russian passengers. I hoped it was my London attire that caused the delay. Probably they had been looking for someone in the balloon trousers and drab, baggy jackets most Soviets wore in those days.

The three of us crammed into their sports car, a handsome vehicle that made me even more pleased to be in my new clothes. We drove along the broad avenues of Berlin, through the first real traffic I had ever seen, to their apartment in the heart of the city. En route I tried out my book-learned knowledge of the capital with casual references about some buildings and landmarks we passed. I must have passed because they asked when I had been there before. For an answer to that I gave a grunt.

That proved an unwise display of mine. The NKVD man responded to my grunt with the statement he knew who I really was, that my right name was Akhmedov, and that I was from the GRU's Directorate. The ambassador, Dekanozov, had told him about me, he said.

I was furious but could not show it. Nor did I retaliate by telling him that he was no more a newspaperman than I was, and that I knew his correct name, too, and for whom he really worked. But that was a fine beginning. I could appreciate how the Gestapo had become interested in that NKVD man in whose car I was riding. What I could not understand was why Dekanozov, known to be so proud of his years of underground work, had opened his big mouth about me.

At the apartment the rest of the *Tass* Berlin setup, all really NKVD or GRU men, too, plus a press attaché whose title was only cover, were awaiting us. Once introductions were made all around, my host announced that the ambassador had instructed him to stay on for another two or three weeks in Berlin while I got my feet on the ground.

As a start that was innocent enough. But as darkness fell and the blackout curtains were drawn, tea and sandwiches were served, and those assembled all became very chatty, too chatty. One of the company whom I found particularly objectionable was my junior, not only in the *Tass* arrangement but in my own division of the GRU, although he fortunately did not know my background. GRU or not, that young man had been suborned by Dekanozov, regarded himself as a favorite of the ambassador's, and therefore was very independent.

Later that uncomfortable evening, marked chiefly by similar efforts of "my staff" to assert themselves and put me in my place, Bogdan Kobulov, the counsellor of embassy, accompanied by his wife, dropped in to complete the process.

Really the chief resident officer of the NKVD, he carefully greeted me by my cover name, even though he, too, doubtless had heard the facts about me from Dekanozov. But there his agreeableness ended. Sipping his tea, he veritably grilled me about my cover background, education, work, acquaintances, and family. His wife even intervened with some pleasantry about my nonexistent mother.

It was a check-out of my *legenda*. The counseller probably knew it just as well as I did, just wanted to see if I would make some mistake that could be used against me later. All that in front of my so-called staff. What an inane and petty operation, and how silly! We all had more important things than that to do in Germany.

At the close of that senseless evening, my host suggested I stay in a spare room in his apartment rather than a hotel until I found rooms of my own. The next morning we left in the sports car for a most strange Soviet settlement and stronghold abroad, our embassy.

A big building, it was a clubhouse of conspirators. The ambassador, the counsellors, the secretaries, the attachés, the trade delegates, the *Tass* and other newsmen, the cipher clerks, the accountants, the drivers, the messengers, the guards, the doorman, and right down to the cook, all looked and behaved like accomplished plotters, which most of them were, in fact. Perhaps even I looked the part, although I, at least, tried not to act it.

As soon as I entered the embassy I felt I was in a small Soviet Union. The ambassador was Stalin. The military attaché was the commissar for defense. The counsellor of the evening before was NKVD. Even the secretary of the embassy Party organization acted as though he were first secretary of the central committee of the Communist Party of the Soviet Union.

The lesser conspirators were divided into two groups: GRU, or military and naval intelligence; and NKVD, or internal security. The latter was the more complex of the two. NKVD was split into intelligence and counterintelligence. And the counterintelligence was further subdivided into SK, EM, and INO sections. SK stood for Soviet Colony, and its function was to watch all Soviet citizens abroad—from the ambassador down to the doorman. EM meant *Emigratsiya*, and its task was to penetrate Russian émigrés for recruitment as well as to collect information about anti-Soviet organizations. INO was *Inostranny Otdel*, or Foreign Intelligence.

All Soviet (and other Communist) embassies are larger than their western counterparts (except in the U.S.A. and other countries requiring pro rata or equal strength of personnel in the respective missions). The reason for that is that indigenous personnel, regarded as security risks, are not employed in Soviet embassies. Another reason is that every slot, including such minor service posts as drivers and kitchen help, is needed for allocation of GRU or NKVD personnel.

As a result the Berlin embassy of those wartime days was a very big one indeed, especially since Germany then ranked as the most important country to keep under surveillance. Therefore the number of conspirators within its walls was also unusually large, conspirators busy at plans for espionage, subversion, and darker matters, such as assassinations.

Those conspirators were in an embassy within the embassy, a real stronghold. That section took up the building's entire top floor, a region secured by solid steel doors and windows equipped with steel bars and shutters. Shielded not only from unauthorized entry, but even from observation from within or without, that top floor was where all the reports and files of the conspirators were kept, where GRU and NKVD cipher work and communications were handled, where all weapons, poisons, secret funds, and secret writing materials were kept. Quick-burning furnaces to destroy all that material in case of emergency were also provided. On that floor I, too, worked regularly, reporting back to the Directorate.

The morning of my first visit to that little fortress on foreign soil, it was teeming with my fellow "newspapermen" and "diplomats." All were awaiting the entry of Dekanozov. It was an uneasy gathering, broken up into small groups, with many whispering to one another and the superiors striking poses of importance.

Almost an hour passed before the ambassador appeared. With his arrival the whispering gave way immediately to dead silence. Like a little Tsar he enumerated tasks to be accomplished and matters to beware of, then dismissed us almost peremptorily. It was a completely unnecessary production and a waste of time. We all had known what we had to do anyway. His performance was just to show us who was boss.

At that gathering I met my current GRU chief, the military attaché, General Tupikov. He told me that in April (about the same time we had received the cable from Prague) acting on information from other sources, he had advised the Directorate that some 180 German divisions were being concentrated along the Soviet frontier. He said he had also duly reported that information to the ambassador as required, adding the Dekanozov had dismissed it airily as a figment of someone's imagination.

Also that morning at the embassy I had run into none other than my predecessor at the Fourth Division, Colonel Engineer Dmitry Konovalov, so admired by the lone female there, Captain Polyakova. He had taken his exile philosophically, had no resentment toward me, and I found him very pleasant and agreeable. Before parting we arranged to have lunch.

We met at a beer hall. He too was operating under a fictitious name, and his cover was that of inspector of the trade delegation. His particular importance to me was that the Czechoslovak engineer at the Skoda plants was his man, under his direct control. When I told Konovalov of Stalin's reaction to the Prague cable, he was terribly surprised, and at first thought I was joking. He was also worried that Stalin's claim that it was a British provocation might be construed to mean that he had had questionable contacts with foreigners. For my part, I did my best to reassure him by telling him that Golikov and all of us regarded the information as genuine. We agreed we had no alternative to following orders and continuing the investigation Stalin demanded. However, we parted of common mind: it was well nigh hopeless to expect to convince anybody in authority that the information was correct once Stalin had rejected it.

Those basics of my real mission under way, I then concentrated on my cover as the *Tass* manager. I also found myself some rooms—just two of them—near the office, in the apartment of an old German couple who were pleased at my command of their language.

In addition to overseeing the routine news I worked diligently on my assignment to determine what made the Nazi party tick, its appeal to the German people, and Hitler's source of power. I regret, however, that factually I made little progress on Hess's defection. I did find support for reports that he was mentally unbalanced, but I did not believe that anybody, even Hitler himself, knew why that strange man had flown to Britain.

Both my cover work and my real mission took many hours daily. Those tasks were often interrupted by air raid alerts, although there was no really serious bombing. As a result I was quite exhausted after my first few weeks in Berlin and welcomed an embassy-sponsored picnic on the Baltic coast Sunday, June 22. Dekanozov had arranged the outing personally and had given almost the whole staff the weekend off.

In high spirits I got up early that Sunday morning. Warm but breezy, it looked like a fine day. We had arranged that my NKVD predecessor—still there—would take me to the Stettin lagoon in his sports car. I walked quite blithely the few blocks from my rooms to his apartment and turned into the building.

On the steps I was met by Gestapo officers. The NKVD man and his wife were being escorted out. The police arrested me, too. They told me that Germany was at war with the Soviet Union.

First I was taken to my rooms. They and my few belongings were searched and, of course, nothing incriminating was found. That over, I was allowed to bundle my clothes into my suitcase before being escorted to Gestapo headquarters.

As I was led into that grim building, another Lubyanka, I prepared myself for interrogation, possible beatings, and torture. I did not expect to leave that place.

To my relief, however, I was taken through the building to an interior courtyard and left. For hours I stood there. I was the first of scores of other Soviets, men, women, and children, who had been rounded up at their homes and brought there. Among them was Konovalov but not Dekanozov, the counsellor, the military attaché, or other high-ranking members of the embassy. Konovalov told me that the ambassador had been asleep when he was summoned to the German foreign ministry and given the declaration of war. Those top officials of ours did not join us in that courtyard. They were probably given the treatment accorded diplomats, which their passports said they were.

As the day wore on we were joined by other Russians, émigrés among them, even an Orthodox priest. We Soviets stayed aloof from that lot, not because of politics, but for fear that some of them might be Gestapo stool pigeons.

The longer we waited there standing, the more depressed all of us became. None of us had any idea of what the future held for us. All the children were frightened and some were crying despite their mothers' efforts to comfort them.

Finally, late in the afternoon, buses with armed SS guards on them were brought into the courtyard. We all were ordered aboard—except for the émigrés—and taken to a camp about two hours' drive from Berlin.

The camp was very well secured. It was completely surrounded with concertina rolls of barbed wire, electrified, and equipped with trip alarms. Machine guns had been positioned all along the periphery which was floodlighted by night. SS guards were at the gates and everywhere within.

We were not the only ones there by any means. As our buses rolled through the camp we passed huts filled with British and French prisoners of war. Those men, who must have built our huts, and who knew well in advance that we were coming on June 22, cheered us and called good wishes as we passed. I had no idea how the other Soviets felt about that, but I, for one, grasped at the support of those westerners, whose war we were now in, too.

At a very new collection of huts we were ordered off the buses. The women and children were separated from us men and taken to another area. We Soviet men were ordered into the huts facing us.

Within were rows and rows of bunk beds made of wooden slats. There we really found we had been expected for some time. Beds had been assigned to each of us. I found mine with great relief. On a board at the head was neatly stamped, "Nikolayev, Georgy Petrovich, born 1906, Tbilisi." It could have carried my correct name, rank, and organization, and that would have marked the beginning of the end for me.

Then we were called out and lined up before the camp commandant in a long, single row. We were inspected one by one, and the camp regulations were read to us. We were told that our daily rations would be two pieces of black bread, a square of margerine, two cups of ersatz coffee, two lumps of ersatz sugar, and a bowl of soup, the latter a very thin substitute for the real thing, I found. We were given reading material, the *Volkische Beobachter,* the Nazi daily. We were allowed to hear news, the camp loudspeaker relay of the Sondermeldungen of the Wehrmacht—the special announcements—already boasting of Nazi victories in our homeland.

Tired and discouraged as I was, it took me a long time to go to sleep that night. I was worried sick about Tamara, alone in the apartment, so near the Kremlin, and such a target for Nazi bombers. As an intelligence officer, I was even sicker about the way Stalin, Malenkov, Molotov, and all the rest had disregarded our warnings and thereby left my people and my country open to sudden slaughter and destruction. My God, we were praised for second-rate information, but when we got something really important, nobody was even allowed to prepare for invasion.

The next morning a representative of the Red Cross visited us to say that there might be negotiations through third parties between the Germans and Soviets to exchange us for Germans held in the Soviet Union. When would that be? Nobody knew, nor were the German camp guards the people to ask.

Later that day I had a few fleeting words with Konovalov, several other GRU men, and some military engineers who had been sent to Germany under cover of trade representatives. We decided that if the exchange negotiations did not work out we had to plan for escape to Switzerland. But we also decided that the Gestapo and Abwehr must have still been unaware of the fact we were not civilians but military—and intelligence for good measure—and that therefore we should not be seen together except when absolutely necessary.

Early on the third day we were again ordered to line up in single file in front of our huts. By that time there were several hundred of us, other Soviet citizens having been brought into the camp from distant parts of Germany. SS guards with machine pistols were posted behind us.

For some time we just stood there. Then the commandant appeared, accompanied by a Gestapo officer with a monocle in his left eye, and by a tall, thin man in civilian clothes and with a scowl on a saber-scarred face.

The civilian started to walk slowly along our row as if reviewing a guard of honor. We had been ordered to look him full in the face as he passed. He stared at each of us carefully. In front of some of us, he snapped out comments that were taken down by the Gestapo man following him with pad and pencil in hand. I thought the civilian must be a counterintelligence officer looking for somebody like me or Konovalov. I was so very wrong!

The exchange of glares finished, the civilian ordered us next to drop our trousers and our underpants, stand with our sexual organs exposed. Were they ridiculing and humiliating us that way? I wondered.

The civilian went down the row again, looking that time not in our eyes but at our sexual organs.

One after the other the military engineers, ten of them, were ordered to step three paces forward. All ten were Jews.

Then I, at the far end of the row, was inspected. I, too, was given the command to step three paces forward.

At the end there were eleven of us in that small forward rank, ten Jews and me, a Moslem. All of us had been circumcised. Our names were written down. All of our cover names were Russian, those of the Jews as well as mine.

Our little roll was called. We were told we were Jews, would be made a separate group among the interned Soviets. We were told we had no right to eat with the rest of our countrymen. While the others were at meals we were to clean latrines and toilets. Our other duties were to clean the barracks, sweep the sidewalks, and police the area.

At first I was terribly angry, but I managed to keep my mouth shut. It would have been useless to explain to those Germans that not only Jews were circumcised, but also Moslems, plus many Christians and atheists, if not for religious purposes, for those of hygiene. And it would have been stupid to have invited even more special attention to myself. Besides, what was wrong with being a Jew? What was Tamara, my love? I cannot say how glad I was then that she was at home, bombs or no bombs. At least they were clean.

So, with my circumcised fellows, I became part of the latrine gang. The real Jews knew that I was a Tatar. They knew why I was with them, but they were often amused quietly as I muttered the curses of a true Moslem when excreta befouled my clothes or person.

I had been filthying myself and my temper for about a week, when suddenly buses were assembled in front of our huts one evening at the beginning of July. We were all assembled; the commandant told us we would be exchanged, via Turkey, for German citizens caught in the Soviet Union.

All of us, uncircumcised Soviets, ten Jews, and one pseudo-Jew, were taken back to Berlin. At the Friedrichstrasse station we were put aboard a heavily guarded special train headed south. On the station platform there was quite a reunion. Awaiting us there to go with us were Dekanozov, the counsellor, the military attaché, and all the "diplomats" who had undergone their internments under guard at the embassy. Just before the train pulled out, a special Gestapo detachment put my predecessor, the NKVD man, and his wife aboard. He had endured more than cleaning latrines, had been under constant interrogation at Gestapo headquarters, and had been badly beaten up. Although none of us particularly liked him—and not because he was a Jew—we made him the special hero of the day.

Several days later, after we had passed Sofia and were nearing the Bulgarian-Turkish border, our train stopped at a small station. When it started again it was going in the opposite direction, back to Germany. Everybody was puzzled. I was even more than that; I was alarmed. Not back to that camp with my circumcision, ever. I would rather have jumped the train and taken my chances with the partisans in the mountains of Bulgaria or Yugoslavia.

Within a few moments, however, the German officer in charge of the train announced we were returning to Nis, just across the Yugoslav border. There we were to await two more trainloads of Soviet personnel coming from Italy and Vichy France.

Two days later all three trains went east, right to the Turkish frontier. Then came the actual, physical process of exchange on a one-for-one basis, so far as the men, not their dependents, were concerned. The Bulgar and Turk signal corps had set up a circuit more than one thousand miles long connecting the Bulgarian-Turkish and Soviet-Turkish frontiers. Over that circuit, it was verified that a Soviet man stepped into Turkey in the west as a German national crossed from the Soviet Union to the opposite end of Turkey.

It was a long, tedious process involving some five hundred nationals of each warring nation. As I waited I reflected on the fact that those figures showed the Germans had had an almost three-to-one superiority over us in the numbers of people stationed in the respective countries at the outbreak of hostilities, quite an intelligence advantage.

Finally the exchange was completed and the Turks took us on buses to Edirne. There, before boarding a train for Istanbul, the internees among us were given the first good meal we had had in a fortnight.

Early the next morning under bright and sunny skies, we arrived in Istanbul, the city of my boyhood dreams. Oh, Istanbul, I thought as I gazed in wonder and in happiness, how blue are your waters of the Sea of Marmara, how beautifully your many minarets pierce the skies, how fine your mosques, bazaars, and modern streets full of gay people. And how long, and by what a tortuous route, it has taken me to reach you.

There in Istanbul that mass of Soviet returnees from France, Germany, and Italy was reassembled. All those from France and Italy, as well as most of those from Germany, were put on other trains a few hours after arrival and sent back to the Soviet Union.

The rest of us, with Dekanozov in charge, were put up at the embassy's summer residence at Buyuk-Dere on the Bosphorus. For citizens of almost any other country that would have been a pleasant opportunity to sightsee in Istanbul, but for us Soviets our stay there amounted to no more than comfortable internment. The ambassador would let nobody off the grounds except himself and the counsellor, perhaps fearing some might not come back.

After a week there, however, we too were put on a train headed home. When we arrived at Ankara, whom should I see on the platform as the train pulled in but a GRU officer I had known well in Moscow. Functioning then as a second secretary, he had come to take me off the train and to our embassy in the Turkish capital.

I was taken in to see the ambassador, Sergey Aleksandrovich Vinogradov, almost immediately. For the first time since leaving Moscow I was addressed by my correct name, as he told me the Director had sent instructions for me to stay in Turkey and work there.

That ambassador was a decided contrast to Dekanozov. A graduate of Leningrad University and of the Institute of the Red Professorate, he was tall, slim, and handsome, and very urbane. Despite his NKVD connections, he really looked and acted the part of a top diplomat, an ambassador. Instead of barking, he smiled as he reminded me of the directive that he be consulted and kept informed of all my GRU plans and operations, that he was the *Khozyain* (boss). At the close of our conversation, he even took me to his quarters and introduced me to his wife, Yevgenia Aleksandrovna, an equally charming person.

I was to retain my *Tass* cover name of Nikolayev, but was given a new cover job, that of press attaché. My permanent residence was to be in Istanbul, since most of Turkey's principal papers were published there. As I received those instructions, I had to remind myself that I was not dreaming. Everything I had put up with over the years, even the internment camp humiliation, suddenly seemed worthwhile. I could not have received better orders if I had written them myself.

Shortly after I had settled into what I imagined would be one of the happiest periods of my life, I got my real orders. They were given me by an old friend, the chief of the Operations Division of GRU, Colonel Sineoky, who had come to Turkey under cover of inspector of our trade delegation.

Basically my assignment was to organize intelligence against Germany. I was to operate from Istanbul, not just for cover reasons, although they, too, were true, but because it was a large cosmopolitan center awash with Europeans of many nationalities and political complexions, many of them refugees from the war. Among them were bound to be natural recruits for our operations. Those people were to be the core of my illegal residencies.

At the same time, I was to seek out other stray Europeans, Poles, Czechoslovaks, Yugoslavs, Frenchmen, Italians, not only in Turkey, but also elsewhere in the Middle East, people willing to go back to their homelands and fight the Germans by joining underground organizations.

I was also given several special and immediate missions. One of those was to cooperate with our military attaché network in locating and mapping proper places for caches near Ankara, Istanbul, Izmir, and other populated areas as well as in open country west of the Soviet frontier. Those hiding places were to be the future repositories of automatic small arms, communications equipment, and money for the possible use of guerrillas. That was standard operating procedure for GRU in every country, but had not yet been done in Turkey.

Another specific task concerned the Yugoslavs alone. My chief smiled as he brought that one up, said the GRU should have had me jump the train from Germany and join the partisans. I smiled back, but did not tell him I had once had that idea in mind. That opportunity missed, the next best was for me to find officers from the routed Yugoslav royalist army, either in Turkey or adjacent countries, and induce them to go to Moscow. There they would be trained as guerrilla commanders and then parachuted into the Yugoslav mountains to lead partisan units.

I also had to familiarize myself with the other GRU nets operating in Turkey and establish liaison with them. Since Turkey was not an industrially developed nation, there were not too many; in fact, in addition to mine about to be set up and that of the military attaché's, there was only one other. That third operation was run out of Istanbul as well, by Aleksandr Akimov, a former regimental commissar with excellent knowledge of Turkish and Persian, whose cover was consul general.

Just before departure from Ankara to get things going in Istanbul, my cover was a bit disturbed. A new NKVD resident chief, Leonid Naumov, a fat and disagreeable man, was sent in. He substituted arrogance for lack of intelligence, boasted of having instructions from Stalin and Beria. Far from an admirable type, his morals were not high. With him, from Moscow, he had brought a young blonde girl, called his secretary, but really his mistress. He had a mean word for everybody, said even of Vino-gradov, "Instead of a formal hat worn on ceremonial occasions, this little man calling himself ambassador should put a barrel on his head." He could have taken any cover he wanted, but decided, perhaps because we were antagonistic almost at sight, that he also would be a press attaché. That put two of us in that masquer-ade, him in Ankara and me in Istanbul. As NKVD chief resident, he also had an office in my city, also at the consulate.

As if that was not enough, he went out of his way to make it quite difficult for me to maintain an effective cover. I did my very best to establish good relationships with the local and foreign newspapermen. He was as rude as possible to all of them, a variance so pronounced it raised numbers of eyebrows.

Naumov's attitude, although it irked me particularly, was typical of, rather than exceptional to, the generally poor relation-ship between the two intelligence services there in Turkey, as I soon found. Except for the ambassador—and he had his question-able moments, too—and a few of my GRU friends, almost every-body was stabbing everybody else; stopping at nothing, includ-ing blackmail; informing the NKVD and the Party; lying. Of course that had its effect on the quality of the intelligence reports. Few risked analyzing data in a detached, objective manner. Instead, the facts, often procured with great effort and risk, were twisted so as to please the opinions of superiors both in Turkey and in the Soviet Union.

As was to be expected, posts at that embassy from ambassa-dor down to drivers and doormen were all held by NKVD or GRU men, no matter what their titles on the diplomatic list were. In Turkey then, however, and only because there was a war on, the GRU held a slight numerical edge, but that was adjusted by giving positions of greater power to the NKVD. The same arrange-ment applied as well to the Istanbul consulate, really an ad-junct of the embassy, and other consulates in Kars, Erzerum, and other cities.

I soon found two of that lot with whom I got along well and with whom I saw eye to eye; that they were also GRU men played its part. One was Akimov, who called Naumov "dirty scum," and detested him for belittling the Red Army. The other was Major Ivan Bukhtin, a jolly, chubby assistant military attaché and once my associate at the Directorate. Although wise in the ways of political survival, Bukhtin was our problem child. It was he who caught a venereal disease from a so-called actress on the train trip from Moscow to Ankara, and who we had to get a local doctor to cure discreetly. It was he who was reprimanded for making bad mistakes as he was learning to drive a car. It was he we always had to pry away from the cabaret girls, before he got in trouble.

Gambling, then women, were the weaknesses of Akimov, otherwise a very able officer. He had an unattractive, nagging wife; worse, most believed his wife was a NKVD informer. In the face of that, his shunning of home life and his peccadilloes were understandable. We made a strange trio, myself, the stiff moralist; the gay Bukhtin; and the old rascal Akimov; but we were close. We could rely on one another.

In August of the opening year of that terrible war, I got a long overdue letter from Tamara, the first from her, although I had written home on an average of twice a month. Her letter was very disturbing in several respects. It had been postmarked at Pervoural'sk, a town in the Sverdlov region, high in the Urals. It was a very short letter, too. All she said was that she had been evacuated from Moscow, giving no reason. The last of those few lines said, "I have had no letters from my parents in Poltava and I wonder what has happened to them. I feel sick and lonely. . . ."

According to our little codes we had arranged to circumvent NKVD censorship before I left for Germany, any reference to her parents meant she wanted to join me. We had included nothing about "sick and lonely." All I could conclude was that she must really be ill and needed me. I could imagine her terrorized by the war, sent to a strange place in the mountains with no relatives, no friends, maybe even without proper housing and enough food.

As fast as I could, I sent off a message to the Director, begging him to make arrangements to send Tamara to me.

My friend Bukhtin was sympathetic but skeptical that Tamara would be allowed to come. He said the red tape for her travel orders, always considerable, would be impossible with a war going on. He reminded me that he had not been allowed to bring his wife and children. "No," he finished, "the NKVD keeps them as hostages. Only Naumov can bring his mistress. Our poor wives! Lost somewhere, far away in the Urals, perhaps hungry, sad, sick, perhaps forced to work in the field to boost production of the *kolkhozes*."

He proved to be right. I sent a second message, a third, to the Director. I got a reply to none of them, nor did I hear anything more from Tamara, either.

I was becoming frantic, but thank goodness work was piling up on me, and I had to do it almost single-handedly. My legal *residentura* was of no practical help at all. That organization consisted of two colonels and a girl secretary. The two officers were masquerading as *Tass* correspondents and spent the greater part of their efforts and time wining and dining Turkish newspapermen, and acting as if they themselves were really newspapermen. The girl was not of much use, either, to a so-called press attaché. She was a graduate of the school for illegals in Moscow. "Illegals" was our term for groups of Soviet intelligence officers operating with non-Soviet and false documentation, who were therefore without the protection of official Soviet installations. These illegal *residenturas* also engaged in the recruiting and handling of foreign agents. The girl secretary would have been more help at my illegal *residentura*, but she had been assigned where she was.

The shortcomings of my legal *residentura* were more than counterbalanced by successes in the illegal field. (Normally, I would not have been operating both the legal and illegal residencies at the same time, but there was a war on.)

In the main my illegals were international drifters. Some worked for money, some for ideological or nationalistic reasons. Others had been recruited in the Soviet Union for the price of getting out of it or its occupied territories.

The most able of mine was a husband and wife team of Swiss origin, but carrying Brazilian passports. He was an expert photographer, an excellent pursuit for an agent. She was a professional governess and tutor, with perfect command of German and French, my candidate for the household of the German military attaché. I met them in a restaurant, had the center run a check on them, and speedily recruited them with the help of wonder-working American dollars. At first I had them report on German nationals in Istanbul, especially those Germans connected with auto touring clubs, a well-used cover for Nazi clandestine operations. Later I sent them on a "vacation tour" to Germany, via Bulgaria, Yugoslavia, and Austria, for a general report on the military, political, and economic situations. Their prime task, which they did well, was to bring me authentic current German documents, identity cards, birth certificates, ration cards. The center needed those documents to prepare acceptable forgeries for other illegals being sent to Germany.

One of my most troublesome illegals, but competent, was a Russian girl traveling on a Polish passport. The daughter of a wealthy Russian family that had escaped to Latvia during the Bolshevik Revolution, she had been recruited when Latvia was "liberated," trained in Moscow, and sent to me in Istanbul. She had not one political idea in her head, but she was pretty, blonde, shapely, and vivacious, and probably imagined herself a kind of Mata Hari. She was the perfect type to plant in bars and nightclubs as a spotter of men with agent potential. She found us many recruits, several of them excellent.

Another of my girls aroused my sympathy and respect. She was a real refugee, an Austrian Jewess who had somehow obtained a Turkish passport. She had big, intelligent brown eyes, carefully groomed brown hair, and a sweet face. She reminded me of a young assistant to a university professor. Her German, of course, was excellent, so was her English, and she also knew some French. She was prowestern and had no illusions about communism. Her motivation was hatred for the Germans, and she had no interest at all in making money via espionage. I used her too as a spotter, but in hotels and better restaurants, and also to check on the Germans. She loathed them, but they had no idea she was a Jewess, and liked her.

I remember a Czechoslovak journalist in the rest of that bag of unfortunates. He also was decently motivated, worked for us because he hated the Germans. And there was a confused Dutchman, too, not a Communist, but a fellow traveler. He posed as an idealist, but he did not forget to demand dollars.

However, my prime work of those months, a task that proved the simplest, was with the Yugoslavs. I started that by making an official call, a courtesy visit to their consulate in my cover capacity as press attaché. Although that establishment was still operated by the royalist Yugoslav government-in-exile, I was welcomed and treated most politely. The consul general, an elderly gentleman, received me, then turned me over to his assistant Vladimir Perich, a former general staff officer of the Royal Yugoslav Army. Both were fine men, dedicated to ridding their country of the Germans.

After our first meeting I took Perich to dinner. Next, he called on me. After that we had lunches and other evenings together. I like to think we became friends; at least I felt that way toward him.

At that point I advised the center of my progress. The reply was to go ahead with my plan, but it added, "Never trust the British." That warning was in reference to British officers, among whom I knew were intelligence people, to whom Perich had introduced me, meetings which I had also reported to the center.

Backed by the Moscow okay, all I had to do from there was to speak frankly to Perich. I told him that we were interested in giving specialized training in guerrilla warfare to Yugoslav officers forced to flee to the Middle East, and that after the training we would get them to Yugoslavia to fight Germans. Perich reacted with enthusiasm. He had half a dozen Yugoslav colonels, he said, all former members of the general staff, marooned in Iraq, good soldiers who would jump at the chance. It was almost as if my Yugoslav friend had been waiting for me to make the offer and had wondered at my delay.

Within a week we had not only located the Yugoslav officers but had them in Ankara. While they were en route, I notified the ambassador of what was going on so that he could have a part in the operation. He personally handled from then on what we called "Shipment of Yugoslav Colonels to Moscow via Ankara," and was very grateful to me. Moscow too was pleased, and promoted me to lieutenant colonel. Vinogradov toasted my promotion and his probable commendation with the best vodka in the world—Polish, not Russian.

By that time it was well into autumn and the November date for the annual observance of the Revolution arrived. The consulate made a big affair of that occasion on that first year of the war. To it were invited the governor of Istanbul, high police officers, local members of parliament, intellectuals, business and professional leaders, newspaper editors and correspondents, Allied representatives, in fact everybody of importance in Istanbul except members of the Axis powers.

Special couriers were sent down from Ankara, bringing many cases of vodka and Soviet champagne, as well as much caviar. Cooks were also sent from the embassy to prepare roasted meats and fowl and all kinds of canapés.

A cook of another kind came, too. Naumov arrived to instruct every Soviet in Istanbul—common procedure at Soviet embassy and consulate functions throughout the world—on the social (actually intelligence) role each was to play and with whom. Previously, of course, the guest list had been checked out with NKVD and GRU.

Each of us was assigned a specific guest on whom to concentrate, and was told what to talk about, what to ask, how to make compliments, whom to ignore, those to whom contempt must be shown, who must be plied with drinks.

Singled out by Naumov for special assignment was a young vice consul, a man of Turkic origin. That poor fellow, one of our GRU officers, was ordered to spare no vodka on his subject, Ahmed Demir, Istanbul's deputy chief of police, in getting him to disclose information of interest to the NKVD.

Unfortunately for Naumov, I recall happily, his plan badly backfired. It was the GRU man, not the Turkish policeman, who got blind drunk. It was also the Turk who gained the information.

He helped the sodden GRU officer to his quarters upstairs and thereby got a good view of the top-secret section of the consulate.

A few weeks after that fine party and finer fiasco for Naumov, on the very last day of November, I was awakened late at night, in my quarters, by a phone call. Vinogradov was on the line and told me to take the next train to Ankara.

As I entered the ambassador's office I noticed he was unusually nervous and uncomfortable. Hardly returning my greeting, he handed me a piece of paper, a short, deciphered cable from the center.

It read: "Your wife died suddenly. Hope you will work even harder for Motherland. Director."

I read again. I thought I was going to faint. I grabbed at a chair for support. Poor, dead Tamara. How did you die there in the faraway, cold Ural mountains? Why? What happened?

Tamara, Tamara. Alone with no parents and no sister near.

Why was the cable sent to the ambassador and not to me? Tamara, did you revolt, perhaps, against unbearable conditions, make remarks and bring the NKVD down on yourself? Did they interrogate and torture you?

Suddenly I remembered the horrible parting words about Jews from Golikov's deputy. Was that it? Poor, poor Tamara. Were your own last words a shout to those NKVD executioners, "Gendarmes, I hate you"?

Was that why they did not tell me how you died? My dear wife, how cruel the world, how terrible I could not get you out. . . .

When I regained control of myself I asked—I demanded—Vinogradov explain the cable. He said he knew nothing more than I did. I begged him to get information about her death. He promised he would do his best.

Then he took me to his wife and she comforted me, the good woman she was.

That night Bukhtin put me aboard the train to Istanbul. He was kind, but there was nothing he could do to help. From the car window as the train started to move, I caught a last, fleeting glimpse of Bukhtin's face. Even that face was the face of a Russian. I was no Russian. Tamara had been no Russian. Thank God, we had had no children. Nothing remained any more for me in that vast, cruel land.

Tamara! Tamara! May you sleep in peace.

# 8

# Decision

The first thing I did on return to Istanbul was to write a long letter to the Director asking for an explanation of the death of my wife. I got no reply to that or to others I wrote him on the same subject. Nor did Vinogradov ever give me an answer.

A week after I had heard of the death of my beloved, my only person in the whole world, radio broadcasts said that the United States of America had entered the war.

The next day I went to the American Consulate General. The consul general received me. He was an elderly gentleman, frail and small. It was cold outside and a cheerful fire was burning in his office. We sat beside it for an hour, smoking and talking.

I did most of the talking. I told him my true name, my true work, my background.

Then I said, "Sir, I am physically fit; I am a skilled technician. I must continue to fight, because we all are now engaged in life and death battle against common enemies. But I have no desire to continue to serve the Soviets. Hitler and Stalin are both dictators. There is no real difference between the Gestapo and the NKVD.

"I also have no desire to avoid taking my share in this war. I am a general staff officer. I want to fight on your side, for your ideas. I am ready to serve in your armed forces, with or without rank, anywhere. Could you help me?"

When I had finished, the old gentleman sat silent for a time, looking at the fire. Then he turned toward me. His eyes seemed sympathetic. He had heard me; he had understood me, he said. At that, he stood up, waited for me to rise, too. At the door he said there was nothing further he could say.

I never did hear anything further from that fine old man. But neither did I hear anything from the NKVD either about my call at his consulate.

The American entry into the war, responsible for my attempt at the consulate, also brought me additional work in my cover post as press attaché. There were several U.S. newspapermen in Turkey, but none of them had called upon me until after America was in the war. Then and only then did they seek me out. They wanted to know about the sufferings of the Soviet people, about battles in the Soviet Union, about our economic and political situations. They also wanted my opinion about the future and about American-Soviet cooperation.

Alas, I wanted to be honest and sincere, but there was little help I could give those men. I could not tell them that the Soviet Union had not, would not, change its attitude to the U.S. and Britain, just because we were all on the same side in the battle against Germany. Least of all could I tell them what I had always known, that any alliance with western powers would be no more than temporary.

On New Year's Day of 1942, at a private party at the consulate for Soviet personnel only, I made the mistake of mentioning my problem concerning American newspapermen. I asked my "comrades" if it were not time to drop old concepts and build real friendship with representatives of the western powers residing in Turkey, especially since we were fighting together. I wanted to know what was wrong with having American and British friends when we were friendly with such lessor allies as the Yugoslavs and Czechoslovaks.

It was Naumov who replied. He almost snarled back, "To forget our old concepts? I really wonder if you understand the Party line. To forget how American financial magnates helped to arm and build the German forces? To forget the close ties between the Thyssens, Krupps, and Wall Street? What you had better not forget is that the United States is the wealthiest, the strongest of all capitalistic countries, is a classic example of imperialism, and as such is, and forever will be, our enemy number one. Yes, now, for the time being, we are allies. This is a temporary thing, a temporary alliance until we defeat Germany. Then, one day we will face the United States of America as our major enemy. You can wine and dine your Americans and British. Smile into their faces and show yourself a pleasant fellow. That is fine. But never forget that they are your enemies of tomorrow."

That retort troubled me. There was nothing new in it, of course. What was news was Naumov singling me out for that kind of blast. I had to be more careful, or before long he would be accusing me of political unreliability.

From that time on, I did my best to avoid the American newspapermen by improving my contacts with the Turkish editors and correspondents. Naumov could not criticize that, the only real part of my cover job. Doing that took me to restaurants, cabarets, museums, theaters, mosques, and universities that were not only a pleasure to visit as a tourist, but were also useful to an intelligence officer with an eye out for possible drops, meeting places, or recruits.

And there was more than that. I truly liked being in the company of the Turks. After all, they were my people, the closest people to me of all, with my family and Tamara gone. Often a Turkish acquaintance would be amused at hearing my correct Turkish in Tatar accent.

Some of the Turks also insisted that I really was a Turk, one from Ana Vatan (Turkestan), and asked me about Turkic peoples in the Soviet Union. With a smile I would remind them that my name, Nikolayev, was a pure Russian name, but most dismissed the name as unimportant and insisted I was of Turkish blood.

The more I saw of Turkey, and the more I learned of its people, the more I admired both. I could understand Father refusing to fight Turks, and I thanked God I had not been ordered to conduct espionage against them. That would have been like spying on one's own home and family.

Once, however, I did come awfully close to doing just that to the Turks. At that time, both the West and the Axis were courting Turkey with might and main in an effort to get her to alter her neutral position. The Soviet Union alone did nothing to try to convince the Turks its cause was just, let alone persuade them to surrender their neutrality. Both the British and Germans had been taking prominent Turkish newspapermen on visits to their countries and to their armed forces. I suggested that the Soviets should do something similar; let the Turks see how the Red Army fought the Germans and at the same time strengthen trade and cultural exchanges.

That suggestion was never acted upon. Instead Vinogradov summoned me to Ankara after receiving it and said, "Comrade Nikolayov, officially to us, Turkey is a neutral country. Note that I said officially. In reality, however, Turkey is not only siding with Germany, but helping her. For that reason, Turkey is our enemy and one day she is going to pay for it. Remember that. For the time being, our task is to swing Turkish public opinion to our side. As press attaché, you have your role in that. It is quite possible that at some future date your present role will be augmented by other more specific tasks of a clandestine nature."

Shortly after I was given that advice and warning, Turkey was rocked by a major assassination attempt that might have altered her international position considerably, had it been successful. It was a blatant act of terrorism that just missed changing the course of the war and resulted in a serious deterioration of Soviet-Turkish relations and brought me, personally, into extreme jeopardy.

On February 24, 1942, an attempt was made to kill the German ambassador, the notorious Nazi Franz von Papen, and his wife, as they were walking near their official residence in Ankara. They had been trailed by a man with a bomb hidden under his coat. The bomb exploded prematurely and the assassin was blown to bits. Some ten yards away, the von Papens escaped with no more than shock and a few bruises, luckily for them and the Turkish government.

Turkish police and security forces reacted immediately and very efficiently. Before the day was over the dead assassin had been identified as a Turkish law student born in Yugoslavia, the scene of a similar deed that preceded World War I. Of Turkish origin, he had fled Yugoslavia in advance of the invading Nazis, had become a Turkish citizen, but had retained his membership in the Yugoslav Communist Party. Three accomplices were speedily rounded up. Two were Turkish-Yugoslavs of similar origin and Party membership. The third was a Soviet NKVD man, Kornilov, operating under cover of our trade delegation.

That was all the general public had been told about that outrage when I went to our consulate the afternoon after the attempt on von Papen. As I approached the building I found it surrounded by Turkish police, both in uniform and plainclothes.

I had to show my identification documents before the Turks allowed me to enter. Within, the consulate personnel were acting as if they were under siege.

Akimov told me that yet another conspirator, Pavlov, had been involved in the Ankara plot and was at that very moment hiding out upstairs in the consulate. He was another NKVD man, with the cover title of junior assistant at the consulate.

Akimov could not stand him and once referred to him as "that *golovorez* [cutthroat], one of the most important operatives of our 'neighbors' because of his long experience in 'wet' [bloody] affairs." My friend had added, "I guess they are cooking up something extraordinary."

No wonder the police were at the door. They were not able to enter because of diplomatic privilege. But neither was the second NKVD murder expert able to leave the building.

That siege went on for two weeks. Both the consulate and the embassy were in tremendous uproar and no real work could be accomplished at either. Long messages were being sent off to Moscow. Long messages came in from there. Naumov was screaming that he would never give up his creature. Akimov wanted the scoundrel out and kept repeating, "You cannot fight the law." Vinogradov was evenly balanced, trying to win time from the Turks and wait for word from Moscow.

Finally, on March 7, the order came to turn our assassin over to the Turks. Naumov had lost his fight but had gained enough time to coach his man in preparation for interrogation and trial.

The trial started April 1 and lasted until June 17, 1942. The two Turkish-Yugoslav defendants made full confessions. They testified that the NKVD men had recruited them in Ankara and Istanbul, had trained them to assassinate von Papen, and had given them explosives. The NKVD expert who had hidden out at the consulate claimed he had been ill with rheumatism and in bed at the consulate from a date prior to the attempt and until he was surrendered to the Turks. A Turkish medical authority countered that lie by establishing that the defendant was in good health and had never had rheumatism. That and the testimony of the two Turkish-Yugoslavs was enough for the court. The NKVD men denied all guilt, of course, and received twenty years' imprisonment. The other two defendants were given lesser terms.

A week or two before that trial had gotten under way, Vinogradov came to Istanbul to see me. First he acted as if he had dropped into my office for a friendly chat—he started by saying he was still trying to get news about Tamara—but he soon got down to the business he had come for. He said:

"Comrade Nikolayev, I am going to give you a new job. It is highly classified, highly important, and was approved by Comrade Molotov. You are charged with recruiting highly respected and recognized Turkish newspaper owners and chief editors. Take your choice from such prominent people as Ahmet Emin Yalman of *Vatan*, Falikh Rifki of *Ulus*, Huseyin Cahit Yalchin or Yunus Nadi of *Cumhuriyet*. Do not bother with Zekeriya Sertel of *Tan*. He is pro-Soviet anyway. Recruit any one of the four I mentioned. By any means. By bribing, by appeal, by clean or dirty methods. Promise mountains of benefit for cooperation with us. Our Party and government need control of an outstanding figure in the news world who can mobilize Turkish public opinion in favor of the Soviet Union."

So that was it, finally. I could not say he had not warned me well in advance at the time he lectured me about the Turks being our enemies—which I knew they would remain, despite that new, "temporary" attitude.

For a moment I tilted back in my chair, thinking. I knew I had to meet that head-on, so I said:

"That is easier to say than to do, Comrade Vinogradov, and I have to refuse your new job for several reasons. First, as you are well aware, I already have a job, the one assigned me by my Director, to conduct strategic intelligence against the main enemy of the Soviet Union, against Germany. Second, I cannot do two jobs. Third, you cannot buy Turks. They are proud people. Fourth, that is work for Naumov, or you, yourself. It is political espionage, the main domain of my 'neighbors.' Finally, until ordered by the Director of Military Intelligence, I will not do it."

My God, he was furious. At each point of my refusal, his face had become paler and paler. At the end, he rose, pounded my desk, and shouted, "I order you to do this job. If you don't, I'll report you to Moscow."

"You do just that, comrade," I retorted, "and remember, I am not your subordinate. Please keep in mind that I am an officer of the General Staff, and never shout at me." My temper was also rising.

He got up, walked out, and slammed the door. That was the end of our pleasant relationship.

Weeks went by. I was so busy I had forgotten the clash with Vinogradov. Then I was told to go to Ankara. Akimov and Bukhtin were also going. The occasion was pleasant. We were to attend a reception and dinner party that Turkish Foreign Minister Shukru Saracoglu was tendering to members of the diplomatic corps. On the way up, the three of us exchanged comments about the type of Soviet "diplomats" the minister would be entertaining.

Before going to the party, we had to report in to the embassy for the usual instructions about whom we should be nice or rude to, to whom we should talk, and about what. At that preparatory gathering was Naumov, looking even meaner than usual. With him was a special visitor from Moscow, a very senior NKVD chief whose department handled assignments of clandestine violence, kidnappings, assassinations, arson; he was in Turkey to find out what had gone wrong with the von Papen attempt. Naumov made a special effort to see that I was introduced to his chief. I was given just the barest of handshakes and a long, searching stare, and then the visitor turned his back on me. Naumov, I thought, must have given a very unflattering description of me.

The Turkish party lasted long into the night. I did not get back to the embassy until about two the next morning. At the door the guard told me I was to go to the ambassador immediately, that he was waiting for me in his office.

Behind the desk, very excited, was Vinogradov. He had been drinking heavily, and his face was flushed. Without even asking me to sit down, without any greeting at all, he snapped out:

"Comrade, I have real orders for you now. You have been recalled. It is urgent. You have two days, no more, to clear up your affairs. Travel alone for you might be dangerous. Two diplomatic couriers are leaving for the U.S.S.R. the day after tomorrow. They will escort you."

I was badly, badly shaken, but I believe I did not show it. As coolly as is possible in a circumstance like that, I answered, "Very well, comrade. I will gladly go back. I belong at the front. I am a military officer. I am sick and tired here with your rivalries, intrigues, with your dull work. But I cannot go on two days' notice because I also have standing orders to get instructions from my Director as to whom to transfer the intelligence networks I have organized. That will take about four or five days. Then I will depart for the U.S.S.R., couriers or no couriers. I can take care of myself."

Surprisingly he agreed to the delay. But he shocked me, too, by telling me that the center had arranged for me to transfer the nets to Akimov. That was a bad piece of information. It meant that the Director had already approved my return with no advice to me.

I got away from that office—and I hoped for the last time—at about half past two in the morning. I went to my room in the embassy and needless to say had no easy sleep.

Some of the work to be wound up was in Ankara, so it was not until the next evening that I boarded the night express for Istanbul. With me was my friend Bukhtin.

Shortly after we had pulled out we went to the diner for dinner and drinks, but mainly for drinking. We ordered strong Turkish *raki* in big amounts and mixed it with water, making the clear liquor whitish, what is called lion's milk. We did not go to our berths. We just got drunk, very drunk, and I did not care.

Somewhere along the Anatolian plateau, Bukhtin turned sad eyes to the window and into the darkness and said:

"Look, my dear friend, you are in big, big trouble. If I were you, I would not go back. I would stay in Turkey or try to go someplace else. You are finished. You are done. You will never see

Moscow as a free man. Perhaps they will shoot you as soon as you cross the border.

"I have heard from my boss—everybody seems to have known the mess you are in before you heard—that the Director has agreed that the NKVD will handle your case. You know what that means.

"All that was done by Naumov, by his chief from Moscow, and by the ambassador. They need a scapegoat for their failure on that fumbled assassination of von Papen. My hardheaded friend, don't you know that was all Naumov was sent here for?

"They said that you told about the plan to kill the German to the Yugoslavs, to the British, and to the Turks. They accuse you of many other things you never did. You have no chance to defend yourself. It is wartime and nobody will listen to you.

"The ambassador accused you of being pro-Turkish, of refusing to carry out special orders of the Party and government. Naumov accused you of collaboration with the American and British intelligence agencies. For months Naumov has collected 'material' on you.

"They established that you visited the American consul general, that you had many meetings with leading members of British intelligence, that royalist Yugoslav officers are your bosom friends, and on and on.

"You are an engineer, have a profession, and technical skills. You know foreign languages. You are of Turkish blood. You don't have a family, or wife, or children, or parents waiting for you back home.

"Again I say, if I were you, I would defect to the Turks instead of going to face the firing squad for crimes you did not commit. People bigger than you, generals and marshals of the Red Army, prominent Party members, and untold thousands of others, have died in NKVD cellars.

"Defect, and say you did it in protest against the terror of the NKVD. . . ."

I was astonished, I was angry, I was disgusted with myself. How naive I had been. There was some truth, enough for the NKVD, in every item of the "case" against me. And Bukhtin was so very right about what would happen.

I looked at him across the table from me. He looked back at me fully, as if pleased I had finally come to my senses. He was my close friend. But could he have been given the job of sounding me out? I believed not, I hoped not, but I could not be sure. In the spot I was in I had to be careful as never before, so I said:

"Thank you deeply, my true friend. It was good of you to bring me to my senses. But understand this: I'm not going to defect to anybody. I'm going to the Director. I'm going to fight for my good name. Besides, they need officers at the front. That is where I belong."

He must have understood what I was not telling him. For when I finished he grinned at me, said, "You old fool. You'll never see the front. They'll shoot you first. Come, let's get to bed while we can still walk there."

Next morning at the consulate I went to Akimov. I found he really had been informed about what was happening to me. He wanted to know when I was going to brief him about my nets and arrange meetings for him with my agents. I told him we would do that the next day. First, I said, I had to write my final report to the Director and straighten out my financial accounts. He agreed to my plans.

Before leaving his office, however, there was something I badly needed information on. I had to find out how and to whom political asylum was granted. In Akimov's rooms were the only volumes of the Great Soviet Encyclopedia. I waited until he was busy at papers on his desk, then pulled down a volume from shelves on the other side of the room. It caught his attention.

"Gregory Petrovich," Akimov called, "whatever are you looking for there?"

Nothing, I told him, just looking up something about Poland for my agent with the Polish passport. *Pol'sha* (Poland) was in the same volume as *Pravo Ubezhishaha* (Right of Asylum). Akimov went back to his papers.

I read. It did not take long. There was very little in those big tomes about that subject, naturally. I learned only that the U.S.S.R. granted asylum to foreigners—"Communists" should be read between the lines—persecuted for defending the interests of the working people, for scientific efforts, or for taking part in national liberation struggles. There was nothing, as I should have known, about other countries' approach to the matter.

I left Akimov's office telling him I was setting up contacts with my agents for him. What I really was going to do was vastly different. There was obvious danger in it now that I was under recall orders, but I had to do it. I had to let independent third parties know my intentions and some of the reasons for them. For my own soul, my integrity, I had to let others know the truth in case I was unsuccessful, died at NKVD hands, or had to kill myself.

A few steps from the consulate, after checking that Naumov's creatures were not on my trail, I hailed the first passing taxi. I got out near the Golden Horn, bought cigarettes at a kiosk, then walked on a few hundred yards. Satisfied that no Soviet security was around, I took another cab over the Galata Bridge and to the first public telephone at the other end.

I made two calls. The first was to my friend Perich at the Yugoslav consulate, the second to a British businessman whose brother was with his nation's intelligence service. I made arrangements to meet both the Yugoslav and the Britisher.

Perich joined me a quarter of an hour later at a small café in the old part of the city. He was not at all surprised about my plans, agreed I had no alternative. In parting we shook hands and kissed each other on both cheeks.

An hour later my British friend was waiting for me at the railway station. I passed him. He followed a few steps behind. I boarded a local train going to the beaches. Once we started moving I walked forward through the cars, found a coach that was empty. I sat, lit a cigarette, and started to read. A moment later my Britisher slid into the seat opposite me. Briefly I told him of the mess I was in and that I was not going back. He too agreed I was right, wished me God's protection from the NKVD. After a brief but warm handshake he got up and left the car. I got off the train several stops later, then returned to Istanbul.

It was then already late in the afternoon. I did not go back to the consulate but went to my apartment, several comfortable rooms rented to me by a refugee, a Jewish woman who had lost all her family to the Nazis.

Sleep that night was difficult. If I was fortunate, before another night I too would be a refugee. My landlady had told me much of her troubles. Mine would be the same, only much, much worse. I would be a political refugee, and therefore a security hazard to my hosts as well. The NKVD would be after me within minutes after I was missing. They would stop at nothing to get me back. Would my hosts be willing to put up with that, to protect me for not just a few weeks, but months, years? I had no way of being sure, but finally I fell asleep from sheer nervous exhaustion.

The next morning I went to the consulate, I hoped for the last time. I shut myself in my room, called the duty office to say that I was not to be disturbed by calls or visitors, that I was at work on urgent messages to Moscow.

Then I pulled up my typewriter and composed two identical statements. One was addressed to my Director, the other to Molotov. I told both that I was breaking with the Soviet government and Party, renouncing my citizenship and my Party membership for political reasons. I stated there was no justice in the Soviet Union, that the private life of every Soviet citizen was always subject to social and political upheaval, that Soviet domestic and foreign policies were utterly wrong, that the country was a police state. I closed by condemning as evil the dictatorship of Stalin and the arbitrary rule of the NKVD.

Next I closed out my accounts down to the last kopek, cent, pfennig, and sou. Even then I could not prevent the NKVD from smearing me as a thief and embezzler, as they do with all defectors.

That done, I put the envelopes containing the statements and the accounts into a large manila envelope and addressed that to my GRU division chief. Before sealing the big envelope I dropped everything else of importance into it: my cipher book; lists of my agents, their names, code names, and addresses; even classified instructions on new radio equipment for agent use.

Everything was in order. I called Bukhtin's secretary to my office, gave him the big envelope with instructions that it was top-secret and was to go to the Directorate in the next diplomatic pouch. As I watched the envelope being taken out of the office I knew I had destroyed the last bridge.

For a last time I looked around my office. In the files were many a top-secret plan or document on GRU installations in Turkey, details of espionage, and other clandestine operations. There was nothing to stop me from taking some of that with me. But I would not. If I could make a new start it had to be with clean hands.

It was about noon. I stopped at Akimov's office, told his secretary I was going to a luncheon meeting, would be back soon.

I stepped into the courtyard. The gates to the street were about twenty yards away. Beyond the gates was another world, something I was noticing for really the first time.

I wanted to run but I had to walk and not fast. The doorman was one of Naumov's creatures.

"Georgy Petrovich," someone called behind me, "Georgy Petrovich." It was not Naumov's voice, not Akimov's. I stopped, looked back. Ah, the naval attaché, a nice fellow. Please, he asked, would I take his typewriter and camera with me back to Moscow? The mail was so irregular during the war. I could have said yes, grabbed his package, and kept on going. But I liked him. I could not disappoint him or cheat him. I had to tell him I would try to do so; but first I had to sort out my own belongings, then I would let him know.

I started again toward the gates. How far away they were, fifteen yards, ten yards, at last only five. Just there, I was grabbed by the shoulder, swung around.

"Georgy, Georgy," Bukhtin panted. "You were going so fast, I thought I'd never catch you. How about dinner this evening, and a nightclub afterwards?"

Not tonight, I told him, the next night maybe. We would see. He was disappointed but left me and turned back toward the consulate.

Finally I was out of the gates. Oh, God, I whispered, I thank you. Again watching for Naumov's men, I got a taxi. Again I went to the old city. Again, still checking that I was not followed, I found a public phone booth.

Closing the door tightly I called the Istanbul Police Department. Identifying myself as a Soviet diplomat, I asked to speak to the chief, personally and urgently.

Another voice came over the wire. It was that of Chief Kamran Chorokh, whom I had met several times at dinners and receptions. Again I identified myself and said I must see him as soon as possible on a personal matter of the utmost importance.

Kamran Bey told me to come to him right away. He added, "Don't worry, we will protect you. My men will be waiting for you and will bring you to my office immediately."

I got another taxi, still checking for Naumov, and went directly to Police Headquarters. There several officers were waiting for me at the main entrance. I was escorted to the office of Kamran Bey.

As I entered the chief came from behind his desk, shook my hand cordially, and offered me a chair. He requested one of my escorts to bring coffee and cigarettes, and then dismissed them. He was doing his best to put me at my ease.

It was not simple for me to start, to wreck everything I worked for so long and so hard, but I knew I had no choice. So with no interruption from Kamran Bey, I blurted out my whole story.

I told him that I was an intelligence officer, that my true name was Ismail Akhmedov, that I was of pure Turkic blood, and that I professed Islam.

I told him I had been ordered home to face a NKVD tribunal, and everything that had led up to that.

At the end I requested asylum in Turkey on political grounds. If that were impossible because of international politics, I asked Turkish protection and permission to travel to other countries that might grant me asylum.

The chief had followed my every word. When I had finished he said, "Ismail Bey," (how wonderful to be addressed by my own name again, and at that moment), "once your country had in Turkey a wonderful man as ambassador. His name was Karakhan, 'Black Khan,' in our language, yours and mine. He was a great friend of our leader, Ataturk, and of the Turkish people. He was respected and loved here. One day your government recalled him and he went. He should have stayed here and become one of us. As you know he was liquidated by Stalin. What for? For being pro-Turkish. Therefore, we understand you.

"I will notify Ankara at once. I hope they will grant you asylum. Meanwhile, and from now on, you will have to be in our custody. It is for your protection and to preserve the good name of my nation. If Ankara will not grant you asylum we will help you to get to another country. On that point I give you my word of honor."

Then we discussed where I should be hidden while waiting word from Ankara. Istanbul, we both agreed, was too dangerous. We settled on Bursa, a pleasant town south of the Sea of Marmara, not far from the coast and in the foothills of Ulu Dag, the Mysian Olympus of the ancient Greeks.

Those provisional arrangements completed, Kamran Bey ordered six officers into the office. They were strapping fellows, young, and trained athletes. All were in civilian clothes, but all carried pistols in concealed shoulder holsters. It was a most impressive escort, one capable of coping with Naumov's thugs.

Kamran Bey warned them about the danger we faced from the NKVD on the trip. If they met Soviet security, he said, they must be prepared to shoot their way out. A boat would be set up for the crossing to the little port of Yalova, from whence we would be escorted to Bursa. Civil and police authorities would be awaiting us at Bursa.

My escort and I left from the rear of Police Headquarters in two cars. First we went to my apartment, where I gathered my things and paid my landlady. The poor woman was terrified by our sudden descent on her, and especially by my escort's warning of direst consequences to her if she gave any information to Russians who would be sure to come looking for me.

That done, we drove immediately to the pier and boarded ship for Yalova. At sea I looked back on Istanbul, her proud towers, minarets, and domes resplendent in the late afternoon sun. Farewell, I said, city of my dreams, city of my shattered hopes, city of my voyage into the unknown, farewell.

# 9

# Exile

All plans for my hideout had been changed, however, by the time we reached Yalova. At the pier we were met by several Turkish army officers who said there had been a flurry of NKVD activity in Bursa, obviously in search of me, and that the idea of keeping me there had been abandoned. Yalova itself had been selected as the place for me to stay until further instructions were received from Ankara and Istanbul.

Also at the pier to meet us was the *Kaymakam*, or county government chief of Yalova. A pleasant young man, he shook my hand and said, "*Marhaba*, Ismail Bey, *hosh geldiniz,* I am your host. It is my privilege to have you as our guest. I hope your stay in our little house will be pleasant and comfortable."

The little house proved to be a handsome villa on the beach. Ataturk had once stayed there. Well separated from neighboring dwellings, it was surrounded by large gardens with roses and other beautiful flowers in bloom. Mountains soared against the horizon to the south, while to the north, as I arrived in the evening, the thousands of lights on the Princes Islands and in Istanbul behind them were beginning to sparkle and twinkle.

The Turks really meant business about my security. Uniformed and plainclothes police were everywhere about the house and grounds, to which, they told me, I was restricted for my own safety. There were checkpoints at the approaches to the area and no one was allowed in it except officials and local residents.

Just before we left the pier for the villa a police boat pulled in and tied up. Off it jumped two men sent as top officers in charge of my security. One was Istanbul Deputy Police Chief Ahmed Demir, the same man who had outwitted Naumov at the Revolution anniversary reception. The other was Halit Tulga, deputy chief of the Istanbul Office of National Security (Turkish intelligence).

172

All of us then went to the villa for dinner, presided over by the pretty young wife of the *Kaymakam*. The meal was superb: *dolmas,* vine leaves wrapped around spiced rice and meat; *böreks,* meat pies; *pilav;* grilled fish; salad; fruit. For drinks, *raki,* Turkish vodka, and excellent local wines were served.

Much as I liked that good meal, it was the atmosphere that went with it that counted most. For the first time in many, many years, I felt that I was among my own people, like a friend among friends, a brother among brothers. And I could talk about anything I chose, and say what I really meant and felt.

The chief topic at dinner and afterwards was the Turkic people of the Soviet Union. I was plied with question after question. What is their number, those people of Turkic stock? How many dialects do they speak? What alphabets do they use? If they were allowed to receive them, would they be able to read Turkish papers, printed in the Latin alphabet since the days of Ataturk? Do they preserve their national traditions? Do they know or remember their own history? Is Islam tolerated as a religion, and if so, to what degree? How extensively are they Russified? How many of them occupy high-ranking civilian and military positions? Are there frictions and misunderstandings between the Russians and the Turkic minorities?

And so it went on until midnight when it was time for bed. My room was spacious and had large windows looking onto the sea. I opened them wide and stood there for a while in pure delight. I breathed in the fragrance of the roses just beyond the window. Beyond them was the beach and the sea, its gentle waves lapping. Somewhere not far away, a nightingale was singing, calling its companion.

Drinking in all that beauty, I felt snug there under the wing of friends, the Turks. For the first time in many, many moons, I began to feel content on that balmy night at the start of July 1942. It was hard to believe that only a year had passed since I was released from the German camp, a dreadful year marked in black with Tamara's death, a year that closed only hours earlier with my flight from the consulate.

And there I was, I told myself, irrevocably cut off from everything and everybody I knew, a political refugee. What now? The start had been good, I had to admit. The attitude of Kamran Bey, the courtesy of my hosts, the fine villa by the sea, even the roses were propitious omens. Perhaps everything would work out.

I dropped to my knees. I prayed. I said the opening sura of the Koran: *"Alhamdulillahi Rabb'l Alemin—Ihdina siratel musta-*

*kim!*" ["Praise to God, the Lord of the Universe—Show us the straight path!"]

Then I went to bed, but not to sleep. I pictured the uproar that must have followed my disappearance. The embassy and consulate must have been in a terrible panic. Naumov, I knew, was certainly not asleep, or even in bed yet. Very soon he would be facing his own, his very own investigation. To have fumbled the von Papen assassination. To have lost two of his best murder operatives to the Turks. And then to have lost me, a lieutenant colonel of the General Staff, a former chief of the Fourth Division of GRU, a former GRU resident in Germany, a GRU resident in Turkey, and a research engineer in military communications. All that gone, just before he was supposed to return me to the Soviet Union. Naumov as a man, as a person, meant nothing to me, but as a representative of the NKVD, those bloody butchers and torturers of thousands upon thousands, I hated him and wished him the worst.

Vinogradov, I mused with some pleasure, must have been having his bad moments too. Probably he was pacing up and down his office taking drink after drink, many more than were good for him, wondering how he, the boss, was going to explain my disappearance to Moscow, and what Moscow was going to say to him.

And I thought of Akimov and Bukhtin, but with concern and worry, not meanness. Perhaps their nights were also uncomfortable. I was sorry. Akimov was being blamed for being my friend and not having vigilance. But he was tough and experienced. He would enjoy fighting Naumov and he would win. And Akimov would forgive me for loss of one night's sleep. He would know that had I not defected there would not have been many more nights for me, awake or asleep.

Bukhtin, my dear friend, his troubles I most regretted. I was everlastingly grateful to him for warning me in time. I hoped he would take the easy way out and denounce me in any way he liked. That was the way we did things as average, normal Soviet citizens. We had seen children and wives denounce fathers and husbands after those poor souls had been arrested by the NKVD on fantastic charges every family knew were false. Bukhtin should have more liberty than they. He was just my friend.

Finally the singing of the nightingale became softer, the splash of the waves gentler, and I slept.

Day followed day at that beautiful haven. On my first morning there, almost the first thing I did was to comb through the newspapers to see if there were reports of my defection. There were none, ever, even years later. I was too hot a case for publicity, my hosts said. Also, they added, with the NKVD looking frantically everywhere for me, the less said about me the better. Officially, I was told, I did not exist. That was right. I could have been in the hands of the Americans, the British, or of any of a number of powers.

Once I had understood my position I relaxed about it. I walked and walked, and admired the roses. I swam for hours in the soft waters of the sea. Always, when out of the villa, I was escorted by three armed plainclothesmen. I too was armed, was never without a Browning pistol in my pocket. At night my hosts and I talked for hours and hours before I tumbled into bed for wonderful sleep. Nevertheless, that good life was not enough. I craved news about my request for asylum and what was going to happen to me, but nobody at the villa knew anything.

Just before midnight of my tenth day there, lights were flashed at the villa from the sea. It was a signal of some sort from a small cabin cruiser a few hundred yards from shore. I could hardly see the boat, let alone understand the signal, but Ahmed Bey had read the flashes correctly. He signalled back with a flashlight, then told me to get ready, that we were to board the boat.

As I went to pack I saw the boat come in and tie up at a little pier that belonged to the villa. The procedure had not been easy. It was a dark and gusty night and the water was rough.

I was quite worried when I went out to go aboard. Ahmed Bey had told me he knew nothing except that we had been ordered to get on the boat. Where was I going? Why all the secrecy? I knew there had been a Soviet freighter tied up in the Bosphorus. Were they going to turn me over to the Soviets, or dump me into the sea? At least they had not disarmed me. I felt the Browning in my pocket. I would kill myself rather than fall into NKVD hands.

On the pier the *Kaymakam* must have seen that I was nervous. He said he could not blame me for being excited and uncertain, but he swore by the Turkish youth and Ataturk that no harm would come to me.

When a Turk makes that double oath, his word is good. I was comforted, enough so that I could make decent farewells and thanks to the *Kaymakam,* his wife and my bodyguards. The *Kaymakam* responded with the wish we would meet again, when I was a free man and a citizen of his country. Then I went aboard accompanied by Ahmed Bey and Halit Bey. Once on, I was invited into the cabin and offered coffee. Our destination, I was told, was Istanbul.

In the very early hours of the next morning we tied up at a pier in front of Dolma Bahche Saray, the magnificent former residence of Turkey's sultans. I was led through hall after hall of that great palace to an ornate room of state. There awaiting me was Kamran Bey, the chief of police.

He greeted me in the name of the governor of Istanbul, thereby making official what he was going to say. With a smile, he said that after a careful check of the circumstances under which I had defected from the Soviets, after a thorough investigation of my background, the Turkish government had decided to grant me political asylum and give me the protection I needed.

That ended the official part. Then, after coffee and cigarettes had been offered, I heard the security part of it, his problem. He said:

"Ismail Bey, the exact place for your permanent residence has not yet been selected. Temporarily we will put you in another villa on the Asiatic side of the Bosphorus. Your movements there will be narrowly restricted and you will be under constant guard.

"The Soviets are searching everywhere for you. Some have been looking for you in Bursa and in Izmir. There have been signs of extreme nervousness, even panic, in the Soviet installations in Ankara and Istanbul. Some of your former friends and colleagues have left Turkey in a great hurry. Please be careful and patient. You are going to have a number of restrictions on your movements, even your social life. It may cause you inconvenience. But you realize, of course, all of this is for your own good, for your security. Your case is very hot!"

I thanked him with all my heart, then left escorted by Ahmet Bey and Halit Bey.

It was still dark when we returned to the cruiser. The minute we were aboard it pulled out and headed into the Bosphorus. We passed the Soviet freighter, but my fears were over. I was so relieved, so happy, I could have taken the sight of a Soviet warship in stride.

Within less than an hour we pulled into an inlet on the eastern shore and tied up at a small pier. There a new trio of bodyguards awaited us. We were led some minutes along the shore, then veered inland into woods and along zigzagging hilly paths until we reached a large villa, low in a valley and surrounded by gardens as big as a park.

I spent about six weeks in that pleasant hideout, roaming my guarded little domain of woods and hills. Then I was transferred again and again under heavy guard, in the first of a series of moves that would have me migrating, like the hunted man I was, here and there across the face of Turkey for eight long years.

That was a large span to lose for life and eventual freedom, but I have no complaint, only perpetual gratitude to my Turkish hosts and guardians. After all, I had tried with the Americans and gotten nowhere. And on that train trip to the beach I had told the British of my position, and received from them no more than a Godspeed.

When the Turks succored me, their nation was in the uneasy position of a neutral surrounded by combatants. Nor was that position eased appreciably by Turkey's belated adherence to the Allied side, bare months before the end of the war. On the very eve of termination of hostilities in Europe, the Soviet Union unilaterally denounced her 1925 friendship pact with Turkey and demanded joint control of the Dardanelles and the cession of large chunks of eastern Turkey along the Soviet frontier. Those demands were not pushed, but neither were they dropped. Twice in those years of my exile, the Soviets also demanded my surrender from the Turks. Both demands were refused. Though unpublicized, that was quite a display of courage and integrity. A weaker nation might have made a deal for me. It would have been easy; nobody knew anything about my case except the Soviets, a few Turks, and me.

My first move to Isparta, a beautiful little town high in the mountains of the southwest, was typical of those that followed over the years.

After breakfast at the villa on the Bosphorus I was put into a car. A police inspector in plain clothes sat with me in the rear, his deputy, similarly garbed, was in front with the driver. Curtains that were on the windows had been drawn and we drove rapidly, but safely, over back roads to Haydar Pasha, the railway terminus on the Asiatic shore of the Bosphorus.

At the station all arrangements had been made in advance. As a porter trailed us with baggage, our trio walked quickly, bypassed the line-ups at the ticket controls, went onto a platform where a train was waiting, and entered a compartment that had been reserved for us. Every effort had been made to avoid crowds in the event a Soviet agent might have been among them.

Almost the moment we were aboard, the train pulled out. The curtains of our compartment were drawn because other passengers were elsewhere in the car. All three of us were armed and did not leave the compartment. Meals were brought to us from the dining car. At each stop the local police chief was on the platform to look into our compartment and advise Istanbul headquarters that all was in order.

At Eskishehir, a little more than a third the distance, our car was detached from the train and connected to another going south to Dinar, a little place locked in the mountains. Some miles south of Eskishehir, the last of other passengers got off, and we were able to raise the blinds and open our compartment to the corridor. At Dinar we changed for a small local train to Isparta, where the railroad track ended.

We were met by the local chief of police, who later introduced me to the governor, who was to have overall responsibility for my safety. It was also arranged that I meet Colonel Abdulkadir Bey, the area garrison commander. My bodyguard was reduced to one, Aziz Bey, who, although constantly armed, posed as my companion.

Only those four men knew my true name and identity. To all others in that town, however, I was known as Ragip Bey, a merchant awaiting shipments of hides from Syria.

For a short time I stayed in Isparta's small and only hotel, until we found, on the governor's recommendation, two bedrooms and a sitting room in the home of an elderly widow.

Once we were settled in, I held council with myself. Forbidden any real job or work, for obvious security reasons, I knew I had to organize a program for myself. I had no idea how long I would be in limbo and appreciated I could fast go to seed in a confined life, if limited to no more than eating, drinking, and sleeping.

Therefore I set myself a daily schedule, one that I kept for years. I rose early, went to bed early. I took up exercising every morning. French and English I made my chief studies, and I also read extensively in several languages. Every day I walked, hiked, or climbed, depending on the terrain, and also set aside time to become acquainted with the local people and their ways. I also avoided excessive drinking, refrained as much as possible from feeling sorry for myself, and tried to comport myself correctly with my fellow men.

I found Isparta a lovely town, and its people most friendly. It is famous for its rose oil and rose water—I will never forget the fragrance of its rose gardens—and for its carpet manufacturing and vineyards. It lies in a green valley sheltered by mountains. To the east is a peak of almost nine thousand feet, perpetually snow-capped, and beyond that lies Lake Egridir, teeming with game fish and rich with snug little coves.

I took many a hike to that mountain and lake, often going beyond the confines set for me by the governor. Aziz Bey, of course, would always be with me on those outings. He knew there was little possibility of a NKVD man being within one hundred miles, and would let me wander far ahead of him, lost in thought. Our arrangement was that if I ran into trouble, I would fire a few rounds from my pistol and he would come running.

As time went by, I met more and more local people and was befriended by a number of them. I was somewhat of a mystery man to them, because of my Tatar accent. And, although no comment was made, most saw Aziz Bey for what he was, not a companion, but a bodyguard. Nevertheless, they were very kind, often invited the two of us for meals, or would chat with us on meeting in the streets.

Frequently we would go to the bazaar, where I had made some friends among the merchants. Also, I liked the hustle and bustle there. After a while, however, we had to avoid the place. My cover story had worn thin. I was asked what kinds of hides I was awaiting from Syria. On what breed of camels were they coming? What arrangements was I making about customs, about currency exchange? We answered the best we could, but nobody believed us.

At the time of those uncomfortable moments in the bazaar, I had been in Isparta about a year. I liked the town, I admired the people, but I felt I had become too much a center of attraction for my own good. I asked to be transferred somewhere else for security reasons. My request was granted and at the end of August 1943, again with two bodyguards, I was put on the train for Bursa.

Before leaving I said farewell to the good governor, who had closed his eyes to my wandering beyond the limits he had set. I said farewell to the police chief, we would drop by several times a week to play cards or chess, to Colonel Abdulkadir Bey, who poured me strong Turkish coffee and tried to keep my spirits high, to fine old Zehra Hanum, my landlady with bright, twinkling eyes set like gems in a face full of wrinkles, who would quietly bring me lemonade or chicken soup when she knew I was tired, depressed, or down with a cold.

I was kept in Bursa for only six months. On arrival there I was taken to a hotel, one which had thermal baths. My bodyguards were sent back to Istanbul and I became the responsibility of the governor of Bursa. I was free to circulate in the town as I wished, but could not leave it without special permission and escort, as I was allowed to do once in January 1944 to go skiing near the summit of Ulu Dag. Since I had no bodyguard at other times, the practice was for the local police to check my hotel twice daily. Besides that, however, they also checked and questioned every person I met or talked with, a technique that was not only embarrassing to my few acquaintances, but annoying to me.

In spring of 1944, just as my nerves were becoming frayed with that surveillance and my friends were beginning to avoid me, I was notified that I was being transferred from Bursa. The reason was logical. The NKVD were thought to be developing a new interest in the town.

Back I was sent to the southwest, yet again by train and with bodyguards. My destination that time was Burdur, a mean little town that became a hateful place to me. What was particularly aggravating was that it was only some fifteen miles west over the mountains from Isparta. Lovely Isparta, nestled in its mountains, with its crooked streets, its gardens, and poplar trees, had reminded me of the Caucasus. Burdur, just a mountain pass away, could have been on the other side of the moon, so great was the contrast. Its flat dusty streets, sand-covered hills, gardens surrounded by walls made of clay, were typical of Arabia. Burdur too had a lake of the same name, a foul sump of alkali, abounding in no fish, no water fowl, but a haven for snakes.

The governor of Burdur was as bleak as the area. He resented my arrival there, feared that a political refugee would cause him nothing but trouble, and said as much. And the police chief was openly hostile. He regarded me as a man who had challenged his government and authorities. For him authority, be it good or bad, was dispensed by God, and any man opposing it was antisocial, a dangerous person.

Somehow I eked out more than a year in that miserable place. All that saved me from desperation was the regimen I had established for myself at the start of my exile. There was no enjoyment, almost no purpose in outings around Burdur, so I concentrated on my studies and my reading to keep sane.

I had only one distraction, one amusement of a sort in all that time. My bodyguard of that period was a fool. The cover story that he manufactured for me was that I was a professor, a geologist. He posed as my assistant, looking for mineral deposits. Within days after that yarn had circulated, my rented house started to fill with rocks and stones of all descriptions, all sizes. Farmers came to me, often from great distances, carrying samples of their property, asking me to assay them. That only came to an end when I told my "assistant" to tell the peasants that the "professor" was sick, too sick to work.

I really was ill. For some time my gallbladder had been inflamed. I needed hospitalization and had requested that as well as transfer to a less godforsaken area, preferrably to Izmir on the west coast.

At last, in August 1945, three years after my defection, I was liberated from Burdur. I was transferred not to Izmir, but to Manisa, the ancient Magnesia, inland and some twenty miles northeast of Izmir.

By the time I arrived at Manisa I had a high fever and acute pain in my back, so I was taken straight from the station to a hospital. For a week I lay unconscious and with high fever, but then began to respond to treatment so well that I was allowed to leave cured and in good health within a month after arrival.

That was a fine modern hospital, built by a Jew from that area who had emigrated to the United States as a penniless youth and made his fortune, part of which he donated so that the people of his land of origin could have good medical care.

The director of the hospital was by no means as fine as the institution or the donor. An American-educated Turk, he had no sympathy for Jews or other minorities, had shown that by changing the name of the hospital. Its correct name had been Eskinazi International Hospital, after the donor, but at the time I was there the director had altered it to Shinazi Hospital. He had also taken Eskinazi's portrait down from the entry walls and put it away in a closet.

In Eskinazi International Hospital I formed a lasting friendship with a fellow patient. He was Remzi Bey, once a deputy in the Turkish parliament and a sugar manufacturer, who later retired to become a gentleman farmer. After we got out of the hospital, he introduced me to many interesting people in the Manisa area. He also recommended to the authorities that I be allowed to work and urged me to apply for Turkish citizenship.

Things loosened up for me a bit when I got out of the hospital, mainly because the war was over by then. The most important change was permission to once more use my real name. For five years, one with the Soviets and four with the Turks, I had been masquerading as somebody else. Another indication of the relaxed attitude toward me was that at Manisa I was no longer the responsibility of the area's governor, but of his deputy.

He had me installed in a small but good hotel, where I could see a bit more of the world and its comings and goings than in an outlying house. And my escort-guard was no longer believed necessary, although the police kept a steady eye on my security. The deputy also, at last, permitted me to seek work, somewhat removing the embarrassment of being a complete dependent of the government, but I was forbidden serious work which would have required references or details of my background. Through the deputy, I also filed application for naturalization.

There was, however, one major concession I was not given, namely permission to travel where I wished in Turkey. I was therefore still a prisoner of a sort, a well-cared-for one, to be sure, but confined to a specific area.

That area was really quite confined, amounting to only a few square miles: the town and its immediate periphery. I could go a couple of miles to the east to admire the statue of Niobe, still sitting and mourning the murder of her children. I could go west beyond the Eskinazi Hospital to wander in ancient Grecian ruins. A walk down to the Gediz River brought me to my southern border. A climb to the top of a mountain above the city was my northern limit.

On the crest of that mountain I spent many pleasant hours lost in thought and dreaming of the past. To the southwest I could look down into the harbor of Izmir on a clear day, and on the blue, blue waters of the Aegean. In the opposite direction I could see far into the Gediz Valley, a crib, if not a cradle, of part of civilization. Beyond was what was once Lydia, and it was along that valley Alexander the Great once conquered and marched on his way to Samarkand and India. In the opposite direction along that same valley had marched the armies of Xerxes en route to invasion and defeat in Greece. It had also been the route of Tamerlane on his way to destroy Izmir, so many times destroyed. And only recently it had been the course of Ataturk and his forces when they drove the Greeks into the sea at Izmir.

On one of those rambles through the hills looking down on Manisa I met a hermit, in fact I came upon his castle. In Manisa, as in many Turkish towns, it was the custom to fire a cannon to signal noon and also mark the time of sunrise and sunset during the holy month of Ramadan. In Manisa it was the hermit who tended the cannon, positioned on a flat rock high above the town. A small stone house nearby, encircled with low stone walls, was his home.

To come upon that hermit suddenly, as I did, was quite startling. He had a Christ-like face, a long beard, hair to his shoulders, a muscular body, lean and bronzed. Although well into his sixties, he looked a score of years younger, his hair and beard still jet black. His most unusual features were his deep, luminous eyes, and his attire, nothing but a breechloth, worn year round in sun, rain, wind and snow. Locally he was called Tarzan, although nobody knew who he was or where he came from, nor would he tell. Some said he was the son of an Arabian sheikh who had abandoned his tribe after a quarrel over a girl he loved. Others held he was a Turkoman who had fled Bukhara after the Revolution. I found he was very familiar with India and the Middle East, but I never learned his identity either. I did note, however, that in his castle he had a medal for fighting in the forces of Ataturk.

Tarzan did more than fire the cannon—and how he did that with split-second accuracy without a watch or any time-keeping device was another mystery. He had planted trees and shrubs along the town's main streets and watered and cared for them regularly. He had converted an abandoned cemetery into a small park, filled with trees, shrubs, and flowerbeds.

The town's little children loved him, followed him everywhere, and he loved them too. He had put his earnings from the town for cannon-firing into a bank, with provision that the small funds left upon his death be given to orphans. To earn his meals he washed dishes at a local restaurant.

He was also the town's unofficial greeter. Whenever he learned, in his unusual ways, of the arrival of a foreign lady, he would bring her wild flowers from the mountains as a sign of welcome.

Tarzan never touched alcohol, never abused anyone, nor cursed. He was a living saint.

He welcomed me as a fellow stranger, like him cut off forever from his past; not only welcomed me to his castle, but also showed me little-known paths in the mountains, hidden caves, waterfalls, and woods. Yah, plants, flowers, and children, you were living goodness, no matter who you may have really been. Peace be with you, my friend.

There in Manisa the year 1945 passed, and then the year 1946. In the course, and thanks to Remzi Bey, I made other friends, too: Hikmet Eginliouglu, the judge; Shemi Bey, a former defense minister; Lufti Karaosmanlu, one of the founders of the Democratic party.

Over the months, the years, restrictions on me were relaxed more and more. I could walk, if I wished, many miles beyond the mountain, or across the bridge to the other side of the Gediz River. In fact, I could go in any direction in the area, even on occasional visits to Izmir, although Manisa had to remain my residence.

With that greater freedom, my loneliness faded away. Many people invited me to their homes and introduced me to their families. From some of those acquaintanceships I got my first work, giving private lessons in English and mathematics to high-school students. I appreciated that teaching, since it gave me my first occupation in years, but my earnings were meager, never more than the equivalent of about fifteen dollars a month. But even though I was happy at being occupied again, the fact that it was at no more than teaching children somewhat depressed me. It was not that I did not love children and teaching them. It was that I could not forget my teaching of years before in Chardzhou and in the mountains of Azerbaidzhan, and wondered if I had another long struggle ahead of me before I had my life in order again. But I could not give up then. I kept on with my little work and my little pursuits. There was nothing else I could do.

The break came, completely unexpectedly, and not until the end of summer of 1947. Passing through the lobby of my hotel I stopped abruptly as I noticed a new face. Guests there were few, and a stranger was always a welcome contact with the outside world for me.

That stranger was quite out of the ordinary. He was tall, big, had red hair, and blue eyes. A cigar in his mouth, he was sitting at a coffee table reading a magazine with his legs stretched comfortably on the table. He was reading *Time* magazine, and I felt sure he, too, was American.

As I approached him he looked up, smiled, and said hello. I said hello too, added, "I am Ismail Akhmedov; glad to meet you."

He said, "I am Porter Mougey from Lima, Ohio, U.S.A. Nice to know you. Where are you from?"

When I told him that originally I was from Russia, he wanted to know if I was a Russian and accepted my explanation that I was of Turkish origin, but born in Russia.

The fact that I spoke English interested him more than my origin. Saying he was glad to find somebody in the hotel with whom he could talk, he called a waiter and ordered *raki* for us both. Soon we were calling each other by first names, but he renamed me Ike because Ismail was difficult for him to pronounce correctly.

Porter turned out to be an engineer who had come to Manisa to install a diesel power plant as part of the Truman Doctrine. Once I had told him that I too was an engineer, and because I knew both Turkish and English, he offered me a job on the spot, to handle translations and administrative problems. He brushed aside my saying I needed permission from the authorities. It was he, he said, who was hiring me, not they.

The next day, however, Porter did get permission from the governor's office for me to work for him. I was so happy. At last, at long last, to be doing something worthwhile and productive again.

And the work itself was fascinating. It gave me a chance to appreciate the practical knowledge and the know-how of American engineers. The diesel had been shipped from the U.S. completely disassembled. It had thousands of parts. Each had to be mounted in the proper place, in the proper sequence. Porter did it all almost single-handedly.

Nor was the Manisa plant his only job. Another station of the same capacity had to be put up in Balikesir, a town about seventy miles to the north, and that project was his task, too.

I became very much attached to Porter and we became very good friends. We were inseparable on the job and off. Forgotten were my solitary hikes and mountain climbing. I no longer had time for that. Besides, Porter was paying me $150 a month, ten times what I had been making teaching.

We spent Christmas of that year and the New Year of 1948 together. From Izmir Porter had gotten a bottle of Kentucky bourbon whiskey and a pound of American bacon. I got eggs in Manisa. Bacon and eggs washed down with bourbon was our New Year's feast. As we were drinking, Porter tried to persuade me to go to America. He said the Turks were fine people and Turkey a fine country, but that I had no future there. He said he would back me in America until I got on my feet.

I was terribly touched. There, I said to myself, my eyes watering, there was a man from thousands of miles away, to whom I had been a complete stranger, unknown until a few months ago, offering to pay the bill for me to get a new start in his country.

My only regret about that work with Porter was that it did not last long. In the spring of 1948 the diesel plant was completed, ready to take over for a decrepit steam generator that had been bilking Manisa with fluctuating voltages and power failures for years. Within two days the governor was to accept our plant officially, a ribbon was to be cut, and speeches of Turko-American friendship had been prepared.

Everything was in order, but to make doubly sure Porter checked everything out once more. We started the motor, but ran it for only a few seconds. It was getting no oil. The oil pump bearings had burned out. During the night, someone—we suspected it was an employee of the old steam plant about to be shut down—had poured sand in the oil line.

There was nothing to do but get a car and drive like demons to Balikesir. We got there about midnight, dismounted the oil pump, which was identical to the one that had been sabotaged, and took it back to Manisa, again at breakneck speed. Immediately Porter set to work making the replacement, and the plant was running for the opening ceremony a few hours later.

That climax also marked the end of my wonderful job. Porter moved on to Balikesir to put the plant there in operation—a matter of just a few days—and then returned to the U.S. Before leaving he shook my hand, told me to "take it easy"—an American expression I had come to know—and made me promise to write.

For me there was nothing left but to return to giving my private lessons. That was a most depressing comedown, somewhat like what happened to Cinderella. I taught as best I could, but with the fear I might be in exile forever. Six long years had passed since I defected.

So things went until August of 1948 when I again ran into strangers in the lobby of my hotel. And again they were Americans, not alone, however, but with several Turks. All were specialists, there to make soil analyses of the Gediz Valley and make surveys for irrigation projects. Every morning they would get into their Jeeps and go out into the countryside, returning in the evenings, tired, sunburned, and dusty, but content with a day's work well done.

As the days passed I came to know some of those people and made some new friends. I was particularly attracted by two. One was the chief soil specialist, an elderly professor from an agricultural college on the U.S. West Coast. The other was a young Turk, an irrigation engineer, who was the conducting officer of the group.

Later the Turkish engineer offered me a job as interpreter for the professor. It was a small job; it paid nothing like Porter's, only twenty-five dollars a month plus board and lodging, but I jumped at it. It was another chance to look in on more of the world than my little work at Manisa afforded.

Day after day I accompanied the professor, tramping over the countryside getting samples of soil, eating with him, and staying in hotels with him in many small towns and villages. In those days that fine old gentleman would tell me about his West Coast, about California, about American education, and about life in general as an American.

Toward the middle of autumn that job came to an end, too. The cold weather made further work impossible, and the group returned to Ankara to await spring before renewing field research. With regret I said goodbye to my friends. I knew I would miss especially the young Turkish engineer who had given me the job. Not only was his home Isparta, the little town I loved, but he was a hard-working and very likeable person. His name was Suleyman Demirel, and later he became prime minister of his country.

That job over, I did not go back to teaching. My morale was very low. I was going into my seventh year as a homeless, paperless refugee, with no word about naturalization, no idea when my wanderings would ever end. As its ward, I had received from the Turkish government the equivalent of fifteen dollars a month, sufficient for board and lodging. I decided that I would make do with that and return to my books, my climbing, and hiking. I was beginning to feel I was a better-clothed Tarzan, but one of much weaker spirit.

# 10

## Kim Philby

Then again the Fates brought me face to face with the KGB (then named the MGB), although at that time I did not know it. For several weeks I was debriefed by Kim Philby and never guessed his real intent.

It was a mild and sunny summer afternoon in 1948. Being rather tired from an early morning mountain climb, I was relaxing in the lobby of the Hotel Ege in Manisa. At this time of year there are few visitors to Manisa, and the hotel where I resided was almost empty. It was quiet and peaceful. The air was fragrant with the many scents and aromas blowing in from the nearby fields and gardens.

Suddenly there was a noise of a car braking, and two men came walking toward me. The man walking in front was a stranger; I had never seen him before. He was a European, perhaps an Englishman, tall, slim and fair-complected. I knew the second gentleman, who was obviously escorting the first. He was the chief of the Izmir Office of the Turkish National Security. I'll call him Mr. R.

Mr. R introduced the stranger to me as a high-ranking member of the British Secret Service who had come to see me on certain matters, but neither his name, rank, nor official position was given. In the world of espionage one gets used to faceless and nameless individuals. The simple fact that the head of the Izmir Office of Turkish National Security brought the stranger from Izmir, located some thirty miles from Manisa, and escorted him displaying all signs of respect and attention, was enough to indicate to me the importance of their journey to this corner of Turkey. We shook hands and I invited them upstairs to my room.

The Englishman asked politely if I could tell him in brief my diplomatic, military, and intelligence background; the circumstances surrounding my defection; and also a short summary of any intelligence information of value I might have.

Sitting there in my hotel room we talked for at least three hours. Rather, I talked and the Englishman listened carefully and took notes. We talked in English, and Mr. R just listened, trying to understand the conversation, for his English was inadequate. After some time had passed, the Englishman suggested we stop at that point because it was getting late.

"Your background is fascinating; your information is also of great value and interest," he said. "We have to sit with you for several weeks and discuss everything in detail. That can only be done in Istanbul, where we would have the proper atmosphere and conditions. I will notify my superiors in London, obtain their authorization to invite you to Istanbul, and also request permission from the Turkish government to interview you. I hope that the Turks will cooperate. You will be notified when all is arranged. Meanwhile, we thank you for your courtesy. It has been a pleasure seeing you." Mr. R was pleased and excited for some reason unknown to me. With that they departed, leaving me with an insatiable curiosity. "Where have they been since 1942? I broke with the Soviets in 1942; it is now 1948! What took the British Secret Service so long to find me? Surely the British were aware long before this that I had defected!" These were the many thoughts that ran rampant through my brain. "Well, times have changed. After the excitement of victory over Germany has subsided, the West is at last beginning to learn and recognize the true face of the Soviets. Maybe now I will find a new home and a job in the West." My hopes started to soar. Hope! Without it a man has nothing. He might as well be dead. He is empty.

Then began the waiting. Slowly, days arrived and passed by, about three months. Then finally the news came one morning. A messenger, a special agent from Mr. R, came with a note. I would leave immediately for Izmir and be prepared for further travel. My ultimate destination was not yet disclosed, but Mr. R had sent his official car with his military driver. This was a benevolence never before extended to me.

In a very short time I arrived in Izmir with the special agent. Mr. R was all smiles. "Here is your own one-way air ticket to Istanbul. You will leave on the first available plane. You will be met at the airport by the deputy chief of our Istanbul Office, Mr. T," (whom I already knew). Mr. R did not know, or at least pretended not to be aware of, the reason for my trip to Istanbul.

The flight to Istanbul takes about one hour. About noon my plane landed at Yeshil Köy, and I was greeted by Mr. T and driven to Istanbul Headquarters of the Turkish National Security, and met by its chief, Mr. J.

There in the beautiful city of Istanbul, a mixture of many cultures, a sort of melting pot, I was formally introduced to the Englishman, the visitor to Manisa. Mr. J presented him as "Mr. Philby, the chief of British Secret Service in Turkey. Mr. Philby is the son of the respected and honorable Arabic scholar St. John Philby, who became a Moslem. It is the desire of Mr. Philby to have a very long interview with you, an interview which perhaps will take several weeks to complete. Mr. Philby specifically asked our permission that none of our representatives take part during your conversations together. This we have granted. You are absolutely free to move in Istanbul and arrange your meetings with Mr. Philby. Here are fifteen hundred Turkish liras, an equivalent of five hundred U.S. dollars, for your expenses in Istanbul. They were advanced to us by Mr. Philby. For your convenience we have reserved a suite in a nice hotel."

Then, there it was. My visitor of the recent past in Manisa was Philby, the head of British Secret Service in Turkey, the son of the famous St. John Philby. Some day in the future I would ask myself: How could I have suspected him of being an agent of the dreaded KGB? His own service did not suspect him, neither did the Turks. He was so courteous and pleasant, always smiling. For me he was a legitimate British intelligence officer interested in Soviet affairs.

It was arranged with Philby that a member of his staff, a nondescript character, would pick me up every morning at nine and drive me to a place for our interview. He would also drive me back to my hotel in the evening after our day's work. Meanwhile, Mr. J—whom Philby would later refer to in his book, *My Silent War*, as an "easy-going Aunt Jane"—relayed to me a private message which read, "Ismail Bey, don't be afraid for your safety. You are under our custody and all necessary measures are being taken to protect your life." That message put me at ease.

The next morning, exactly at 9 a.m., the nondescript character drove me to the place of our meeting. It was a luxury apartment building in Jihangir, overlooking the Bosphorus and Marmara with a wonderful view. The door was opened by a giant Kurd of dark complexion. One look at this ruffian on a dark corner at midnight would have given a person quite a scare. He gave a servile look to my escort and glanced at me with a look full of unexplained hostility. "Well, well," I said to myself, "this one could easily strangle a person and carry his body away in a bag to the Bosphorus." We entered the apartment. This was Philby's safe house. I have seen many safe houses in my lifetime, but this one was more than the usual run-of-the-mill type. Above all else it was very comfortable, richly furnished with taste and understanding. The floors were covered with expensive oriental rugs, and in the center of the living room floor there was a polar bear skin of good size. As soon as we entered the living room I was met by Philby, who introduced me to a young and charming English lady who was going to act as our hostess and stenographer for the days ahead. The nondescript Englishman retired with the reminder that he would pick me up in the evening.

Philby was all smiles and courtesy: the impeccable English gentleman full of attention. For starters we had a drink, and then got down to business, business which was going to last approximately four weeks—each day from nine to five, with short interruptions for lunch, which was served in the same room.

Oh, my God. If I had only known that this smiling, courteous Englishman named Philby was the man who had tipped the KGB about Soviet Vice-Consul Konstantin and had him sent to certain death!

If I had only known that here in this most luxurious apartment I was actually sitting in a KGB den and was being interviewed by a KGB agent!

How could I? Even so, when my interviews were completed and I left immediately for my return to Izmir by boat, I had some vague misgivings about this man Philby, but I managed to subdue them. To whom could I tell and discuss my misgivings? To suspect a senior officer of the British Secret Service was one thing, but to talk about it was suicide. Who would listen and even if I could find someone to listen—who would believe me? One would immediately accuse me of causing a Soviet provocation, or of being slightly "off my rocker." And what proof had I except rationalizing? Therefore, on my return to Izmir, I made up my mind to keep my misgivings about Philby to myself until the proper time.

Now, looking back in retrospect and reviewing my conversations with this master of deceit, and after so many years, I see certain flaws in the strategy Philby used in questioning, certain flaws in Philby's behavior, and most vividly of all now, the biggest mistake he made in my case.

Of course from our earlier, brief conversations, Philby had learned the scope and value of my information. Much, much later it became clear that while seeing me in Istanbul, Philby had received KGB instructions to learn my motivations, how much I

knew of the Soviet military, diplomatic, intelligence, and technological secrets, to whom and on what I talked on these matters.

Accordingly, the program of my interview was outlined by
Philby approximately as follows:

- My background and biographic data.
- My motivations for defection.
- Step-by-step details of my defection to the Turks.
- All Soviet high-ranking military officers and other public figures
  known to me, and their characteristics and style of working.
- Soviet High Command, the General Staff, the political directorate of
  the Soviet army and navy, their organization, policy, control, strategy,
  and doctrine. Military schools and academies. All personnel known by
  name, and their characteristics. Soviet military, scientific, and
  research organizations, their tasks, personnel, and their characteristics, and so on.
- Signal corps of the Soviet army.
- Border troops.
- Purges in the Soviet armed forces; Soviet invasion of Finland in 1939.
- Soviet military intelligence—functions of the GRU, strategy, operations, tactics, its history, chiefs and deputies, and organization. Intelligence objectives, political aspects; that is, the relationships between
  the Party, Soviet government, and the GRU. Finances, operational
  doctrine, and methods of operation, agent handling and modus operandi, and communications. Soviet diplomatic, commercial, and some
  other establishments, such as *Tass*, as cover for Soviet espionage
  activities. Professional standards, efficiency, security, and so on;
  training establishments.
- KGB history, organization, the relationship between GRU and KGB.
- GRU activities abroad, the legal and illegal networks in Turkey,
  Europe, U.S.A., Asia.
- The state of my mind and my plans for the future.

All conversations took place in a smaller room, a sort of
anteroom, with my chair placed behind a glass door leading to a
balcony overlooking the Bosphorus. I believe we were on the fifth
or sixth floor, and the narrow cobblestone street was far below—
an ideal spot for a so-called suicide jump.

The charming young English lady took notes in shorthand,
but I felt certain the place was wired, and perhaps somewhere in
the front of me there was a concealed microphone.

Our discussion of my background and the talks covering my
biograhic data were surprisingly short. Perhaps they would add
up to a few hours. As a rule, any intelligence service (and certainly
the KGB) would take a long look into a person's background.
Nothing is overlooked in this respect. A complete family history
of parents and relatives would be taken. Then a thorough interrogation covering friends, associates, education, professional

skills, languages, military duty, names and dates of schools attended, service record, classmates, transfers, and moves from place to place; everything would be examined and sifted to the most minute detail. It would take several days, sometimes a week or more, to effectively evaluate a person of interest. The more mature the person under scrutiny, the more information he has; the more experienced he is, the more time it takes to discuss and evaluate him. This is done in order to understand him, to establish his *bona fides*, to evaluate the materials and information he provides.

In short, it takes a great deal of time to check out a person from all angles. Yet, here I was, the former chief of the Fourth Division of the GRU, a Soviet General Staff officer, a lieutenant colonel, sitting face to face with the head of the British Secret Service in Turkey, and he showed virtually no interest in me, my background, my *bona fides*. I was both puzzled and hurt, because I had hoped that this high-ranking British intelligence officer would understand my problems and perhaps be able to assist me in my plans to go to the West.

Many years later it would become clear to me why Philby had not the least interest in my background. It was already fully known to his masters in Moscow, and Philby had no reason to spend much time on the subject. This was the big mistake made by both Philby and his masters. Every game must be played all the way, according to the rules. And of course on this point, he would never have helped me leave Turkey. On the contrary, he would and did do everything to prevent my move to the West.

Even though my personal history was just touched lightly, Philby did not forget to ask about my close relatives in Moscow. He wanted their names and addresses; when I mentioned the name, address, and place of employment of my sister-in-law, a most charming and beautiful lady of high culture, Philby immediately asked if I would write her a short letter. "Someone from the British Embassy in Moscow will find her and deliver your note." Delighted with the opportunity to inform her of my freedom, I wrote a short note and gave it to Philby. She and her husband were in opposition to Stalin's dictatorship, though they were not anti-Soviet. Much to my sorrow, I realized years later that this dirty trick was used by Philby to victimize a poor innocent lady.

In speaking of high-ranking Soviet military officers, Philby was successful in getting from me the names of several hundred officers and engineers who were, at one time or another, associated with me, either at a school, an academy, or on assignment.

I volunteered this information in order to show the free world that there were a number of senior Soviet military officers realistic and wise enough to understand the evils of Stalin's domination in all spheres of Soviet life; officers bright enough to have arrived at a real understanding and an eventual mutual cooperation with the people of the western world. They were men like myself, men who could show the West that not all people of the U.S.S.R. are dogmatic or content to be used as antiwestern tools by Stalin and his henchmen.

Fate is cold and cruel. Once Philby was exposed, it became clear to me that all this material was interpreted by the KGB masters in their usual way. One need only review the press and come to the conclusion that Stalinists were promoted to higher and higher ranks and positions while the others were demoted and disgraced.

While neglecting my background, Philby showed an intense interest in my reasons for defecting, in the circumstances surrounding it, in how I was handled by the Turks, and finally in the attempts, if any, of the KGB to whisk me out of Turkey or to liquidate me. He was obsessed with learning the smallest details of the Turkish handling of my protection. I made no bones about letting him know how politically motivated my defection was, how much I disagreed with Stalin's leadership, how I did not approve of the existing political structure of the U.S.S.R., did not agree with the dominance of the KGB in all phases of Soviet life.

I related to him how the GRU was able to detect and produce in advance data clearly showing the preparedness and strength, the concentration, of the German armed forces ready to invade the Soviet Union, to find out the strategic plans of the German High Command, and the approximate dates of the forthcoming invasion of the Soviet Union. I emphasized that all our reports on these matters were rejected by Stalin and the generals close to him. Stalin, in not accepting the validity of the GRU information on the German invasion, chose to stamp all news of this sort as products of British provocation. I also explained that Stalin and some of the senior military officers close to him underestimated the strength and power of the German army and, as a result, made wrong decisions on fundamental strategic measures. When one speaks—provided, of course, he is a person of intelligence—he usually can tell, by the facial expressions and immediate reactions of his listener, by the interest displayed, and by the type of questions asked, just how much and how deep is the understanding of the listener. This was obvious to me. Philby indeed did not display much understanding or desire to grasp the tragedy of those struggles within the Soviet General Staff on the eve of the invasion. I told him of the deep-rooted suspicions held by the Soviet leadership toward the Allies while the war was going on in 1942. Stalin's motto was, "Our number one enemy is the United States. After victory over Germany, we will take an uncompromising position against the United States."

Finally I told him of my recall to Moscow by the Soviet government in May 1942. Of course I had no intention of becoming the scapegoat for the bloody butchers of the Soviet secret police.

Years later, in looking back on these tense moments of relating all my thoughts and reasons for defection and then my notice of recall, I can remember seeing a temporary flash of anger in Philby's eyes behind his false smile. I remember that I wondered: Why? Maybe it was anger for me and the way in which I was unjustly treated? These were the thoughts running through my mind on that summer day in 1948. How wrong I was! How could I know that this man, this highly respected senior officer of British intelligence could be, and was, a wolf in sheep's clothing?

However, I did notice that he had some difficulty in grasping the whole significance of many of the military terms I used— strategic echelon, operational depth, initial period of the war, operational art as an independent part of stategy, and so on.

"He is not a military professional, he is a civilian," I told my questioning mind.

As for the protection given to me by the Turks, I told him that it was excellent, beyond all expectations. "I am always escorted by bodyguards. Even when I am free to move around, they take their own measures to protect me against the unexpected. You seem worried about my safety here in Istanbul. I have excellent protection." I continued by telling him of the past. Immediately after my defection the KGB tried to spot me in order to kidnap or assassinate me, but they failed in their attempts. Again, I detected that momentary flash of anger in his eyes.

The days tumbled by without much color. We were somewhere in the middle of our schedule. One day, discussing the agent-handling methods used by the GRU, Philby suddenly asked: "Tell me, please, how do the Soviets treat their double agents?" My answer was, of course, a long one, and I could not possibly remember each word, but I will give the gist of it: "The Soviets do not like double agents. They look upon them as something dirty, working strictly for material rewards. In Soviet intelligence the word 'double' is a dirty word; one must work for the cause," I said. "It is for the cause that so many Soviet military officers in the GRU and in other branches of the armed services tried to oppose the domination of one single person over every aspect of life in the U.S.S.R. It is for this cause that so many well-known Communists such as Nikolai Bukharin, Grigory Zinoviev, Karl Radek, Tomski, Gamarnik, Tukhachevski, and so on, have suffered torture and death.

"This is why an honest citizen in the Soviet Union, be he a military or political figure, or a government employee, a farmer or peasant, hates with heart and soul the KGB—the evil successor of the Tsarist Okhrana. It is the KGB that extensively uses doubles, informers, and the other scum recruited from among Soviet citizens and foreigners," I said. "Look at the long list of Cheka-OGPU-NKVD-KGB top officials I have given you. All of them were disgraced, shot, liquidated, or disappeared in their struggle for power. There was no cause."

Philby's face became masked with a very strange expression, one filled with anxiety, fear, anger, and misery. We stopped for a short time to have a strong drink, and then Philby asked, "Please, tell me again, according to current doctrines of the GRU, how the Soviet intelligence treats foreigners working for them."

"You should know that there has been a very strong phobia about foreigners in Russia since the time of the Tatar invasion. For a very short time during Lenin's time this phobia declined and foreign Communists, even fellow travelers, found a safe haven in Russia, were trusted to a degree, and offered jobs. Since the purges, however, everything has changed. Now Soviet intelligence agencies see each foreigner as a spy. They suspect their own citizens who have contact with foreigners of being spies. The GRU, using one pretext or another, called back almost all foreign agents and many were liquidated. The smart ones avoided the call by staying abroad." This was my reply, and to fortify my point I related many facts pertaining to this question. We had another drink and again Philby had this fearful, distant look in his eyes. The look was not caused by the strong drink. While sipping my scotch and soda I reflected on how little these foreigners knew of Soviet realities.

The days slipped by almost unnoticed. Philby and I had come to the end of our talks. On the last day Philby asked me if the Turkish authorities had used all the information I had given to him. "No," I replied. "As a matter of fact, the Turks never interrogated me. Of course they asked me detailed questions about who I was, what I was doing in Turkey working as a press attaché, and what Soviet intelligence networks were in Turkey, but they showed no interest outside their own sphere."

Philby was delighted with this. "That is wonderful!"

"Intelligence services are always jealous of each other and want all the information only for their own use," I remarked, sipping another scotch. Our talks were at an end. I say "talks" because our meetings never took the form of formal interrogations. This was hardly possible since I was too big a "fish" for any highhanded treatment in conversations. Our meetings were more a mixture of discussions of wide-ranging intelligence and a sort of cleverly directed interrogation. Philby could not put forth expert questions related to GRU organization, doctrine, military, and political problems. He was not a professional on these subjects. But, I may say that he was thorough and meticulous on counterintelligence matters both within and outside the U.S.S.R. He was extremely interested to find out how much I knew about Soviet espionage activities in England. Here he tried his best to grill me. Of course, I did my best to tell him everything I knew of all those matters, because I wanted to expose the scale of Soviet worldwide espionage activities conducted through all channels. Also, I was hoping, as a result of our long association during these meetings, that he might help me settle in England. I told him that the Turks were very kind and protective toward me, but that life in Turkey was like exile, and I would much prefer to live freely in Europe and make my living as a professional in some technical field.

Philby told me that getting to England was impossible, out of the question, and suggested that I continue to live in Turkey, exile or no exile. This is the best place for you, he said, and he handed me the equivalent of five hundred dollars in Turkish liras to cover my personal expenses.

That was the last I saw of him. Many years later I learned that Philby had submitted only a small part of the reams of material obtained from me to the British and American intelligence services. The important fact to remember is that Philby saw me in 1948, at a time when everything was very fresh in my mind. I am sure he made voluminous reports as a result of our meetings and sent them posthaste to the Russian masters of his double life.

Now that he has been discovered and exposed for what he truly has been and is, all this can be told. He made, however, another grave mistake. Imagine interrogating a former lieutenant colonel of the GRU and sending home only a minimum amount of information obtainable from such a source! Here he trapped himself and was eventually caught.

Years later the western world was shocked and surprised as a result of Philby's exposure. The Soviets granted him citizenship and gave him the Order of the Red Banner. This honor is usually reserved for military men for gallantry in combat. What a sad commentary that the KGB succeeded in awarding a human hunter this coveted order. Philby is presented as a great champion for the "cause."

For me, this is all so much hogwash. This traitor was never a fighter for the cause. He was, and still is, a sick alcoholic weakling. The real fighters for the real cause, the cause of freedom, democracy, and human dignity, are the Soviet officers who defected to the West, severed all ties with the Communists, and revealed the ugly reality of the Soviet police state. Other true fighters are the contemporary Soviet writers, the poets and those military officers who are demanding a change in the Soviet system. The old Bolsheviks who fought Stalin and suffered all kinds of torture in the Cheka and KGB cellars, some murdered because of their dedication, are the true champions.

Philby was recruited into the web of OGPU counterespionage under the rule of the notorious Menzhinski. He was filled with socialist dreams. Once one is caught in the KGB network, it takes tremendous courage, wisdom, foresight, and a deep understanding and sympathy for human dignity to leave it. Philby had none of these qualities. He secretly worked for the Soviet secret police, which was ruled successively by Felix Dzerzhinsky, Yakov Peters, Vyacheslav Menzhinski, Genrikh Yagoda, Nikolay Mezhov, Lavrenty Beria, Sergei Kruglov, Vsevolod Merkulov, and company, all of them bloody executioners of the Soviet people.

After many years of leading this treasonous double life, years of selling his countrymen and allies down the drain, betraying the trust of his loved ones, finally in January 1963 when faced with a new interrogation by Britain's MI 5, he disappeared into the Soviet Union. This time he knew the circle was closing.

His third wife, Eleanor, the woman he was courting while his second wife lay on her deathbed, says of him in her book, *Kim Philby: The Spy I Married*, "He never complained, nor uttered a word of criticism of Soviet life." How could he? His criticism would never have reached the free world. He is not free. Everything done in Philby's name is purely for propaganda.

To completely close the circle he will pass into oblivion, into an empty abyss during one of his drunken hours, as did Burgess, and join the company of butchers, henchmen, headhunters—call them what you will—the despised enemies of the unfortunate Soviet people still yearning for their freedom.

# 11

## Peace

There was one good thing, just one, in that low period into which I sank in early 1949. Restrictions on me were again lifted to the extent that I could go to Izmir whenever I wanted and for indefinite stays.

As soon as that permission was given to me, I went to that beautiful city on the coast, determined to stay until spring. I wanted an escape from the depression that obsessed me.

I had not been at the sea more than a few days before my spirits revived. I spent hours at the port watching ships sail and arrive, passengers of many nationalities come and go, meerschaum for pipes and cigarette holders and Turkish tobacco being loaded, cargoes of infinite variety from all parts of the world being discharged. The more I watched, the more that I felt I was once more part of the world.

By then I was forty-five, but I felt years younger, almost a boy again. In that spirit I gladly accepted an invitation to the house of friends in Izmir, an invitation to a party. Before I had been there very long, I saw a pretty girl on a sofa in a corner. Her face was a mixture of Slav, Tatar, and Turk. She was a brunette, with a secret smile on her lips, and had dark brown eyes that seemed to me to reflect nights of the warm south. Her posture was ladylike and her figure attractive.

I asked to be introduced to her. She was as charming as I had imagined from a distance. Her voice was soft and gentle and had the sweetness of a singer. She was self-possessed and made me feel at home as soon as we started to talk. Her name was Muazzez, which means beloved. Her family name was Parlakses, meaning one who has a sweet and brilliant voice. At sight, to me, she indeed deserved both names.

That lovely and beautiful young woman was a graduate of Gazi Terbiye Institutesi (teacher's college) in Ankara. She had majored in literature, specializing in English classics, but also was familiar with the great Russian writers in translation. She knew no word of Russian except "da" and "nyet." Her spoken English was poor because, as she said, she had had "no chance to practice, to improve it."

I decided to improve her knowledge of both languages. We became friends and saw much of each other that winter and spring of 1949. In May she came to Manisa to visit me. By then I knew I was in love with her. I took her for a walk, out to the statue of Niobe. There I proposed to her, and she accepted.

We became engaged by exchanging rings at a small family party in Muazzez's home in Izmir on June 1, 1949. At that gathering I got to really know her father, an elderly gentleman with fine features, a man well traveled in the Near East, with fluent command of Arabic and Persian, and who could quote many passages from Turkish and Arabic classics; and her mother, Ihsan Hanum, her hair the color of silver and her mind full of wisdom. They accepted me as their own son. I had a home again after all my wanderings. At last I once again had something to live for and loving people to live with.

Nor was that my only good fortune. Suddenly luck appeared to be heaped upon me. Just before our engagement I had been notified that I was free to move about all of Turkey, to go to any city I chose, including the capital, and that work, real work, might await me in Ankara.

And as if that were not enough, after our engagement I was told that my naturalization request had received favorable consideration. That proved a bona fide report. In Ankara, August 6, 1950, after more than eight years as a political refugee, I was made a Turkish citizen by decision of the Cabinet of Ministers, number 3/11678.

I was given a Turkish passport. I could go anywhere in the non-Communist world I chose. I was finally a free man.

---

As I write this, forty years have passed since I defected at Istanbul.

Life has been good for me in the free world. I married Muazzez, of course. We have two children, Huseyin, named after my father, and Ayshe, named in honor of my wife's grandmother. A few years after our marriage Muazzez and I emigrated to West Germany, where Huseyin was born. Later we moved to the U.S.A., the birthplace of our Ayshe. Although our daughter is American by right of birth, the rest of our family became American by naturalization.

No matter how our citizenship was obtained, all four of us are very, very American, of modest means. Muazzez glories in her modern kitchen with its garbage disposal unit and other labor-saving devices, but still makes fine cups of good Turkish coffee. After our children finished high school and went to college, Muazzez, a linguist, turned to teaching. Ayshe is just as American as any of the girls next door, except that she had to learn some of the art of Middle Eastern cooking from her mother. After graduating from the University of San Francisco, she became an English teacher and is now married. Huseyin, when well into his teens, did what many other average American boys tried. With the family cat he ran away from home en route to the South Seas, and had hitchhiked as far as Los Angeles and enrolled himself at a university there before we caught up with him. As it turned out, he graduated from Boston University in 1973 with a degree in anthropology. He later gave that up for civil engineering and now is a home builder.

As for myself, after the Philby interview I was thoroughly debriefed by the FBI, CIA, and Pentagon officials in Istanbul in 1949. In 1950 Muazzez and I moved to West Germany, where I began to work for the Pentagon as a consultant on various Soviet military matters. In 1953 we came to the United States, where I testified publicly on two occasions before the Senate Judiciary Committee investigating Soviet espionage. I also continued my work with the military until 1970, when I retired.

Because I was well past fifty when I was naturalized, I am probably not as typically American as my wife and children, but at least I have an air-conditioned sports car. I shudder to think what my father might have said about that effete type of transportation!

In retirement I have both the time and the opportunity to pursue such hobbies as fly-fishing, swimming, and hiking in nearby mountains. I also do much reading, writing, and traveling.

Since coming to America, I have also had the chance to cross paths again, directly and indirectly, with some of the people who helped me during my years of stateless exile in Turkey. I have visited Porter Mougey, who installed the power plant in Manisa. No longer at "Lima, Ohio, U.S.A.," he has quit the engineering profession to run a farm in great contentment in the South. In Denver I picked up traces of Suleyman Demirel, the young Turkish engineer who got me the work with the soil-analyzing team. He had been sent to that Rocky Mountain city under an American government grant to continue his technical studies. While busy at that, Demirel lived in a small, one-room apartment where he did most of his own housework. He fascinated his landlord by saving every glass jar and container in which his food and commodity purchases had been packed. They were too good to throw away, in the opinion of the young Turk, who later became prime minister of his country.

Only once have I run into agents from my intelligence past. That single occasion was quite startling, and I want no repition. It happened several years ago when I was traveling in Central America by air. When we had become airborne after an intermediate stop, I suddenly noticed a group of Soviet citizens a few seats away from me. One of them was a GRU man who had been an assistant of mine in the *Tass* cover operation in Berlin. From our seats we looked at each other warily. He whispered a few words to the Russians with him. I struck up a conversation about nothing with passengers near me, all complete strangers. I had some fear that my former assistant and his group might be after me. He too probably feared that I and my fellow passengers might be after him. A nervous hour or so later we landed to part in crowds at the airport without incident. I never knew who was bluffing whom, but did learn later that my one-time assistant was the current Soviet ambassador to Castro's Cuba.

By means of the Soviet press and periodicals available in the West, I have maintained a limited knowledge of what happened to some of the more important people of my Soviet past.

Mekhlis, the commissar of the Ninth Army who almost had me court-martialed, died a natural death, one of the few of his background and position to do so.

Chuykov, who intervened for me with Mekhlis, gained world renown for his leadership of troops in World War II. Made a Marshal of the Soviet Union, in the postwar period he served as one of the deputy ministers of defense, and until his recent death was chief of the ground forces of the Soviet Union and active in a capacity unknown to me.

Golikov, my chief at the Directorate, also distinguished himself in World War II and was likewise made a Marshal. Until a few years before his death, he was director of the main political directorate of the Soviet army and navy.

Of my more immediate colleagues I have learned very little. In fact I have heard about only one, Captain Polyakova, my female assistant in the Fourth Division of the Directorate, and I have no proof of the authenticity of the information about her. There were reports, but not substantiated, that she had been retired from all work because she was a Jewess.

So far as I am concerned, my friend Bukhtin, who warned me in time, my lesser friend Akimov, who did not warn me, our KGB opponent Naumov, whom I escaped, all have disappeared without trace. I imagine that all three, friend and foe, were among those Russians whom the Turks had told me had departed posthaste for the Soviet Union after my defection. Bukhtin and Naumov in all probability were speedily purged after their arrival home. Akimov, a tougher character, may have survived, but with his career finished.

Of those Russians concerned with my fate in Turkey, only the ambassador, Vinogradov, continued on the surface. His next important foreign post after Ankara was as ambassador to France. Later he was transferred to Cairo, where he must have played a major role in Soviet penetration of the United Arab Republic and other Arab states, as well as in Arab hostility to Israel. I presume he had just as good an explanation for the rout of the Soviet-equipped Egyptians in the Sinai peninsula as he earlier had for my defection. He is dead now.

My continued interest in those people of my past is no stronger than that with which others follow the ups and downs of former classmates. It certainly betokens no nostalgia for my land of origin, because for me, a Tatar, it never truly was my land, but was Russian. And with the death of Tamara, I lost the only person there I could claim as my own.

Nevertheless, one cannot have been alive in that vast land of my birth during the throes of the Revolution and Stalinism and lose all interest in it. My concern on being out of it involves what some of those there, especially the new breed of writers young and old, might be able to do to make it a better land to live in.

And for me, a not-so-newcomer to the U.S.A., comparison between the country of my birth and the country of my choice is also constant. Both girdle continents, both are immensely wealthy. Both are involved in the world about them and both, at the same time, have problems at home. The main difference between the two superpowers is that everybody in the whole wide world knows about American foreign policy and American internal troubles, while only a very few Soviet hierarchs are truly informed about Soviet external and internal affairs. With all its widely publicized shortcomings, America is an open society, constantly changing, while the Soviet Union remains a closed society, balking at change.

True, as an American, I am distressed at the drain on life and fortunes in the far corners of the world, at the slums in American cities, at the struggle of black Americans and other minorities for civil rights and equal opportunity. But as a one-time Soviet citizen, I am amazed at the protest, the violence, and the occasional political Communist-lining attendant to those problems. I know how Moscow would handle such problems, particularly those of a minority people. That I learned the hard way—as Americans say—in the Soviet Union.

But my days of learning are coming to an end. It is time now for the young people of my land of birth and of my land of choice to learn, too. *Alhamdulillahi Rabb'l Alemin . . . Ihdina siratel mustakim!* (Praise to God, the Lord of the Universe . . . Show us the straight path!)

# Glossary

**Amtorg.** Russian. Abbreviation for *Amerikanskaya Torgovlya,* American Trade. A trading corporation; a joint stock company created by the Soviets in May 1924 in New York, as an import and export trade operation headquartered in Moscow. A real and legitimate business enterprise, having commercial operations with many trading institutions, it was an ideal cover for Soviet intelligence operations, both RU and OGPU. For example, Brigadier General Vartanyan of the RU worked under the umbrella of Amtorg in the mid-thirties in New York as an intelligence operator. At that time, shareholders' equity totalled about three million dollars. At its height, Amtorg employed about nine hundred men and women, some 250 of them leftist or Communist Americans. Its employees had a chance to travel across the U.S.A. and visit plants and companies in many cities. *See also* RU, OGPU.

**Ariks.** Turkish. Plural of *arik,* an irrigation ditch in Central Asia, many parts of the Middle East, and the Transcaucasus. Acres of rice fields, orchards, and cotton fields in these areas require huge amounts of water for irrigation. Nearly two-thirds of the Soviet Union's cotton is raised in the Uzbeck S.S.R.—in Turkmenistan, for example, irrigation water is brought from such rivers as the Zarafshan, the Syr Darya, and the Amu Darya (all originating in high, snow-capped mountains) into many canals, and finally is distributed into innumerable irrigation ditches, the ariks.

**Ataman.** Tatar. Literally, "I am father." (*Ata,* father; *man,* I.) The commanding officer of a Cossack military district. In pre-Revolutionary Russia, there were eleven Cossack military districts, located in outlying areas of southern and southeastern Russia and southern Siberia. Cossack (also a

Tatar word) means free man, and the Cossacks were set apart from the serfs, who worked as slaves for the nobility. In the fifteenth and sixteenth centuries, Cossacks were established as a military class, were organized into military units, and settled in the above-mentioned areas, were given the best lands, were charged with guarding the borders of Russia, and were made the elite cavalry forces in the service of the Tsars against domestic and foreign enemies. Cossacks reported to military service with their own horses, outfits, and side arms. In reward for their services, Cossacks enjoyed local autonomy. The majority of Cossacks were of Russian origin and were Orthodox Christians, but there were also some of Tatar origin who were Moslems, especially the Orenburg Cossacks.

**Basmachi.** Turkish. The root of basmachi is the verb *basmak,* to raid; therefore, a basmachi is a raider, a highwayman, a bandit. The word was coined by the Soviets to denote anti-Soviet fighters in Uzbekistan, Turkestan, and Khiva. In this context, *basmachestvo* means counterrevolutionary banditry in Central Asia in the 1920s. In reality, *basmachestvo* was a popular uprising against the Soviets in general, and against Russians in Central Asia in the 1920s in particular.

**Beg, Bek, Bei, Bey.** Turkish. Sir, superior, chief, ruler. The term is in great use in Central Asia and the Middle East. Affixed to the first name, for instance, Ahmed Bey, Suleiman Bey, it denotes "Sir," and is much used in Turkey. A polite way to address a man.

**Belsh.** Tatar. Food; a pie filled with meat, potatoes, and carrots.

**Böreks.** Turkish. Plural of *börek.* Food; a flaky pastry stuffed with cheese, ground meat, or some other filling.

**Caravanserai.** Turkish. Caravan plus the word *serai;* a palace. An inn for caravans built along the roads of Central Asia, Iran, Afghanistan, Turkey, Pakistan, and the Transcaucasus. Usually consists of rooms for travelers and a closed court for their horses, camels, and donkeys.

**Chapan.** Tatar. An oriental robe of many colors and patterns, made of silk, cotton, or satin, depending on the wealth and social status of the owner. Some are of great beauty, others of depressing, dark colors. All are comfortable in hot climates. They originated, perhaps, in ancient China. Are worn by both sexes in many countries of Asia and Africa.

**Chaykhane.** Persian. *Chay,* tea; *khane,* house. A teahouse. In the Middle Eastern Moslem countries, these are visited by men only, to have a tea; to relax; to make deals; to play backgammon, cards, chess; to gossip. Chaykhanes are trademarks of Turkey, Iran, Afghanistan, Central Asia, Egypt, Saudi Arabia, and Pakistan.

**Cheka.** Russian. Abbreviation for *Chrezvychaynaya Komissiya po Borbe s Kontrrevolutsiyei i Sabotazhem,* Extraordinary Commission to Combat Counter-Revolution and Sabotage. Precursor of the KGB. *See also* KGB.

**Chekchek.** Tatar. Food; a sweet kind of dessert, something like granola bars, made of fried flour balls held together with honey. Made during religious holidays and for weddings.

**Cherkeska.** Russian. An outer garment of the mountaineers of the Caucasus, U.S.S.R. A long-waisted Circassian coat.

**Chetvertoye Upravleniye.** Russian. Fourth Directorate. *See also* RU.

**Chistka.** Russian. Cleaning; in the political sense, a purge. The first general purge of the Russian Communist Party of Bolsheviks (RKPb) was carried out in 1921. In 1925, Communist cells in state institutions and schools of higher education were purged. In 1926, a partial purge was carried on in village Party organizations. The second general purge of the Communist Party was carried out from 1929-1930. The late thirties witnessed the bloodiest purges.

**ChON.** Russian. Abbreviation for *Chasti Osobogo Naznacheniya,* Special Forces. Created in Soviet Russia during the years of the Civil War, 1918-1921, to fight the counterrevolution. Formed exclusively by recruitment of members of the Communist Party and Komsomol. Disbanded in 1924. *See also* Komsomol.

**Dacha.** Russian. A country cottage, especially a summer house, owned by those of some means in pre-Revolutionary Russia. During the Revolution, many were deserted and some were requisitioned by the authorities. Later, new dachas were built for members of the ruling clique. When an ordinary Soviet boasts of a dacha, he usually is speaking of a shack, cabin, or hut without running water, electricity, or phone, erected on a small lot.

**Dechkan.** Persian. A peasant of Central Asia.

**Dolmas.** Turkish. Plural of *dolma.* Food; fresh vegetables such as tomatoes, green peppers, or grape leaves stuffed with rice or ground beef.

**Duma.** Russian. Representative assembly established by Tsar Nicholas II in 1905.

**EM, INO, SK.** Russian. Abbreviations of KGB terms for operations conducted in foreign countries. EM is an abbreviation of *Emigratsiya,* Emigration. Term for espionage and counterespionage conducted among active white Russian émigrés in foreign countries, especially in world capitals, with the object of recruiting agents for the KGB, and of controlling or destroying existing anti-Soviet organizations. INO is an abbreviation for *Inostranny Otdel,* Foreign (Intelligence) Department. Term for operation of espionage and counterespionage carried out by KGB officers working under the Foreign Intelligence Directorate of the KGB in Moscow. SK is an abbreviation of the Russian words for Soviet Colony. This section maintains internal security; every aspect of the life of a Soviet citizen working abroad is constantly controlled by KGB officers. *See also* KGB.

**Golovorez.** Russian. A daredevil; a son of a gun; a cutthroat.

**GRU.** Russian. Abbreviation for *Glavnoye Razvedyvatelnoye Upravleniye,* Main Intelligence Directorate. Main Intelligence Directorate of the General Staff of the Red Army. *See also* RU.

**Haram.** Arabic. That which is forbidden by Islam; that which is illegitimate, unlawful, or wrong, such as to commit murder, to drink alcohol, to acquire property or money in unlawful ways, to commit adultery.

**Havuz.** Turkish. An artificial basin or pond.

**Hosh Geldiniz.** Turkish. Words of welcome.

**Illegals.** English equivalent of the Russian name for a Soviet agent operating independently in a foreign country. Illegals have no connection with legal *residenturas,* Soviet intelligence networks under the cover of officially recognized Soviet establishments such as embassies, consulates, trade delegations, *Tass,* Aeroflot. Illegals have their own networks, their own funds, their own means of direct communication with Moscow. In some instances, the chief legal resident (head of a network) could have contact with an illegal resident or individual illegal agents. *See also* Residentura.

**Imam.** Arabic. A Moslem prayer leader, a successor to the prophet Muhammed; a Caliph, according to the Shiite doctrine; a religious leader; a chief of a sect; a religious teacher.

**INO.** Russian. Abbreviation for *Inostranny Otdel,* Foreign (Intelligence) Department. *See* EM.

**Inorodtsy.** Russian. Foreigners.

**Inovertsy.** Russian. A heterodox; one who departs from church dogma.

**Kafir.** Arabic. An infidel; an unbeliever.

**Kalpak.** Turkish. A fur cap; a triangular women's hat.

**Karakul.** Turkish. Fur prepared from the skins of very young (two- to three-day-old) lambs of karakul sheep, most of which are reared in Central Asia. Their fur is characterized by extreme lightness and durability, and the sparkling, silky hair comes in several curly forms. The furs are used as apparel.

**Kaymakam.** Turkish. Chief administrator of a district in Turkey.

**KGB.** Russian. Abbreviation for *Komitet Gosudarstvennoy Bezopasnosti,* Committee of State Security. An administration overseeing political security, espionage, and counterespionage. After the Revolution, around 1918, Cheka was set up to oversee these operations. In the early twenties, Cheka was upgraded and renamed V Cheka *(Vserossiyskaya Cheka),* the All-Russian Cheka. It was again upgraded in 1922 and took the name GPU, State Political Administration. At the end of that year GPU was further upgraded to OGPU, *Ob'yedinnoye|Gosudarstvennoye Politicheskoye Upravleniye,* the United State Political Administration. In the mid-thirties, the organization was reorganized and was made part of the People's Commissariat of Internal Affairs, the NKVD. As a commissariat its sphere of responsibility was widened, and it took on the administration of police duties. In 1946, when the Soviets changed the commissariats into ministries, NKVD dropped "Commissariat" and became the Ministry of Internal Affairs, the MVD, *Ministerstvo Vnutrennykh Del.* Thereafter, the responsibilities of the MVD were split between it and the newly created MGB, the Ministry of State Security, *Ministerstvo Gosudarstvennoy Bezopasnosti.* The MVD retained the administration of police, prisons, and similar tasks; the MGB took on espionage, counterespionage, and internal security.

After Stalin's death and Beria's execution, the Politburo downgraded the MGB from a ministry to a committee, the KGB, in an effort to decrease its size and power. Neither of these ends was accomplished. *See also* Cheka, NKVD, OGPU.

**Khan.** Turkish. The title of rulers in the countries of Central Asia and the Middle East. Rulers of the Mongol Empire, such as Ghengis Khan, Kublai Khan, and Bati Khan; also of the Golden Horde, of the Crimean Tatars, and of the Kazan Tatars. The sultans of Turkey also had the title of Khan.

**Khozyain.** Russian. Master, boss, owner, proprietor. Used by the Soviet intelligence community to indicate the Soviet ambassador. Took on this meaning in 1941, when, by a secret directive of Stalin, Soviet ambassadors were charged with the supervision and coordination of the intelligence activities of both the GRU and the KGB. This was done to nullify any unhealthy competition between the GRU and KGB, and to streamline intelligence. Ambassadors, however, were in charge only of the end result, intelligence information. They were not authorized to learn operational details, such as the names of agents and the details of networks. How intelligence information was procured was the business of the GRU and KGB. *See* GRU, KGB.

**Kishlak.** Turkish. *Kish,* winter; *lak,* quarters. Winter quarters used by nomads and their animals.

**Kolkhoz.** Russian. Abbreviation of *Kollektivnoye Khozyaestvo,* a collective farm. According to Soviet theory, a kolkhoz is a voluntary union of peasants formed to farm land owned collectively. The reality is quite different. It is well known that Soviet peasants never had a special love for socialism, and after the Revolution of 1917 had dreamed of having their own land to farm. It is also well known that Lenin was afraid of this trend, and declared, "Either we control the peasants or they will overthrow us." To prevent the danger of such an overthrow, the Fifteenth Congress of the Communist Party of the Soviet Union decided in 1927 to collectivize the agriculture of the U.S.S.R. This was carried out forcibly, with bayonets and machine guns; in the process, thousands and thousands of peasant farms were destroyed.

**Komandirskiye Zvaniya.** Russian. Officers' ranks; officers' titles.

**Komsomol.** Russian. Abbreviation for Young Communist League.

**Kumis.** Tatar. A nutritious drink, a liquid food, made from mare's milk or camel's milk by the process of fermentation. It contains lactic acid, vitamin C, protein, fats, natural sugar, and a small percentage of alcohol. Kumis has medicinal qualities, is very nutritious, and because of its slight alcoholic content, is pleasantly intoxicating. It is not forbidden to Moslems—as are drinks such as vodka, whiskey, and wine, considered not food but poison, filled with empty calories, and bad for the health—because the alcoholic content is so low, because it is healthy food, and because of its medicinal value, especially for those suffering with TB. Kumis has been known since antiquity in Central Asia.

**Kursant.** Russian. In this case, a student of a military school; a cadet.

**Legenda.** Russian. A legend, a story. In Soviet intelligence parlance, a legenda is a fictitious biography backed by solid, verifiable details, given to intelligence agents to conceal their true identities. A legenda is not as simple as it sounds. Usually the minute details of legendas are worked out by the agents themselves, subject to the approval of their superiors. Some agents spend months living in a country procuring birth certificates and other documents, and becoming familiar with street locations, schools, churches, cemetaries, and so on, to back up their stories. Military attachés, career diplomats, trade representatives of the U.S.S.R., well-known correspondents, and persons well-known in other fields are exempt from having legendas, as there is no need for them to have a cover story.

**Maidan.** Arabic. An open space, a public square. For example, Harb Maidan is a battlefield, Kizil Maidan is Red Square.

**Marhaba, Merhaba.** Arabic in origin. Phrase meaning hello; good day; how do you do; greetings; welcome. Used as a greeting in all Moslem lands.

**Medrese.** Arabic. A Moslem theological school; a high school; a college.

**Mezar.** Arabic. A tomb; a grave.

**MGB.** Russian. Abbreviation for *Ministerstvo Gosudarstvennoy Bezopasnosti.* Precursor of the KGB. *See also* KGB.

**Mulla.** Arabic. A theological student, a doctor of Moslem law.

**Muska.** Turkish. A written charm enclosed in leather; a triangular thing shaped and worn like an amulet.

**Muzhik.** Russian. A peasant.

**Nazir.** Arabic. A minister; a superintendent.

**NEP.** Russian. Abbreviation of *Novaya Ekonomicheskaya Politika,* New Economic Policy. Adopted by the Soviets between 1921 and 1926; characterized by granting permission for private property, private capital, and free trade.

**NKVD.** Russian. Abbreviation for *Narodny Kommissariat Vnutrennykh Del.* People's Commissariat for Internal Affairs. Precursor of the KGB. *See also* KGB.

**OGPU.** Russian. Abbreviation of *Ob'yedinnoye Gosudarstvennoye Politicheskoye Upravleniye,* United State Political Administration. Precursor of the KGB. *See also* KGB.

**OO.** Russian. Abbreviation for *Osoby Otdel,* Special Section. KGB office in the armed forces, charged with counterespionage among military personnel. *See also* KGB.

**Opergruppa.** Russian. In this case, a punitive group of operational size used by Soviet security organizations against anti-Soviet movements.

**Paranjas.** Turkish. Plural of *paranca.* A distorted form of the word *ferace,* a dustcoat formerly worn by women in Turkey and Central Asia when out. Still worn by Moslem women in Saudi Arabia, Iran, Afghanistan, and Pakistan, and in the countryside of Egypt and Morocco.

**Peremech.** Tatar. Food; ground beef or lamb meat closed in a pastry shell and deep fried.

**Periis.** Persian in origin. Plural of *peri,* a fairy. A good *djinn;* figuratively, a beautiful girl.

**Pervy Dom NKO.** Russian. *Pervy,* the first; *Dom,* a house or building; *NKO,* an abbreviation of *Narodny Kommissariat Oborony,* the People's Commissariat of Defense. Prior to World War II, the main components of the Soviet military establishment were housed in two buildings. In the First Building of the NKO, on Znamensky Street, were housed the General Staff, including its Intelligence Directorate; the Political Administration of the Armed Forces; and the Department of Foreign Relations. The other directorates, the Directorate of Signal Communications, the Directorate of Armored Troops, the Directorate of Chemical Warfare, and so on, were housed in the Second Building (*Vtoroy*

*Dom)* of the NKO, located east of the Red Square, facing the Kremlin.

**Pilaus.** Persian. Plural of *pilav.* Food; boiled rice prepared with butter or meat fat.

**Pirozhki.** Russian. Plural of *pirozhok.* Food; pies filled with meat or vegetables.

**Podpol'naya Rabota.** Russian. Underground activity; secret work.

**Pravo Ubezhishcha.** Russian. Right of sanctuary.

**PRP.** Russian. Abbreviation for *Pogranichny Razvedovatel'ny Punkt,* Border Intelligence Post (or Point). A PRP conducts intelligence activities in neighboring countries adjoining Soviet borders. They are subordinate to the intelligence department of border military districts.

**Raki.** Turkish. Turkish brandy, an alcoholic drink.

**Razvedka.** Russian. Intelligence; reconnaissance.

**Razvedupr.** Russian. Abbreviation of *Razvedyvatel'noye Upravleniye,* Intelligence Department. *See also* RU.

**Residentura.** Russian. A residency; in Soviet intelligence parlance, an intelligence network. A *resident* is an intelligence agent or intelligence officer who runs a residentura, that is, runs an intelligence network.

**RU.** Russian. Abbreviation for *Razvedyvatel'noye Upravleniye,* Intelligence Department. (*Razvedyvatel'noye,* adjective of the noun *razvedka,* intelligence or reconnaissance; *Upravleniye,* administration, directorate, command, control, tactical control. Also abbreviated *Razvedupr.*) RU was the Second Directorate of the General Staff. The First Directorate of the Soviet General Staff was the Operations Directorate. Historically, Razvedupr was created by Leon Trotsky in 1918, and thereafter underwent a number of reorganizations and changes. At the beginning it was called the Registration Department, then the Second Directorate, then the Fourth Directorate, then the Seventh Directorate, then simply the Intelligence Directorate, and finally, at the beginning of World War I, in accordance with the consolidation of the military establishment, RU was upgraded to the GRU *(Glavnoye Razvedyvatelnoye Upravleniye),* the Main Intelligence Directorate. The American counterpart is the DIA (Defense Intelligence Agency).

**Selam Alekum, Salam Aleikum.** Arabic. Correctly, *Selamun*

*Aleikum.* Formal greeting of Moslems, "Peace be with you." The formal reply, *Va Aleikum Salam,* "And unto you also be peace." (Correctly, *Ve Aleikumusselam.*)

**SK.** Russian. Abbreviation of the Russian words for Soviet Colony. *See* **EM.**

**Uyezdny Gorod.** Russian. An *uyezd* was an administrative and territorial unit, part of a province, in pre-Revolutionary Russia. The uyezdny gorod was the chief town of a *uyezd.* For instance, Orsk was the uyezdny gorod subordinated to the Orenburg province.

**Yurt.** Turkish. The portable, round dwelling of the nomads of Central Asia and adjoining areas. Known to the Mongols before Ghengis Khan. Consists of a sliding wooden lattice frame with a dome-like top. This construction is covered by thick felt. The floor of a yurt is covered with carpets, rugs woven mattings, and is further furnished with blankets, pillows, and hides. There is no furniture other than richly ornamented chests. To eat, the occupants sit around a metal tray that serves as a table. First water is brought, and all wash hands. A grace is said, and then eating may begin. Spoons are used, but knives and forks are not.

**Zagranitsa.** Russian. *Za,* beyond; *granitsa,* border. Foreign lands. Zagranitsa has a special meaning for the Soviet people. It conveys to them the freedoms of the U.S.A., Canada, and Western Europe, and the high standards of living in these countries. For the people of the Gulag Archipelago, these are a magnet, a beacon of hope.

**Zastava.** Russian. Gate; outpost; security detachment; border post. In this case, a border post manned by border troops.

**Zaytsi.** Russian. Plural of *zayits,* hare. In the figurative meaning, a ticketless passenger, a stowaway. In the early twenties, these were thousands of uprooted children and teenagers who were wandering from one end of Russia to another in search of some work and a home.

# Index